AUTISM SPECTRUM DISORDERS

in the Mainstream Classroom

Barbara Boroson

SCHOLASTIC

New York • Toronto • London • Auckland • Sydney
Mexico City • New Delhi • Hong Kong • Buenos Aires

Dedication

To Lou and Florence Boroson
with admiration and love

Acknowledgments

I am lucky to have been surrounded by many steadfast supporters while writing this book. Together they are a testament to how a community, filled with the spirit of caring collaboration and positivity, can make anything happen.

With fondness and appreciation, I thank: Ann Horowitz, Jennifer Magnani, Marla Levine, and Terry Dunn for keeping me writing, believing, and laughing; Leah Tahbaz and Elyse Varos-Pollack for their artful turns of phrase; and Una Murray for her hard-won wit and wisdom.

With reverence and deference, I offer my appreciation to all teachers who strive to both reach and teach; most notably to Gail Sider and Cathy Schaeffer who set the bar so tantalizingly high. I am grateful for and humbled by the stories of triumph and despair contributed by many dedicated teachers.

Thanks also to the overwhelmingly responsive and creative team at Scholastic: Executive Editor Joanna Davis-Swing, Editor-in-Chief Virginia Dooley, and designers Jorge Namerow and Sarah Morrow; and to my prescient agent at Writers House, Susan Cohen.

Finally, with all my love and gratitude, I thank my family:

Lou and Florence Boroson for their generosity, unshakeable confidence, and on-call ingenuity—and for their standing offers to sit;

Martin Boroson, for his exhaustive edits, his inexhaustive support, and his exhausting ideas;

Joseph Rutt, for holding me up and backing me up, every single day;

Sam Boroson Rutt for inspiring me . . . literally;

and Leana Boroson Rutt, for inspiring me . . . literarily.

✳ ✳ ✳

The art on pages 48, 54, 57, 61, 66, 121, and 165 was created with Boardmaker software, which was developed by DynaVox Mayer-Johnson, 2100 Wharton Street, Suite 400, Pittsburgh, PA 15203 Phone: (800) 588-4548 Fax: (866) 585-6260.

Cover Designer and Artist: Jorge J. Namerow
Editor: Joanna Davis-Swing
Interior Designer: Sarah Morrow

Copyright © 2011 by Barbara Boroson
All rights reserved. Published by Scholastic Inc.
Printed in the U.S.A.
ISBN: 978-0-545-16876-2

2 3 4 5 6 7 8 9 10   40   17 16 15 14 13 12 11

Contents

Introduction

If you don't have a student on the autism spectrum in your class today, you will soon. The prevalence of autism spectrum disorders is at an all-time high, and more students on the spectrum are being placed in mainstream classrooms every year.

As of the publication of this book, 1 out of every 110 children is believed to have an autism spectrum disorder—and that number has been rising dramatically for decades. (U.S. Centers for Disease Control and Prevention, 2009.)

In combination with national movements toward least restrictive programming in schools and recession-era budget cuts, these statistics mean that you'll see many students on the spectrum crossing the threshold of your suddenly inclusive mainstream classroom.

In other words, students with autism spectrum disorders are coming your way. You need to stay current. You need to be ready.

The prospect of including these students in your mainstream class may fill you with anxiety: You may dread having to exert the extra effort. You may resent what feels like an intrusion on your comfort level and expertise. Or you may welcome the inclusion of these students as an exciting challenge and an opportunity to explore new territory and expand your professional horizons. Most likely, you find yourself vacillating somewhere in between. That's your spectrum, and wherever you find yourself on this autism-spectrum-support spectrum, help is in your hands.

Within these pages you will discover what makes students on the spectrum tick (as well as what makes them *tic*). You will learn to identify spectrum disorders, recognize what drives the responses and behaviors of students on the spectrum, and find out how you can help steer them toward success. You will learn how to hold it all together and how to keep your whole class running smoothly and your whole self feeling steady. And you will see that while this will be a year full of new challenges, it will also be a year full of powerful, emerging new perspectives, for you and for your entire class, about seeing and being in the world. Really.

Individuals Together

Students on the autism spectrum may share common traits and may appear alike from a distance. But just like stars in the sky, each of these students possesses unique characteristics we can see only when we magnify the details. One of the fundamental goals of this book is to help you look closely enough to see and appreciate the distinct singularity of each student.

Every individual functions in and experiences the world differently on the basis of his or her own history, creativity, flexibility, adaptability, sensitivities, and sensibilities. There is no correct way to experience life. Some of us are excited by the taste of cayenne pepper; others find it overwhelming. Some of us meditate or read a book to relax; others relax by jogging or dancing. Some of us tend to get anxious; others get angry. Some of us feel and react passionately; others are stoic. None of these experiences or coping styles is right or wrong, just individual.

But we must all strive for the flexibility and adaptability to *feel when we need to feel, and deal when we have to deal.* We must strike this delicate balance in order to be true to ourselves while functioning effectively within the context of the social world. Though many of the strategies in this book will help bring students on the spectrum closer to "mainstream" or typical functioning, all of your students will need to make the effort to adapt to the diverse culture of your classroom.

So while this book seeks to highlight the brilliant and singular sparkle of each individual student, it also seeks to guide your efforts to create a *cohesive classroom community* that embraces and draws together all kinds of learners and doers, thinkers and feelers, workers and players, walkers and talkers, actors and reactors, movers and shakers. With this book, you will learn how to help all students showcase their strengths and cope with their challenges within the context of the multifaceted classroom community. An inclusive classroom is a community built around mutual understanding, acceptance, and support. This is what inclusive education is all about and, when done well, every student grows and benefits from the experience.

The Spectrum of This Book

Every one of these unique students in your class possesses an assortment of strengths and challenges. Some of those strengths and challenges may be fairly typical and familiar to you; others may be quite remarkable and unfamiliar. The chapters in this book will familiarize you with the numerous idiosyncratic strengths, challenges, and factors that drive the functioning of students on the spectrum. Many examples and strategies are offered to help you prepare and respond effectively. In combination, the information in these chapters will help you lay the foundation to build a learning environment that is inclusive of and beneficial for every member of your class.

But no single chapter stands alone in guiding academic instruction. This is because academic instruction is possible only within the context of all of the issues in all of the chapters. You really cannot begin to teach students on the autism spectrum if you haven't taken into consideration their challenges related to anxiety, sensation, socialization, engagement, regulation, organization, communication, and all the rest. When any of those systems is amiss, challenging behaviors may arise, so it is crucial to look *beyond* problematic behaviors to discover what is fueling them. Each chapter of this book will describe common triggers for behavioral reactions and offer ways to respond simply and effect lasting change. So please read the book all the way through at least one time, keeping your specific students in mind.

You'll see that most of the strategies in this book reflect a *way of thinking,* more than specific ways of doing. As you read, you may want to focus less on implementing general strategies and more on looking at your students through this investigative lens. Once you become familiar with the underlying sensitivities and challenges students on the spectrum face, differentiated problem solving may become second nature to you. And even if at first you make adaptations or modifications with only one student in mind, once you start thinking along these lines, you'll see just how powerful creative thinking and new styles of instruction can be for every learner in your class.

In the meantime, here are lots of preventive and responsive strategies. Preventive strategies will be the most important tools in your box, both philosophically and practically. They will guide you toward thinking in a proactive, positive way. They will help you keep the heat down and keep problematic situations from occurring and recurring. That's important because once a cycle of reaction has begun, it can be especially difficult or truly impossible to recover the day for your students on the spectrum.

So go ahead and implement whatever preventive strategies seem relevant and useful. But please don't try to use all of the strategies. You will be doing your students a disservice by not differentiating their needs, and, worse, you will use yourself up. Grab what makes sense today, and then put this book down. But don't put it far: The issues these students face and the ways they cope with them comprise an ever-changing landscape. So the parts of this book that feel irrelevant today may be life-savers tomorrow.

Ten Things You Can Do Before Day One is a quick checklist you can use to prepare yourself and your classroom before students on the spectrum join you. If you have limited time, try to implement the simple but critically important ideas on this list, even if you don't yet understand why they're so important. For now, just trust that these steps will pave the way to a smoother start. The rest of the book will put them into meaningful and compelling contexts for you.

Chapter 1, *Terms of Engagement,* defines and explains many of the terms and acronyms you will encounter on your journey with students across the autism spectrum. This chapter also offers an overview of the special education referral and placement process.

Chapter 2, *The Power of Positivity,* offers suggestions to help you bring out the best in your students, in your colleagues, and in yourself. Progress for students on the spectrum can be almost imperceptible. You may feel frustration and discouragement rearing up against your every effort. If you feel frustrated and discouraged, imagine how your students feel. This chapter will show you how to recognize and celebrate your students' strengths and how to keep yourself afloat even when you feel you're drowning.

Chapter 3, *The Simmering Pot,* describes why students on the spectrum cling to routine and consistency. Always guarded against unexpected input, these students live in a permanent state of high anxiety. Learn how to structure a classroom to keep the weather calm and cool, enabling students to relax and rely on your systems to support their feelings of safety and fuel their independence.

Chapter 4, *Body and Soul,* illuminates the sensory systems of students on the spectrum. Discover why their systems may be on high alert in many ways you might not expect or even recognize. This chapter will describe the broad range of sensory experience, common sensory triggers, and other factors affecting self-regulation. Learn how to create an environment that nourishes each student with just enough—and not too much—sensory stimulation.

Chapter 5, *The Inner Sanctum,* uncovers why students on the autism spectrum, immersed in the comfort of reliable rules and static topics, may struggle to engage in the learning environment around them. You will learn how to find the *hook* to capture their interest and keep them on board.

Chapter 6, *Meeting of the Minds,* introduces you to one of your most valuable resources: students' families. Find out where the families of students on the spectrum are coming from and how you and they can walk in lockstep on the journey you are now on together. Combining your educational expertise with their whole-child, historical perspective, you will make a formidable team.

Chapter 7, *That's What Friends Are For,* dissects the struggles of students on the spectrum to read and interpret the feelings and intentions of others. Their need for sameness makes adapting to the unpredictable dynamics of interaction painfully elusive. Meanwhile, your other students may struggle to tolerate the quirks and behaviors of students on the spectrum. This chapter will help you make it work for everyone as you create a classroom community of support and acceptance.

Chapter 8, *Say What?,* explains the communication challenges that limit the capacity of these students to process and utilize language. This chapter articulates common areas of communicative challenge for students on the spectrum and offers strategies to support both receptive and expressive language, as well as nonverbal communication.

Chapter 9, *Boiling Up and Over,* details what can happen when circumstances deviate too far out of the comfort zones of students on the spectrum. Sensory systems overload and the anxiety that always simmers within erupts. Inside the student flares a sudden chaos of confusion, inadequacy, and panic. Outside we see a breakdown of coping skills and a loss of control. This chapter explores what is really being communicated by intense behavior. You will learn how to restore equilibrium with confidence and competence, how to find and address the true antecedents of behaviors, and how to help students develop more adaptive means of coping and communicating.

Chapter 10, *Info In, Info Out,* explains that conceptual processing and learning may happen in unusual ways for students on the spectrum, and offers strategies to support assimilation and generalization of new information and skills. But Chapter 10 won't help you if you haven't read all of the chapters that come before. Only *after* you have attended to the full range of other issues can you begin to actually teach curriculum. That's why the chapter that pertains to curricular instruction comes last. Don't do it; don't jump ahead. You'll be fiddling with phonetics while Rome is burning. It is only after the sparks settle, the climate is cool, and the forecast is stable that you can begin to teach academic curriculum to students on the spectrum.

It's all here for the taking; take it as you need it; use it as you like. This book is not meant to be prescriptive. It's just full of ideas for you to think about and make your own. Pick and choose for yourself, as you consider the ongoing and evolving needs of each member of your dynamic classroom community. Some strategies will resonate with you for some of your students; some may spark new and different ideas; others may sound ridiculous. Some may take a bit of work to create or implement, but trust that an initial investment of time and effort will pay off for months and years to come. By taking the time to recognize, address, and support the strengths and challenges of students on the autism spectrum, you will discover ways to feature ability rather than disability. You will unearth innovative approaches that breathe fresh life into your curriculum and teaching methods to benefit all of your students. And as you develop your understanding of different ways of being in the world, you will open up new dimensions in your classroom constellation and inspire a panorama of remote stars to begin to shine.

Ten Things You Can Do Before Day One

Every student on the autism spectrum will enter your classroom bearing a backpack full of worries. If those worries can't be put down on Day One, then toting that heavy load will become a way of life at school, a learned behavior. Each day those students will return burdened and compromised by the worries on their backs. Instead, seize this moment to help them offload their worries by preparing a classroom that exudes comfort, clarity, and consistency, even on Day One.

Here is a basic list of what you can do before Day One to lighten the load for students on the spectrum:

1. Reach out to families. Well in advance, send home a questionnaire about strengths, challenges, anxiety triggers, and comfort anchors. (See Chapter 3 for a sample questionnaire.) Encourage parents or caregivers to get in touch with you to discuss any specific concerns. Consider carefully whatever anecdotal information emerges from these contacts as you plan for Day One and beyond.

2. Talk to colleagues who may have had experience with these specific students so that you can benefit from both their successful and failed efforts.

3. Arrange a visit. (Read about the visit in Chapter 3.)

4. Use collected information to determine optimal seating arrangements: Which peers might be good choices to partner with these students, and which peers are best avoided?

5. Avoid seating these students near probable distractions or possible sensory provocateurs, such as the loudspeaker, the gerbil cage, the bathroom, the windows, the microwave, and so on. (Get a sense of sensory considerations in Chapter 4.)

6. Prepare a visual schedule for the first day. (Learn all about how and why to do this in Chapter 3.)

7. Keep classroom decorations to a minimum, at least for a while. (Learn why in Chapter 4.)

8. Set up the classroom with clearly organized, plainly labeled spaces. (Find out why in Chapter 10.)

9. If possible, designate a small corner of your classroom as the Cozy Corner or Sensory Corner. For now, soften it up with some basic comforts: pillows, a small rug, a few stuffed animals, and a few books and magazines. If you've learned what might specifically comfort these students, add that, too. All students may welcome some chill-out time in the Sensory Corner. (Learn more about sensory corners and sensory tools in Chapter 4.)

10. Brush away your doubts and polish up your confidence. You can do this. (Find out why you should believe that in Chapter 2.)

Autism Spectrum Disorders in the Mainstream Classroom

Chapter 1

Terms of Engagement

Spectrum and Special Education Terminology

Individuals with autistic traits have been perceived and identified in myriad ways over time. Despite evolving trends of ignorance, discrimination, questioning, research, clarity, and ambiguity (in that order), a straightforward explanation of autistic-type disorders that really makes sense is hard to find.

In the past, the term *autism* most commonly described only very remote individuals, people who were unable to communicate or engage with the world around them, who were inscrutable and unpredictable, lost in their own selves.

Since the early 1900s, several similar but functionally different variants of *autism* have been identified. Therefore, the term *autism spectrum disorder* has more recently become an umbrella term, beneath which all the varied and related symptoms huddle. This cluster of symptoms is now believed to be *neuro-developmental* in etiology, which means that autism spectrum disorders:

- involve the brain and nervous systems
- emerge during childhood and alter the course of a child's development

Across the spectrum one can find a colorful collection of individuals who demonstrate similar autistic-type characteristics, but may function in different ways and at different levels. The image of a spectrum evokes the *associated-differentness* among the subtypes of autism spectrum disorders.

Autism Spectrum Disorders Today

Today, more students are being diagnosed with spectrum disorders than at any time in history. Many possible explanations for this increase have been proposed over the years, and controversy swirls around them all. One popular theory asserts that the mercury added to vaccines throughout the mid-to-late 1900s may have contributed to the dramatic increase in prevalence over the years. Other theories portray autism spectrum disorder as an autoimmune response or a nutritional deficiency due to incomplete and inadequate digestive processes. Still others suggest that spectrum disorders are the combined result of a neurological predisposition that gets triggered by exposure to environmental toxins. While many of these theories are compelling, none has been scientifically substantiated.

Another possibility to consider is that the increased frequency of diagnosis may not reflect an increased prevalence so much as a broadening of the definition. Because the autism spectrum now includes varying levels of functioning, individuals are diagnosed today who never would have met the narrower diagnostic criteria of the past.

But none of that speculation or information really helps you as you stand before a classroom full of students, wondering what to expect from those who arrived with all the evaluations, alerts, and acronyms accessorizing their school files.

This chapter will define common terminology you will encounter in your work with students on the spectrum, so that you'll be able to talk the talk, as you learn to walk the walk.

What Are Autism Spectrum Disorders?

What follows is a summary of the five clinical subtypes of autism spectrum disorder. Read it over. Get a sense of it. Then we'll start talking about real kids.

First, the Textbook Version

The United States Department of Health and Human Services' Center for Disease Control and Prevention Autism Information Center (2009) seeks to answer the question *What is autism?* with this explanation:

> [Autism spectrum disorders] include autistic disorder, pervasive developmental disorder—not otherwise specified (PDD-NOS, including

5 official subtypes:
1 Autism,
2 Asperger's
3 Rett's
4 Childhood Disintegrative Disorder
5 Pervasive Developmental Disorder
PDD-NOS

atypical autism), and Asperger's Syndrome. These conditions all have some of the same symptoms, but they differ in terms of when the symptoms start, how severe they are, and the exact nature of the symptoms. The three conditions, along with Rett Syndrome and childhood disintegrative disorder, make up the broad diagnosis category of pervasive developmental disorders.

Got that? If it helps any, this definition is remarkably consistent with the similarly befuddling explanation in the current version of the American Psychiatric Association's Diagnostic and Statistical Manual (DSM) IV (1994).

And believe it or not, these are all significant improvements over the judgmental and punishing explanations of autistic behaviors years before.

But don't despair: some good can come of this confusion. If you read these classifications enough times, you'll find your brain goes into information overload; the words begin swimming before your eyes, and things you thought you knew vanish from consciousness. Your attention veers off toward something more manageable like what you have planned for Saturday night. You might feel compelled to slam the book shut just to restore your equilibrium. Before long you may experience a total meltdown. System overload. Nothing's getting through. _Now_ you are beginning to get a functional understanding of autism spectrum disorders.

In Other Words

Let me try to clarify. Here is a brief description of each of the five "official" subtypes of Autism Spectrum Disorders.

1. *Autistic Disorder* (what I prefer to call *Classic Autism*) is a term used to convey profound obstacles to functioning in the social world. A diagnosis of Autistic Disorder always reflects significant challenges in the areas of behavior, socialization, and speech and language.

Key Behavior Issues

- preoccupations with certain activities and interests

- profound dependence on routines and sameness

- repetitive and stereotyped motor mannerisms

Key Socialization Issues

- minimal eye contact
- limited development of peer relations and interactions
- ineffective social communication and comprehension
- lack of socially or emotionally shared experience

Key Speech and Language Issues

- delayed, limited, or absent expressive and receptive speech and language development
- idiosyncratic use of language

Astonishing Savants

Savant qualities are exceptional abilities or talents that stand dramatically apart from typical functional levels. In the movie *Rain Man*, Dustin Hoffman's character, Raymond, exhibited extraordinary calculation skills when he glanced quickly at a mess of hundreds of spilled toothpicks and instantly assessed exactly how many were scattered about the floor. Savant qualities are present among about 10% of people with autism spectrum disorders (as opposed to among less than 1% of the general population), and when they appear they can be quite astonishing. Students on the spectrum who have savant qualities almost always demonstrate remarkable memory and often possess uncanny abilities in music, math, technology, calendar calculation, or other areas.

---

2. *Asperger's Disorder* is characterized by most of the same social and behavioral challenges listed above. *But in contrast to students with Classic Autism, students who meet the diagnostic criteria for Asperger's have had no clinically significant delays in language or cognitive development.* These students usually possess average or above-average intelligence. Because students with Asperger's *do* struggle with preoccupations and social blindness but are *not* limited in verbal expression, their repetitive thoughts and preoccupations flow, unfettered, right out of their mouths. These students will expound on their area of interest or knowledge, *ad infinitum*, regardless of whether or not they have anyone's attention or interest. And despite the absence of delays in language development, students with Asperger's often use language in idiosyncratic ways.

Asperger's Disorder, also known as *Asperger's Syndrome*, is a relatively new diagnosis. First identified by Hans Asperger more than fifty years ago, the diagnosis didn't come into broad use until the 1980s, and wasn't officially recognized by the American Psychiatric Association until 1994. Prior to that time, before autism disorders were seen as a spectrum, most individuals who functioned at this relatively high level remained undiagnosed.

Under the Radar

Because of their strong cognitive and speech and language skills, individuals with Asperger's Syndrome can often cope fairly well in certain contexts. It is not uncommon for them to pursue higher education in their specific areas of special interest and expertise, and to meet with success in related careers. Often their chosen occupations are the sort that do not require the nuance and unpredictability of social interaction. You might find individuals with Asperger's writing technical programs behind a computer screen, calculating numerical figures in a CPA's office, or researching interactions between light and sound in a physics lab. You are less likely to find individuals with Asperger's working successfully in customer service positions or collaborative team environments that demand social savvy.

Chances are, there are adults in your life with Asperger's, who may or may not ever have been diagnosed. Do you know someone who is bright and personable, but never seems to be having quite the same conversation with you that you think you're having with him? Where you're sort of *just missing* each other? That could be someone with Asperger's Sydrome.

Some students may be described as having *High-Functioning Autism,* which is not an official DSM diagnosis. These students may have been diagnosed with Autistic Disorder earlier in their development. But now they are believed to have progressed significantly beyond their earlier language, cognitive, and other delays to the point that they no longer meet the specific criteria for the Autistic Disorder diagnosis. However, because those delays were exhibited at some point, they do not meet the official criteria for an Asperger's diagnosis either. The clarity and usefulness of the terminology is hotly debated by experts in the field, and as of now, many believe the two terms can be used interchangeably. For your purposes, students with High-Functioning Autism present

Chapter 1   Terms of Engagement: Spectrum and Special Education Terminology much like students with Asperger's Syndrome; just be aware that they may have traveled a very different developmental route to your door.

girls

3. Much less common is *Rett's Disorder*, also known as *Rett Syndrome*, which occurs most often in girls. This condition, which is believed to be due to an alteration on the X chromosome, is also a relative newcomer to the diagnostic world. Rett's Disorder is characterized by a period of at least five months of typical infant development followed by a significant deceleration in certain aspects of development and/or loss of previously acquired skills. Rett's Disorder is frequently characterized by compulsive hand movements, such as wringing, tapping, clasping, and touching. The repetitive interests and need for sameness that appear in the above-mentioned subtypes do *not* figure prominently in a diagnosis of Rett's Disorder.

4. *Childhood Disintegrative Disorder* is another less common subtype of autism spectrum disorder. Individuals who meet the criteria for this disorder demonstrate

DID YOU KNOW . . .

As of this writing, the American Psychiatric Association (APA) is gathering data for a revision to the current Diagnostic and Statistical Manual (DSM-IV), which hasn't been updated since 1994. Several important changes in the area of autism spectrum diagnosis are in the works.

Rather than list autism spectrum disorders as five separate subtypes, DSM-V may consolidate them into one single term: "Autism Disorder" or "Autism Spectrum Disorder." If the proposed changes are implemented, there will be no more "Rett's Disorder," "Childhood Disintegrative Disorder," or "Pervasive Developmental Disorder," and no more "Asperger's Syndrome." Instead the broad, stand-alone term "Autism Disorder" or "Autism Spectrum Disorder" would be crafted in such a way as to be inclusive and representative of all of these constellations of symptoms.

The impetus for this highly controversial proposal relates to the ambiguous differentiations among the various subtypes. The APA suspects that difficulty applying the criteria has led to inconsistent diagnoses among practitioners. Many practitioners are inclined to embrace this movement toward clarification, consistency, and simplification. However, many clients and their families fear oversimplification, and worry that the significantly variable functioning levels among the subtypes may get lost in the consolidation. If you're interested, check www.barbaraboroson.com for updated information and revised classifications.

typical development for at least the first two years of life in the areas of socialization, speech and language, play, motor development, and self-care. But between the ages of two and ten years old, these children show a clinically significant loss of previously acquired developmental skills in those areas, leading them to look very much like a child with classic autism.

5. The fifth subtype of autism spectrum disorder is *Pervasive Developmental Disorder Not Otherwise Specified (PDD-NOS)*, including Atypical Autism. This is the one that seems to cause most of the confusion in terms of nomenclature. Something of a catch-all, loosely defined category, PDD-NOS describes individuals who possess *some* of the characteristics usually found on the autism spectrum, but either do not exhibit enough of the traits or the traits exhibited are not to a significant enough degree to meet the official diagnostic criteria.

Students as People

If you can keep straight the subtle and not-so-subtle distinctions among the subtypes of autism spectrum disorders, good for you; and if you can't, that's okay, too. In my work, I have encountered many children on the autism spectrum whose precise address along the spectrum is unclear or inconsistent. And what I've discovered is that the name of their diagnostic subtype does not dictate the details of their functioning, education, or identity.

The details are in the individuals. Your success with any student on the spectrum ultimately depends on the same factors on which your success with any other student depends: the whole person each student brings to the table; how you respond to him and how he responds to you. Each student with an autism spectrum disorder is as unique as any other: He has his own strengths and weaknesses, his own likes and dislikes, his own patterns of action and reaction, his own past and future, his own personality, his own potential, and his own dreams.

FIRST IMPRESSIONS

Some students in your class will have been identified as *students in need of special education,* as *students on the autism spectrum,* or other similar designation prior to arriving on your doorstep. They may be first introduced to you via their Individualized Educational Programs (IEPs) and packets of evaluations, test scores, and recommendations. (See more on IEPs on pages 22–23.) Some will bear a painful personal history of failure, the cause of which has never been adequately identified or addressed. Still others will have issues that are first emerging as problems only now, as the academic and social demands at school intensify. Regardless of where they've been or what paperwork accompanies them, your journey together begins now. The weather forecast calls for variable sun and clouds.

Partly Sunny With Some Clouds

Since every student is so different from every other, you really can't know what to expect when you first meet a student on the autism spectrum. One student on the spectrum, for example, may present as surprisingly poised and related, greeting you with direct eye contact, a confident *Nice to meet you,* or an impressive exposition on the weather. You may find yourself wondering why she has been identified as she has—she seems totally typical. But any of these factors may also be at play:

- The challenges for this student may be in such specific areas that they don't necessarily manifest in brief encounters.
- This student may have memorized the rote and predictable elements of a conventional greeting.
- This student may be very bright and highly articulate, but only on a specific topic *of her choosing.* You may not realize at first that despite the fact that she provided you with the long-range meteorological forecast, she is unable to carry on a two-way conversation on this or any other subject.
- She may be able to blend into the crowd seamlessly until something on her rigid roster of rules goes awry; then suddenly her "autism" shows in a big way.
- She may seem absolutely typical as you get acquainted conversationally. But tomorrow she may try to engage you in exactly the same conversation she had with you today.

Partly Cloudy With Some Sun

On the other hand, some students on the spectrum wear their challenges on their sleeves. They may have a peculiar rhythm or cadence to their speech, their language may be incomprehensible, they may make no eye contact, they may flap their hands, rock in place, grimace, chirp, or exhibit other idiosyncratic mannerisms. You may find yourself wondering why these students have been placed in your class and how you will possibly break through.

Remember that these students may be unavailable to you in conventional ways because they are busily preoccupied trying to manage their anxiety, adapt to their sensory surroundings, curb their impulses, or keep their hands still, and simply cannot do all of that and carry on a conversation, too. These students may actually be capable of engaging in academic, esoteric, or other pursuits, but not in the context of overwhelming stimulation and not in a socially conventional way. They may be very aware of the social world around them, while profoundly unaware of how to enter it.

CLIMATE CONTROL

Regardless of how your students on the spectrum present themselves, the forecast for success in the classroom will depend largely on you. You are the weathermaker. You determine not only the seating arrangement and elements of the curriculum, but you also create predictable routines to keep the heat down. You set the barometer for social acceptance. You use sensory strategies to protect against sudden blustery squalls. And you keep your eye on the horizon, always watchful for the subtle signs of heavy storms brewing in the distance, and ever at the ready with comfort and shelter when the rains come pouring down.

The Special Ed Process

Now that you understand some of the basic terminology of diagnosis and a bit of what to expect, let's look at the details of the process through which supports and services may be provided for students on the spectrum.

Given that the average age of diagnosis for Autistic Disorder is three years old, you may have students in your classroom who were diagnosed with a spectrum disorder quite a while ago. These students may have many years of special education support and individualized services behind them and arrive in your classroom with various supports and services already in place. (See the section on Intensive Therapeutic Programming later in this chapter.)

Other students, however, may not yet have been identified as having special needs when they come to you. In fact, the average age for diagnosis of Asperger's Syndrome is between seven and eleven years old (Howlin & Asgharian, 1999; Mandell, Novak, & Zubritsky, 2005). These students may be so articulate and bright that they have been able to function adequately at school in the early years—presenting as a bit quirky, perhaps, but not raising any red flags. Yet as they move through the elementary years, the curriculum begins to require abstraction and higher-level thinking, and socialization begins to demand spontaneity and reciprocity. So now, in the mid-to-late elementary years, "quirkiness" descends into "dysfunction," and the academic and social gaps become apparent and problematic.

Whether you are working with students who are already known to be on the autism spectrum or students you *suspect* are on the spectrum, you can be sure they will need more support than do typical students. They may need ongoing specialized instruction and individualized supports, both inside and outside the classroom, to enable them to function successfully in the mainstream.

Fortunately, there are many federal, state, and district guidelines and systems that exist to help. As you embark on this journey, know that having students on the spectrum in your class does not imply that you need to have all the answers or solutions. It does not mean that you should be staying up all night creating a parallel or modified curriculum for one or two students. It does not suggest that you must single-handedly carry the burden of the diverse and intense needs of your whole class. Instead, make use of the services and supports that are out there. Rather than expecting or pressuring yourself to be a hero or a savior, try thinking of yourself as a champion, an advocate who can help students on the spectrum get what they need. Join the charge, along with the parents or caregivers and the multidisciplinary team at your school, to advocate for the programming and supports necessary to help these students find success.

Here is a description of some of the systems and supports that may be available and how to gain access to them. Going to bat for your students on the spectrum will rally a team of supporters around them and around you, and help make this placement work for everyone.

Response-to-Intervention (RtI)

Most likely, when you perceive skill or performance deficits in students, intuition guides you to modify your classroom or instruction slightly to compensate for the deficits. Under the Individuals With Disabilities Education Improvement Act of 2004 (IDEIA), this previously intuitive approach has gone legislative. Response-to-Intervention (RtI) is an initiative that directs teachers to collect data over time, intervene and adjust instruction as needed, and monitor responses, all according to a tiered system.

While details can vary from district to district, a Tier 1 RtI plan usually indicates time-limited, in-class supplemental instruction to address minor skill and performance gaps among students considered to be at-risk based on standardized testing. But if skill and performance deficits are shown to persist in certain students, RtI directs teachers to shift to a Tier 2 plan. In these instances, specific interventions are designed on a case-by-case basis by the school's multidisciplinary, child-study, or RtI team and then implemented and measured. The interventions at this level can extend beyond the classroom to include instruction from reading or other academic specialists, or related services that can be offered in school by specially trained professionals, such as speech and language therapy, occupational therapy, physical therapy, and school counseling. Responses to these Tier 2 interventions are closely monitored and adjusted as needed.

If a student's skill and performance base is demonstrated as not responsive to Tier 2 interventions, a greater level of support is indicated. At this point, a multidisciplinary evaluation process is recommended to determine the presence of a disability, and the need for Tier 3 special education intervention, which offers a more intense level of support than can be provided at the Tier 1 and Tier 2 levels. Many districts require schools to provide documentation of their efforts at Tier 1 and Tier 2 RtI-based interventions before a referral for a special education evaluation will be accepted.

You will find that students who are or may be on the autism spectrum will likely need the more intensive supports that a Tier 3 special education qualification provides. When used in combination, differentiated strategies and special education provisions can make your classroom a fertile and responsive learning environment for all kinds of students. What follows is an overview of the steps necessary to obtain special education supports.

The Evaluation Process

A district-level, Tier 3 multidisciplinary team will determine which of the following evaluations to conduct for any given student based on the challenges you have documented.

Psychological Evaluation: A psychologist assesses the student's intelligence (according to IQ testing) and emotional coping skills. The psychologist or other clinical professional may also meet with parents or guardians to assemble a social history, which would include developmental milestones, birth and family data, living circumstances, and any other potentially relevant personal information.

[handwritten: IQ PROJECTIVES SOCIAL HIST. BACKGROUND]

Educational Evaluation: An educational evaluator assesses academic achievement in terms of broad and specific math and reading skills. These skills are scored according to age- and grade-equivalent norms.

[handwritten: ACADEMIC ACH.]

Academic achievement findings can be especially informative when compared to the IQ scores. A significant discrepancy between achievement and potential raises a red flag that there may be an important disconnect between the student's *capacity* to learn and his *actual* learning that could indicate the need for a different style of instruction.

[handwritten: Disconnect between ability and achievement]

Physical and/or Occupational Therapy Evaluation: A physical therapist assesses gross-motor skills (such as climbing stairs, jumping, running, and so on). An occupational therapist assesses fine-motor skills (such as gripping a pencil, cutting

[handwritten: P.T.]

Bringing the Family on Board

Be sure to keep parents or guardians up to date throughout the entire process. Share with them the persistence of behaviors, the data you have collected, the interventions you have tried, the impressions of other professionals in the building, and the recommendations of the team. Encourage them to share their own interpretations of the issue. But be aware that this may be very emotional territory for parents or guardians. Some will welcome your efforts while others may reject your observations. Take a look at Chapter 6 before broaching new concerns with parents and guardians.

Written consent from a parent or guardian is required to initiate a referral to the multidisciplinary team for Tier 3 evaluations. You or the school counselor should explain the evaluation process to parents or guardians (as described below), assuring them that a referral is a means of determining the best ways to support their child's success. Share that students tend to enjoy the individual attention and the activities they do with trained evaluators. And assure parents or guardians that evaluations are conducted individually and confidentially and can be provided by the district at no cost to the family.

with scissors, manipulating small objects) and sensory integration (the way sensory input is received in the brain). In many cases a student's overall academic or behavioral functioning may be significantly compromised by matters of coordination or sensory integration. (See more on motor issues and sensory integration in Chapter 4.)

Speech and Language Evaluation: A speech and language therapist or pathologist evaluates the student's ability to receive and express information via the use of speech and language. Often even a student who is quite articulate can have significant delays or distortions in his processing of language. Conversely, students who have very limited speech may in fact have strong language comprehension skills that might otherwise have been overlooked. (See more on speech and language in Chapter 8.)

Results of Evaluation

When all evaluations have been completed, a meeting of the team is convened to synthesize all results and paint a complete picture of the student's functioning in terms of strengths, challenges, and needs. (Typically these meetings include the classroom teacher, the student's parents or guardians, all contributing evaluators, a special education teacher representative, a psychologist, the committee chair, and sometimes other professionals or family members as well.)

The goal of the evaluative process is to ensure that every student has access to a Free Appropriate Public Education (FAPE). If the process determines that the student's current educational program is not appropriate to meet her needs, program placement must be changed or modifications and accommodations must be enacted, in accordance with the IDEIA.

As a result of this process, an assortment of the following recommendations may be put into place.

DOCUMENTATION

504 Plan: Students who are found to have a *discrete physical or mental challenge* that directly impedes their ability to function at school (for example, challenges related to walking, breathing, seeing, hearing, speaking, writing, reading, and so on) may qualify for a Section 504 Accommodation Plan under the Rehabilitation Act of the Americans with Disabilities Act (ADA).

This civil rights statute protects students from discrimination on the basis of impairment, and thereby grants certain accommodations to allow them equal *access* to education. A Section 504 Plan, which is individually crafted by the team according to ADA regulations, essentially levels the playing field, granting compensatory accommodations such as preferential seating, large print texts, a ramp into the school building, adaptive technology, and so on. Once provided with such tools, these students can reap the full benefit of their educational program. (See more on adaptive technology in Chapters 8 and 10.)

IEP: In contrast, an Individualized Education Plan (IEP) is a legal document under the auspices of the IDEIA. If the student in question is determined to be a student in need of special education (also known as being *identified* or *classified*), the team creates an IEP according to IDEIA regulations.

IEPs are reserved for students who need more than a leveled playing field. Preferential seating or large print texts would not be enough to give these students equal access to education. These students have conditions that require specialized instruction and support systems in order for them to learn and function in an educational setting. All provisions that might have been granted in a 504 Plan may be included under the broader reach of an IEP.

Based on the determinations of the evaluative team, an IEP does the following:

- classifies a student as being in need of special education
- mandates a type of classroom or school program and a student/teacher ratio
- mandates the types, frequencies, and student/teacher ratios of supplementary services
- grants specific program accommodations and modifications (see below)
- presents long-term goals and short-term benchmarks for every aspect of the student's program

The IEP is a blueprint for a student's learning environment and must be followed closely and updated every year. The student's progress toward meeting his or her IEP goals will depend on your efforts to do the following:

- actively pursue the acquisition of academic, social, and behavioral benchmarks with an eye toward long-term goal achievement
- oversee the implementation of accommodations and modifications
- keep data regarding progress and concerns
- stay alert to specific conditions or circumstances that affect this student's ability to function
- facilitate collaboration and continuity among all members of the team, including the family
- report on the student's progress at multidisciplinary team meetings

ACCOMMODATIONS AND MODIFICATIONS

Accommodations are changes made to a student's program that allow for equal access to instruction or assessments. Accommodations do not alter the standards of learning; they only seek to reduce the effect a disability has on the student's access to education. Accommodations can be granted according to the following four categories:

- *presentation of information*, which provides supports such as "talking textbooks" or "directions read and clarified"

- *response options*, which could allow students to fulfill assignments in alternative ways, such as orally or using spell check, or other adaptive technology

- *setting considerations*, such as "preferential seating" or "separate location for testing"

- *timing and scheduling adjustments*, such as extra time to complete their work, or periodic breaks during work activities

Modifications, on the other hand, refer to changes made to the actual curricular standards in order to meet the needs of the student. Some modifications are intended only for use during certain kinds of testing; others apply across the board. Common modifications include reducing the amount of class work and/or homework or simplifying the content of the curriculum to meet a student's level.

You will be expected to consider and recommend specific accommodations and/or modifications for your students who have 504 Plans and IEPs. Most districts use 504 Plan- and IEP-generating computer programs that offer menus from which to select appropriate accommodations, modifications, and relevant academic goals. All of these options are considered and discussed by the evaluative team before they are approved as a part of the official document.

PROGRAM OPTIONS

The evaluative team is obligated to pursue placement in the *least restrictive environment (LRE)* based on each student's specific needs. This means that every student must participate in mainstream programming and assessments, learning alongside typical students, to the greatest extent possible. For every student, the team is required to consider all placement options, beginning with least restrictive. When an appropriate placement recommendation is agreed upon, reasons for rejecting all less restrictive placements must be justified on the IEP.

Educational placement options for students on the autism spectrum range from least restrictive, such as a mainstream classroom setting, to most restrictive, such as homebound instruction or in-patient hospitalization. In between lies a wide variety of options mandated on the basis of the student's specific strengths and challenges. (Students in *any* placement may qualify for accommodations and modifications to their program.)

Here is a list of program options, beginning with the least restrictive.

Mainstream Program: A mainstream program is a full-size class run by one credentialed regular-education teacher.

Supplementary Services: Regardless of educational placement, most students on the autism spectrum qualify for supplementary pull-out or push-in services in conjunction with their program. These mandated services may include occupational therapy, speech and language therapy, physical therapy, counseling, consultant teacher support, resource room, reading support, and more. (Whether or not students qualify for in-school supplementary services, parents or guardians may opt to obtain these services privately outside of school, at their personal expense.)

Integrated Co-Teaching Program (also known as *Inclusion*): This model integrates typical students with those who have special needs in a full-size class, and provides full-time collaboration of a credentialed regular education teacher and a credentialed special education teacher.

Integrated settings offer the advantage of full-time special education in the context of the general population. Many students on the spectrum benefit from participating in a typical social and academic environment with the support of the special education teacher, and this model is quickly gaining popularity.

Special Class Program (also known as *Self-Contained*): A special class program is a small, self-contained special education class with a student:teacher:assistant ratio of 12:1:2 or even 6:1:2. These classes offer more specialized instruction and protection from the mainstream than inclusion classes do, but, by the same token, less access to the social modeling of typical peers.

One-to-One Support: To support success in any of the above settings, some students are appointed a full- or part-time one-to-one aide. An aide's role is to provide individual academic, social, and behavioral support, while at the same time fading into the background whenever possible to facilitate independence. Aides may be appointed to support students on the spectrum in their efforts to engage, attend, communicate, transition, socialize, and modulate their reactions.

Out-of-District Placement: Often smaller public school districts, which have relatively small numbers of students needing special education, establish a system of reciprocity with neighboring districts. In these arrangements, special education services, resources, and funding are shared and available to students in both districts.

Non-Public Placement: If the district's evaluative team determines that the public school system does not have the ability to provide the kind of programming a student needs, they may suggest a non-public placement, which is a privately run, publicly funded, special education day school. Since all of the students in this type of program have special needs, this is a more restrictive placement than any of the aforementioned. Non-public placements can be fully self-contained day schools or hospital- or clinic-based day-treatment centers.

Residential Treatment: Students who are unable to be kept safe or function successfully in their restrictive school setting or at home may qualify for a residential treatment center where they receive clinical supervision around the clock.

Homebound Instruction or In-Patient Hospitalization: For crisis or other extreme situations, some students may qualify for temporary homebound instruction or be referred for in-patient psychiatric hospitalization.

In addition to the program options listed above, some students may have received private therapeutic programming from a very early age. The next section is a brief summary of several popular interventions.

Intensive Therapeutic Programming

Parents or guardians of young students on the spectrum may opt for intensive treatment programs that seek to address global autism spectrum symptoms, such as responsivity, flexibility, regulation, socialization, and more. Students on the spectrum may have received many years of treatment or training prior to joining your class or may continue to receive intensive support outside of school.

Although each program features a different emphasis and approach, they all seek to help students learn and unlearn certain behaviors, in the service of reaching developmental milestones and pursuing independence and engagement in the world. Some of the most commonly used home-based approaches include Applied Behavior Analysis (ABA), Pivotal Response Treatment (PRT), DIR/Floortime, and Relationship Development Intervention (RDI).

Providers of intensive treatment programs must be specifically trained and certified to practice each methodology. Although such programs are not designed to be implemented by mainstream classroom teachers who are untrained in the techniques, you may find it useful to be aware of these methods, since some of your students on the spectrum may be participants in or graduates of these extracurricular programs. (To learn more about any of these intensive programs, please visit www.barbaraboroson.com.)

The TEACCH Program

TEACCH (Treatment and Education of Autistic and Communication-related handicapped CHildren) is somewhat different from the programs listed above because it is school-based and is built on the belief that students on the spectrum have the capacity to function productively and independently in a *highly structured environment*.

Though the TEACCH program can be implemented only by trained TEACCH instructors, many of the structured teaching elements of TEACCH are woven through the pages of this book, and can be implemented simply in any kind of classroom.

STRUCTURED TEACHING

Some of the basic principles of structured teaching address the following:

- individualizing instruction and intervention (more on individualizing instruction in Chapters 5 and 10)

- organizing the physical classroom space in order to minimize distractions, maximize organization, and facilitate independence (more on organizational and sensory strategies in Chapter 4)

- adhering to visually presented schedules and routines to reduce anxiety, facilitate independence, and help students understand what is expected of them (more on visual cues in Chapters 3 and 8)

Alternative Therapies

Some parents or guardians pursue medication or other alternative therapeutic interventions, outside the school environment. Listening Therapy programs (based on the work of Alfred Tomatis) can be purchased or provided at specific listening centers to help build new sensory connections and desensitize problematic reactions to auditory stimuli. Vision Therapy, provided by a Developmental Optometrist, works to improve visual processing and visual motor coordination through the use of eye exercises. Additionally, Chiropractic Therapy, CranioSacral Therapy, Biofeedback, Hippotherapy (therapeutic horseback riding), nutritional strategies, and other approaches have all been suggested to offer benefits. While these therapies are time-consuming and often very expensive, many parents and guardians believe strongly in their effectiveness.

Now that you have a sense of who students on the autism spectrum are and where they may have been, it's time to prepare for what will be. Chapter 2 will help get you in the best frame of mind to approach the challenges ahead.

The Power of Positivity

You Can Do This!

As you begin this journey with students on the autism spectrum, you may be nearly as anxious as they are. Even though you likely have better developed coping skills, greater flexibility, and savvier social instincts than they do, the prospect of attending to the needs of each individual student in your diverse class probably feels pretty overwhelming. Maybe you don't even feel up to the challenge. This chapter will explore ways to help you stay hopeful and to use your optimistic attitude to set an example for everyone around you, especially the students themselves. Your belief in their ability to grow and your efforts to make it happen will be the most powerful catalysts for success.

Keeping Yourself Going

If you had wanted to be a special ed teacher, you would have become a special ed teacher, right? Presumably, integrating students with significant special needs into your mainstream classroom was not what you bargained for when you signed up for gen ed.

I would love to tell you that despite the challenges you and your students on the spectrum face together, the growth and development you see over the year will be breathtaking and rewarding; that by year's end you will be bursting with pride and basking in a bright spotlight, showcasing evidence of your stunning success, your miraculous ability to coax a butterfly from a seemingly empty cocoon.

I would love to tell you that. But I can't. It's just not going to be that flashy. Instead, progress is more likely to be resoundingly quiet, conspicuously subtle. If you don't look carefully, you might even miss it. But don't let yourself miss it because the progress you do make will be more powerful and more gratifying than anything you've ever done, as long as you tune in to a new set of personal goals and expectations. When your personal goal is to capture those brilliant moments that happen when you make a connection with a student on the spectrum—those fleeting moments when you reach *and* teach—you will catch a glimpse of that butterfly and you will be awed and renewed.

The Power of Progress

The ability to look for and recognize progress in unusual and unexpected places will go a long way toward helping you sustain yourself through your journey with students on the spectrum. Achievement and mastery of conventional goals may be elusive. So as you work to adapt your program to address the needs of these students, you will also need to adapt your idea of *progress*—expanding your own personal definition of what individual student progress looks like and what teacher progress feels like. Look carefully for huge victories in small places. For example, several months into kindergarten, Damien still drops his backpack on the floor in the middle of the classroom, where other students trip on it until he is prompted to put it in his cubby. When the day finally comes that Damien independently drops his backpack on the floor right in front of his cubby and *no one* trips on it, this *non*-event might go unnoticed. Even though Damien's backpack has still not quite made it into his cubby, for him this is terrific progress. Look closely or you might miss it.

THREE STEPS FORWARD, TWO STEPS BACK

In some cases, progress will feel, at best, as though you're taking three steps forward and two steps back. You may need to walk certain students over the same two steps dozens of times, adjusting terms and expectations as you go, before you can move forward together. It takes patience. It takes hope. And it takes belief in your students and yourself.

It Takes a Village

There will be days when you just can't find anything to feel good about. Nothing seems to be getting through. Nothing. Remember that you are not alone. As you rally a team of support around your students on the spectrum, you are also rallying a team of support around yourself. No one person can address the myriad needs of a student with "pervasive" challenges. Lean on those who have been there, who have had similar experiences, who have pushed through the frustrations, who may even be able to help you find something good to take from the day. Rely on colleagues who may be able to offer practical support: the occupational therapist, the speech and language specialist, the school counselor, a special education teacher. Look through the pages of this book. And visit www.barbaraboroson.com for more ideas, tools, strategies, and supportive words to help keep you going.

Keep an Open Mind

Most of the time, big struggles can be ameliorated by small fixes. When big struggles leave you feeling discouraged and depleted, try to hold on to the fact that very often the resolution is surprisingly simple once you determine the purpose of the challenging behavior. All behavior serves a communicative purpose. Behavior is a way all students can signal that something is amiss. Many behavioral triggers that are common among students on the spectrum can be easily addressed and smoothed over. Approaching behaviors according to this way of thinking will help you ride out the big struggles with competence and confidence.

By the time you finish reading this book, you'll be adept at figuring out what might have sparked a behavioral reaction or what is standing in the way of learning. You will be able to implement simple tweaks, quick adjustments that will make all the difference. Once you learn to recognize the antecedent of a challenging behavior, resolving the issue may be as simple as restating instructions in more concrete terms, changing some elements of the physical space in your classroom, or offering diverse tools or systems to your diverse collection of learners. Open your mind to creative ideas; your efforts have the potential to generate a lifetime of possibility for students on the spectrum and a world of difference for your entire classroom community.

If you keep watch for small signs of progress and trust in the ultimate potential for net growth among students on the spectrum, you will become a believer. And as long as you believe, anything is possible. Even if yesterday one of your students on the spectrum took ten steps back, even if his pot boiled over, and even if you got burned, begin today as a brand new day, full of potential and promise. Thinking positive will keep you feeling positive, which will be the best predictor of success.

Spotlight on Strengths

Let's face it: the innumerable challenges of working with students on the autism spectrum jump into our minds unbidden, and vent readily out of our mouths. But if we focus only on the negative, then, just like the students themselves, we run the risk of becoming pessimistic, getting lost in the struggles, and never finding our way out. What hope is there for struggling students when the people around them don't celebrate or even note their strengths?

This section will help you emphasize strengths so that you can maintain an optimistic outlook and model it for your students and for everybody else around them.

First . . . Then

Each of the remaining chapters of this book (Chapters 3–10) describes an area of struggle—and they all come *after* this chapter, which is all about strengths and positivity.

PUTTING STRENGTHS ON THE TABLE

There are always strengths, even if they are only relative to areas of challenge. Look for competence in unexpected places, because otherwise, in the face of all the challenges, you might overlook them altogether.

For example, in Sasha's nursery school class, the students were being taught to recognize their own names. The teachers had labeled each seat with the name of a student. Every morning, when students arrived for school, they were expected to find their names and sit in their designated chairs. However, later in the day, the chairs were redistributed around the rug for circle time and students were told to sit in any chair. Three-and-a-half-year-old Sasha routinely elbowed other students out of her way at circle time to get to the chair with her own name on it: she would not sit in any other chair, and no one could sit in *her* chair. Sasha would then direct Mira to the chair that said *Mira* on it, pointed Michael toward the chair that said *Michael*, Marcie to the *Marcie* chair, and so on.

Sasha's teachers were frustrated with her "inflexibility" and "aggression" and "inability to follow classroom rules," and they asked me to come in for a consult. Indeed, Sasha had been showing some rigidity and impulsivity in other areas that warranted further investigation. But in this particular circumstance, I first pointed out that the on-again, off-again assigned seating system was, in fact, confusing. We resolved that problem easily by putting the students' names in fixed positions *on the tables* instead of on the chairs. Now the labels had consistent value, and the chairs were freed up for more flexible use.

But another issue had become apparent as well. While focused on maintaining order in the classroom, all three teachers had completely overlooked the fact that Sasha was demonstrating, at three years old, that she had learned a dozen sight words: not just her own name, but the names of every student in her class. That fact, no one had noticed.

WHY ACCENTUATE THE POSITIVE?

The struggles of students on the autism spectrum pervade most areas of their functioning. There is little that they do that is not made more difficult by their wide array of challenges. This compilation of overwhelming experiences and failures is relentlessly stressful and anxiety-provoking for them. It is also a tried-and-true recipe for low self-esteem, depression, and self-destructive behavior. Those debilitating secondary conditions are frequently seen in adolescents and adults with autism spectrum disorders.

Paradoxically, individuals who are higher functioning on the autism spectrum are at even greater risk for depression than their lower functioning peers on the spectrum. This is, in part, because higher functioning students on the spectrum are both blessed and cursed with awareness of their condition and their differences. My own son, who is on the spectrum, cried many nights in bed as he reflected on the hurts of the day, coming to terms in painful increments with the facts of his disability and his deepening feelings of differentness.

All students arrive in your classroom already in possession of specific strengths. Among students on the spectrum, these strengths, remarkable as they may be, are often overshadowed by concomitant challenges. As a teacher, you know to look for strengths, but others in their lives will not look past their obvious quirks and inadequacies. The world around these students will offer a steady stream of negative feedback, failure, and rejection.

While the special strengths or interests of students on the spectrum may not be in conventional academic areas, they are still worthy of admiration and recognition. Find them and *use them*—even if they don't specifically fit into your curriculum—as a way to blaze a trail of respect all around those students, weaving it among their families, among their peers, among your peers, and within themselves.

Special Interests and Abilities

Here are some common strengths students on the spectrum often possess. Find out whether students in your class have any of these or other exceptional strengths. Then read on to see how to use those strengths to promote an atmosphere of positivity, acceptance, and respect.

STRENGTH: THE EXPERT

Some students on the spectrum become experts in areas of special interest to them. They may excel in assembling jigsaw puzzles or solving mazes, or demonstrate a remarkable sense of direction. Others may have exceptional talents in the arts, such as painting, sculpture, musical performance, or acting. Some have in-depth understandings of the intricate inner workings of cars, planes, computers, or any other type of technology.

They may be internal schedule keepers, keeping track of anything from your classroom schedule, to classmates' birthdays, school holidays, city bus schedules, or lunar phases. They may know the date of every Thanksgiving going back to the Kennedy assassination, or keep track of what television shows aired on each network during prime time hours dating back twenty years. You will find that some have an astonishing capacity for memorizing information such as mathematical facts, movie trivia, classroom rules, historical dates, state capitals, maps, species of dinosaurs, baseball statistics, train routes, international flags, and more.

> **ON THE OTHER HAND . . .**
>
> See Chapter 5 to learn about the social challenges that result from preoccupations with special interest areas and what you can do to help.

STRENGTH: THE COOPERATOR

Chances are, no one will be more invested in your classroom rules and schedule than students on the autism spectrum. These students will cling to your classroom structure as a lifeline for guidance and reassurance. By providing a clear structure of expectations, you enable them to anticipate and mentally prepare for whatever comes next. It is truly their pleasure to adhere to—and enforce—your rules and schedule. When they know exactly what's expected of them, students on the spectrum recognize a rare opportunity to strive confidently for success.

So you may find students on the spectrum to be extremely eager to please and cooperative. *As long as your schedule is clear*, these students will likely be first in line—always aware, for example, of when it's time to move out to music class. *As long as your expectations and organizational systems are clear*, they'll be reliably prepared, always wearing their sneakers on physical education day, always ready in their seat when the bell rings to start the day. *As long as your rules are clear and routines are consistent*, they may well be Jiminy

> **ON THE OTHER HAND . . .**
>
> See Chapter 3 to learn about the challenges related to rigid rule-following and what you can do to help.

Crickets on your shoulder—reminding you that take-home books are supposed to be returned to the homework bin and not put back on the shelf, or that you forgot to collect the pencils before reading time.

STRENGTH: THE TRUTH-TELLER

Lying is a tool that some people use purposefully to evoke specific reactions in other people. To lie, we need to first anticipate how another person will react to our words, and manipulate those reactions to our own benefit. We have to consider: *If I tell the truth, I might hurt her feelings.* Or *If I tell the truth, I might get in trouble.* Or *If I tell the truth, everyone might laugh at me, but if I make up something cool, everyone will like me.*

ON THE OTHER HAND . . .

See Chapter 7 to learn about the social challenges related to honesty and what you can do to help.

So, believe it or not, being *dishonest* requires the ability to understand and predict the feelings, thoughts, and reactions of others—a skill that is often quite limited in individuals with autism spectrum disorders.

Without the capacity to *put themselves* inside other people's minds and anticipate reactions, many students on the autism spectrum are incapable of dishonesty or manipulation. Recognizing no reason to lie, perhaps even unaware of the concept of lying, they are naturally, spontaneously, and often refreshingly honest. (See more on *mindblindness* in Chapter 7.)

Honesty is a great strength to celebrate with students on the spectrum. Enjoy your faithful truth tellers. Though unmitigated honesty may not be socially savvy, let us remember that honesty still is, technically, the best policy.

Using Strengths to Blaze a Trail of Respect

Since students on the autism spectrum are not always able to put their best foot forward, here are some ways you can showcase their strengths to help them step out in style.

Promoting Positivity Among Classmates

Your attitude toward your students on the spectrum will shape how they are viewed and treated by peers. If you allow yourself to focus on challenging behaviors, other students certainly won't be able to see beyond them either. Classmates have the capacity to see their peers on the spectrum from many perspectives: They may see them as weird or annoying, as scapegoats or victims, or even as geniuses—depending in large part on how you set the tone. If you demonstrate how much you value and appreciate the strengths of your students on the spectrum, and represent them as people who are more than their challenges, your words will grant them status as contributing members of your classroom community, and you will be modeling an atmosphere of true acceptance. (See more on building classroom communities in Chapter 7.)

Take a moment to consider what strengths your students on the spectrum can contribute, and actively look for ways to utilize those strengths publicly, by assimilating them into your classroom language. Here are some examples:

- If a student's strength is schedule-keeping, demonstrate your confidence in his skill: *Ravi, please tell everyone what we will do right after science.*

- If a student's strength is memory, show the class that you trust her: *Jessica, what was the name of that man who showed us around the museum last month?*

- If a student's strength is knowing the state capitals, consult him as an authority: *Antoine, help me out here: What's the capital of Wisconsin?*

Creative thinking and conscious effort on your part will open and establish new channels of association between your students on the spectrum and their classmates.

Promoting Positivity for Parents and Caregivers

Ravi cannot stop wiggling his fingers in front of his eyes. Jessica's handwriting is illegible. Antoine can't find his way around the school building. But when talking to parents and caregivers, try opening with remarks like these:

- *Ravi is right on top of the schedule. He is always where he's supposed to be.*

- *Jessica has an amazing memory. I count on her to remind me where we left off every day.*

- *Antoine is our best geography player.*

These kinds of comments are important in several ways. Your acknowledgment of students' strengths gives their parents and caregivers something to feel proud of. They will be pleased to hear how their children can incorporate atypical skills into useful classroom tools. Remember, these parents and caregivers probably have not had many gratifying moments when discussing their children with teachers. Your positive presentation will not only warm their hearts; it will also foster a positive relationship between you and them, which will facilitate the parents' or caregivers' ability to hear, accept, and collaborate when you go on to present your concerns.

Promoting Positivity for Your Team

Team meetings and impromptu collegial conversations are valuable opportunities to vent negative feelings and bounce ideas off each other—and that's important. Whatever frustrations you're feeling, chances are other professionals who work with students on the spectrum share them, too. Meanwhile, offering anecdotes of positive experiences helps uphold the perspective that these students are more than their challenges. Your effort to look for and talk about strengths will reflect your optimism and ability to see the whole child. As the primary teacher, you are in the best position to model positivity for the team, just as you do for your class.

Promoting Positivity for Students on the Spectrum

The greatest benefit of being positive in the classroom is the message you're sending Ravi or Jessica or Antoine. Even though Ravi can't stop wiggling his fingers long enough to catch a ball, he knows exactly what time recess begins and ends and what will be served for lunch in the cafeteria each day. Although Jessica's handwriting is illegible, she is a great resource for historical information. And while Antoine can't find his way to the nurse's office, he has an impeccably organized filing system of state capitals in his head. Imagine how good students on the spectrum will feel when they are given the opportunity to offer their skills to the class; when they get singled out for what they *can* do, and not only for what they can't.

Laura, a third-grade teacher, knew that computation was an area of strength for one of her students. Juan had memorized the times tables before the school year began and knew multiplication facts instantly. Even though he was struggling socially and was way behind on reading comprehension, Laura saw an opportunity to let him shine. One day, when Juan had completed his multiplication worksheet before anyone else had, she asked him to have a seat at her desk. She told the other students to hand in their worksheets to Juan, gave him her red correcting pen, and invited him to help her out by correcting the worksheets. Juan was thrilled not only to be singled out to correct the worksheets, but to be given a seat of honor in which to do it. Years later, Juan still remembers that moment as his favorite experience of elementary school.

PRAISE THE PROCESS

There are many opportunities to criticize and correct students on the spectrum. When we look closely at their strengths, we begin to notice that frequently the work they produce is not reflective of their potential because they so often get derailed along the way. They may lose focus or misunderstand instructions. They may be hindered in their efforts by sensory, social, language, organizational, motor, or other challenges. Don't wait until the worksheet or the project or the interaction is completed to comment on it, because the final outcome may not seem praiseworthy. Once you check the math test, you may find that many of the problems were done incorrectly. At that point, the student's good effort will have been overshadowed by a poor outcome, and an opportunity for praise and encouragement will have been missed. You and they will get discouraged.

✳ **Catch the Moment:** Whenever you see a student on the spectrum working diligently, sitting quietly, listening attentively, interacting appropriately, reacting calmly—whenever you catch them *in the moment* of doing the right thing—that's the moment to comment on. Praise the *process.* For example, *Ravi, you are really trying to keep your hands still. Jessica, I see you being careful with your handwriting.* This will inspire students to keep on doing their best and will signal to them that their excellent effort is valuable in and of itself, and will not be negated by a less-than-excellent outcome.

The Language of Positivity

As we look for and emphasize strengths, we need to be mindful of the language we use regarding students on the spectrum. These are not just semantic nuances to help you be diplomatic or politically correct. Instead these distinctions represent key ways of thinking that will inform the relationships between you and your students and between your students and everyone else. By being mindful of how you think and what you say, the degree of acceptance your students on the spectrum achieve is in your hands . . . or really, in your mouth.

What follows are some simple ways to use positive language that will inspire and reflect your positive attitude and inclusive approach.

✳ **Speaking of Strengths:** Consider that the inverse of *strength* is not necessarily *weakness*. The inverse of *strength*, in my book, is *challenge*. Again, this is a semantic difference that packs a big punch. The word *weakness* has a negative connotation and implies permanency. The word *challenge,* on the other hand, reflects a belief that a struggle is fluid and surmountable. A *challenge* is an invitation to work harder and an opportunity to grow.

✳ **So Typical:** Consider the commonly used word *normal* and its inverse, *abnormal*. Anything that is not *normal* must be *abnormal*, which means *defective*. Though students on the spectrum may be different from your other students in many ways, it serves no one to think of them as abnormal or defective.

Typical and its inverse *atypical,* however, are much kinder and more accurate descriptors of students or behaviors that are different. *Atypical* is more neutral and accepting than *abnormal,* implying difference rather than defect. Surely you already use the word *unusual* instead of *weird* for the same reasons.

✳ **What We've Got Here Is a Failure to Communicate:** Students on the spectrum often speak or act in ways that are incomprehensible to others. Sometimes we cannot understand the verbalizations of these students because of their profound articulation challenges, or because their linguistic constructions are inscrutable, as in, *Who put the bus?* **Who put the bus?** Other times students on the spectrum use their bodies in ways we don't understand—flapping their hands, spinning, and so on.

In many cases these expressive efforts seem to be non-communicative, disconnected from the topic at hand or disconnected from our reality. And so, because they are not *apparently meaningful,* professionals tend to dismiss them as *meaningless*.

While indeed these seemingly non-communicative words and behaviors do not conform to conventional definitions of meaning, they do hold meaning for the students who use them. So just because *you* don't know why a student is doing what he's doing, that doesn't mean his words or actions are without meaning. The problem is not an absence of meaning; it is a *failure to communicate meaning*.

✳ **Moving Beyond Tolerance:** Consider the difference between *tolerance* and *acceptance*. A fifth-grade teacher with the best of intentions eagerly told one parent that her son's classmates were "really learning to tolerate him!" Why did this not make the parent feel good? Because the word *tolerate* does not mean *accept. Tolerate* means "to endure without repugnance; put up with." Is that our goal? Is that the best we can do? No. We must strive for *acceptance,* which is a full-on welcoming as an equal member of society—or in this case, the classroom.

✳ ✳ ✳

Creating a positive atmosphere around all of your students and within yourself will keep everybody optimistic. And staying optimistic will optimize progress, thereby fueling the positive atmosphere. It's an upward spiral. As you read each of the remaining chapters, hold on to your strengths-first outlook as we examine how the many challenges of students on the spectrum will manifest in your classroom. Learn what they are trying to communicate and how you can address their needs calmly, confidently, competently, and . . . positively.

The Simmering Pot

Keeping the Heat Down on Anxiety

Starting with this one, each of the remaining chapters in this book addresses a specific area of challenge and offers strategies to help you prepare for, prevent, and respond to it. We begin here, with anxiety, because students on the spectrum carry it with them to every situation, every minute of every day. Continually braced against unfamiliar situations, ill-equipped to handle whatever might come next, anxiety almost always simmers just below the surface, and boils over in a flash.

This chapter will help you recognize what students' anxiety may be communicating and guide you to prepare yourself and your classroom to keep things cool, even before Day One.

Why So Anxious?

The challenges that result from having an autism spectrum disorder pervade nearly every aspect of students' lives as they try to function in the social world. The term *social world* here is not meant to imply a world full of birthday parties and play dates. Instead, *social world* refers to the communal context in which we each live an individual life while necessarily participating in the lives of others.

In the context of this social world, we are all confronted by innumerable influences that are beyond our control. These unpredictable elements range from the words, actions, and reactions of other people to the whims of technology, culture, health, weather, transportation, and many others. Really, we never know what's coming next. Yet, generally, we are able to adjust our functioning automatically from moment to moment to cope with new situations or changes to our expectations.

As you'll see throughout this book, the assortment of challenges students on the spectrum bring to the social world leaves them seriously compromised as they approach nearly any novel situation. Significant obstacles often stand in the way of socialization, engagement, communication, sensation, organization, abstract thinking, learning, self-regulation, and many other areas. Moreover, since their coping skills are inadequate to compensate for their challenges, these students learn from experience to doubt their abilities. So anxiety is always on the burner.

The next section will explore common triggers that spark anxiety for students on the spectrum and will describe how and why these students may cling tightly to certain anchors for comfort and safety.

Anxiety Triggers

Consider your own sources of anxiety. Maybe you bristle at the sound of interference on the radio or the feel of wool on your skin. Perhaps you can't stand being late or you feel uneasy leaving home without double-checking the door locks. Individual flexibility and tolerance levels vary across the many experiences we encounter in a day, but any situation can cause anxiety for someone who is sensitive to it. Generally, most of us are able to manage our reactions to our anxieties. We cover our ears, scratch our itches, take a different route, and reassure ourselves about nagging doubts.

But for students on the spectrum, when all is not in order, senses are heightened, flexibility and rationality fly out the window, and reactions can be intense, boundless, and uncontrollable. The triggers for unexpected behaviors are as variable as the potential reactions to them. Every day, the senses of these students are relentlessly assaulted, every deviation from expectation threatens equanimity, and social demands force students out of their comfort zone into perilous territory. Conventional means of verbal and nonverbal communication are ineffective, and self-regulation relinquishes control over impulses. Most likely students on the spectrum are unable to alert you to their mounting distress along the way. Sometimes their only form of communication is behavior.

For example, in his memoir *Look Me in the Eye* (2007), John Elder Robison, an adult with Asperger's Syndrome, recalls playing with blocks as a young child: "I never mixed my food, and I never mixed my blocks. Blue blocks went with blue blocks, and red blocks with red ones. But Doug would lean over and put a red block on top of the blue ones. Couldn't he see how wrong that was?! After I had whacked him, I sat back down and played. Correctly. Sometimes when I got frustrated with Doug, my mother would walk over and yell at me. I don't think she ever saw the terrible things *he* did. She just saw me whack him" (p. 7).

In the situation Robison describes, his behavior does not effectively communicate his anxiety to his mother. She makes no connection between the anxiety trigger and the behavior. And why would she? Who would have guessed that mixing the colors of blocks would trigger such a reaction? But it did. One of the most valuable strategies to use when working with students on the spectrum is *to look past a behavior to find what's behind it, what's fueling it, what the behavior is communicating.* Many sources of distress can account for difficult behaviors, such as sensory challenges, social challenges, and more. These are discussed in each of the following chapters of this book. But even behind most of those sources of distress, anxiety is brewing.

Comfort Anchors

To cope with their ever-simmering anxiety, many students on the spectrum rely heavily on certain elements of their lives to provide the consistency and predictability they crave. These are anchors that can help them feel more sturdy and in control. For example, one student may need to wear the same pants every single day. Another may need to be greeted in the same way every morning. Another may feel that all is right in the world as long as she has a baseball card in her pocket—but only if it's Derek Jeter on Mondays, Wednesdays, and Fridays, and Jose Reyes on Tuesdays and Thursdays. Equilibrium may depend on those specific anchors.

LOCAL COHERENCE

Kamran Nazeer, the author of *Send in the Idiots: Stories From the Other Side of Autism* (2006), calls the act of finding comfort in the familiar "local coherence." In his book, Nazeer describes walking into a party with his friend Craig. Both men are highly educated adults, both of them articulate and worldly, and both on the autism spectrum. Despite their achievements, being at this large, posh party is very stressful for them. They don't know exactly what to expect. They move among clusters of conversation, but find none to be on topics about which they are well versed (or really, well rehearsed). Their anxiety builds.

But Nazeer has been in this type of situation enough times that he has a plan, an ace in the hole, or more specifically, a clip in his pocket. Nazeer goes everywhere with an "alligator clip" in his pocket. Like a binder clip, this is a small clip that can be squeezed on one end and opens and closes on the other. When Nazeer feels overwhelmed, he invisibly shifts his mental focus to the clip in his pocket.

He recalls, "I opened this clip and I closed it. I opened it and held it open. I put a finger between its jaws and let go its sides . . . The alligator clip provided . . . local coherence. I could focus on what I was doing with the clip and other matters could become just a backdrop. I didn't have to worry about what I was achieving at the party. I could take a break and worry about the clip instead, which was a simpler thing to worry about, a simpler thing to understand and manipulate" (pp. 121–122).

TRIGGER SAFETY

Trigger safety in the classroom involves recognizing and respecting not only the sources of anxiety for your students on the spectrum, but also the comfort anchors they cling to and rely on. That's why you're going to want to find out about your students' specific anxiety triggers and comfort anchors before Day One. Learning as you go may be tempting but would probably prove a costly choice. You really can't afford to wait until simmering anxiety boils over. Fragile equilibrium is very difficult to restore, especially because a loss of control sometimes sets off a chain reaction of disruptive events: because he is upset, a student on the spectrum may unwittingly violate his own precious external or internal rules; the class schedule may get delayed; and other things he relies on for consistency may suddenly go awry. *The disorganization of the situation snowballs.* And by then, trust between you and this student may be gone for good.

That's why the goal of this chapter is to help you tamp down problematic situations before anxiety ever flares up. More than in any other area, when it comes to anxiety, prevention is overwhelmingly your best strategy. (Later in the book—in Chapter 9— we'll look at how to cope when, despite your preventive efforts, anxiety causes the pot to boil over.)

Common Anxiety Triggers and How to Avoid Them

Clearly, getting through the day—getting through even a moment—can be painfully challenging and anxiety provoking to students on the spectrum. Chances are, as you read this, your anxiety is bubbling up, too. Life at the helm of a roomful of students is demanding enough without having to be always braced against students' seemingly unpredictable eruptions.

Unfortunately, the fact is, many circumstances can set off anxiety reactions in students on the spectrum. This section will introduce you to common anxiety triggers for these students and will help you prepare your classroom, even before Day One, to include steady anchors for support. Even if these strategies seem time-consuming now, your investment of time in advance will save you and your students hours of anguish throughout the year by keeping anxiety on a low burner, and may very well make the difference between success and failure.

Since anxiety triggers are unlikely to be mentioned on students IEPs, this information will need to be collected anecdotally. Here are two general suggestions to ease the way.

✳ **Ask the Families:** Send home a form *before* students on the spectrum join your class, inquiring about areas of strength, sensitivity, and challenge. Parents and caregivers will likely welcome your proactive, individualized approach and be more than happy to warn you about what they've learned the hard way. Request that completed forms be returned to you quickly so you'll have a chance to plan accordingly.

This questionnaire may be the most important tool you have to get the year started on the right foot. This form will clue you in to each student's unique strengths, challenges, hot spots, and anchors, allowing you to plan and prepare for them before any triggers get pulled. You'll see that your efforts to implement many of the strategies below will be based on information you obtain from this form.

✳ **Ask the Team:** If possible, even before you meet your students on the spectrum, consult with their school support team (school counselor, occupational therapist, speech and language therapist, and so on), and previous teachers. Ask about the students' anxiety triggers. What has helped? What hasn't helped? Prepare yourself to

---

Parent/Guardian Questionnaire

Dear Families,

Please fill out the following questionnaire and return it to me by _____. Thank you for your support.

Child's Name: _____ Nickname? _____
Parent(s)/Guardian(s):
_____   _____

Phone numbers: Best times for me to reach you:
#1: _____   _____
#2: _____   _____
#3: _____   _____
#4: _____   _____

Siblings (names and ages):   _____
_____   _____
_____   _____

Please tell me some of your child's *specific* strengths and/or special interests (eg. technology, arts & crafts, history, pets, sports, books, etc.):
_____
_____
_____

What does your child find most challenging? (eg. math, reading, taking turns, listening, etc.) _____
_____
_____

What kinds of situations make your child anxious or upset? (eg. loud noises, transitions, large crowds, etc.) How does he/she tend to react? (eg. crying, yelling, running, hiding, striking out, etc.) _____
_____
_____
_____

What comforts your child when he/she is anxious or upset? (eg. quiet time, a favorite toy, etc.) What makes it worse? (eg. being asked questions, a touch on the shoulder, etc.) Please be specific: _____
_____
_____
_____

Please share any specific goals, hopes, or dreams you have for your child this year (eg. social, emotional, academic, etc.): _____
_____
_____
_____

Are there any other concerns or issues you would like me to know about or to watch out for? (feel free to continue writing on back)
_____
_____
_____

The best way for you to reach me is via _____ at:

Thank you. I look forward to working with you and with your child!

For reproducible versions of these forms, please visit www.barbaraboroson.com.

approach this student using tried and true productive tools to establish continuity and, of course, try to avoid known provocations and pitfalls.

Once you have familiarized yourself with what to expect from these new relationships, give your students on the spectrum that same opportunity by easing their transition into their new classroom, as described in the next section.

Facing Something New

One of the most overwhelming new situations students on the spectrum can face is a new school year. Everything they grew comfortable with last year is now upended. New room, new faces, new routines, new rules, new expectations—all at once.

But a little preparation can minimize the unexpectedness of it. When you take care to address specific anxiety triggers ahead of time, students on the spectrum will recognize that they are starting off on solid ground. This is particularly valuable because students on the spectrum tend to associate certain environments with certain feelings. Those associations can become imprinted. If the first day of school feels overwhelming, then a high level of anxiety may become associated with school. This association is a learned behavior and so it can be unlearned over time, but that's a bumpier road. A better bet is to make the first impression as positive as you can.

✳ **Arrange a Visit:** Offer students on the spectrum the opportunity to stop by for a visit a day or two before school begins. Students will be very reassured by familiarizing themselves with practical information such as what you look like, what the classroom looks like, where they will be sitting, and how to find the bathroom. Students with specific sensory needs may be comforted by exploring what the classroom smells like, what they can see from their desk, what kind of chairs are available, what kind of clock is on the wall, whether there are rugs in the room. Plus, any of these elements can serve as comfort anchors, reliably awaiting the student's arrival on the first day. Take a little time to chat with students, answer their questions, show them around the room, and learn about their anxieties. And best of all, send them home with (or send in the mail) a copy of the first-day schedule, as described below.

What's Next: Life on Schedule

Even once students have seen your face, heard your voice, and explored the classroom, the actual events of a day in your class are still unknowns. Most students on the spectrum function best when they know exactly what is coming next. That's where visual schedules come in. Read here about what they are, how to create them, and why you'll want to have some version of a visual schedule in place before Day One.

An ideal day for students on the spectrum might be like the movie *Groundhog Day*—every day the same as the day before. So the best way to start out is to try to create an environment that is as predictable as possible (given the circumstances), to minimize the likelihood of surprises and unexpected turns of events. The more preparation students have for any new experience, the less anxiety they will bring to the table.

Since most students on the spectrum are primarily visual learners, visual daily schedules are essential tools to add predictability to the day. Visual schedules can be used to help students *see* what's coming next. When the environment remains predictable, students know what to expect and can learn when and how to respond to it. Each time a familiar stimulus arises, they know they can be successful by using a previously learned response.

> *If I can't picture it,*
> *I can't understand it.*
>
> —Albert Einstein

The schedule is a comfort you can provide to enable students to function easily and effectively throughout the day. Fortunately, in most cases students on the spectrum have both the capacity to learn a classroom schedule and the motivation to adhere to it, though some modifications may be required. This section will address how to help students calmly navigate the many twists, turns, and transitions they face in a school day.

TYPES OF MODIFIED VISUAL SCHEDULES

The presentation of your typical schedule may need to be modified and expanded for specificity and clarity in order for it to be useful to students on the spectrum. The goal is to make the schedule concrete and straightforward. Specific modifications will depend on each student's level of functioning. You may choose to integrate elements of several styles. You may choose to adapt your whole-class schedule, or you may prefer to keep your whole-class schedule as is, and create individual schedules for students who need the extra support.

Regardless of the approach you choose, a daily schedule should be in place before the students arrive at school every morning. Individualized schedules can be posted alongside the whole-class schedule, or on a wall, on desks, in manila folders, in three-ring binders, on clipboards, or in relevant locations around the room.

Schedules that use removable and reusable icons allow you the most flexibility as you try to manage multiple schedules. They also allow students to interact with their schedules, posting the icons themselves, or perhaps removing icons after an activity is complete. Invest in strips of Velcro and be prepared to use them. Once you have a stash of icons outfitted with Velcro, you can simply reuse and rearrange them as schedules dictate.

Which kind of schedule would suit your students on the spectrum best?

✳ **Concrete:** For some young students who cannot read and are extremely concrete, you might need to post actual objects on the schedule. Using Velcro, mount a pencil on the schedule to denote journal writing time; a tiny ball to represent physical education, a plastic fork to indicate lunch time, a linking cube for math, and so on. This format provides a concrete and realistic representation of each activity, and offers visual and tactile options to pre-readers or multisensory learners.

✳ **Photographic:** If you think a student does not require absolutely concrete representation on the schedule, post photographs of the student himself doing the expected task. Photos offer a student very specific visual representations, by enabling him to see himself doing the expected activities. But this format also offers greater challenge because he will have to infer that the photographic objects represent real objects, before he translates that information into real action.

✳ **Representative:** Most students on the spectrum who are in mainstream elementary classes will be able to utilize a schedule comprised of representative line drawings accompanied by words. These stick-figure-like pictures are less concrete than photographs—they only vaguely look like real people with real objects. Many icons of this kind already exist. You can purchase pre-made icons, print them from downloadable programs, or draw them yourself. (For links to resources for supplies like these, visit www.barbaraboroson.com.)

My Daily Schedule

1 unpack 6 math class
2 morning work 7 lunchtime
3 calendar 8 recess
4 reading 9 science
5 specials 10 social studies

The Picture Communication Symbols ©1981–2010 by Mayer-Johnson LLC. All Rights Reserved Worldwide. Used with permission. Boardmaker™ is a trademark of Mayer-Johnson LLC.

✳ **Written:** A long-term goal for students on the spectrum is to follow a schedule written in words. But if your students don't achieve that this year, that's fine. The first goal is to find a schedule format that works for each student right away. Some may use the same schedule all year. Others may be able to move slowly toward more abstraction as the year progresses.

Success With Schedules

Despite having made what may feel like significant modifications, do not take for granted that the meaning of a schedule is self-evident.

✳ **Clarity:** Explain exactly what each icon on the schedule represents and implies, and then check for understanding. For example, clarify that a pencil on the schedule means that it is time to use a pencil for journal writing, and not for sharpening, drawing pictures, or poking peers. Verify that a student understands the icon by asking her to restate the meaning in her own words or demonstrate to you what she will do when she sees that icon on her schedule.

✳ **Specificity:** If your students on the spectrum seem lost and confused, despite the schedules you have made, don't give up on schedules. Instead, streamline them, concretize them, make them even clearer to ensure that they are understood.

✳ **Consistency:** Try keeping a *Check Schedule* icon in your pocket. When a student comes to you for guidance, refer her to the *Check Schedule* icon. This will remind and empower her to find the answer to her question on her schedule—and on her own.

Off-Roading: Planned Deviations From the Schedule

Of course, life is not a movie, and no matter what we do, we cannot rewind and replay the same day over and over. Nor should we, because again, our ultimate goal is to help students on the spectrum adapt to the ever-changing social world. So there will

---

Be Hyper-Vigilant for Hyperlexia

When choosing a schedule type, be aware that some students exhibit extraordinary decoding skills that can mask very poor comprehension skills. There can be as much as a four-grade discrepancy between decoding and comprehension skills. This disparity, known as hyperlexia, can affect up to 10% of the autism spectrum population. Examine reading strengths and weaknesses very closely and consult with your school's reading specialist for assessments to uncover reading comprehension needs across the board and to determine interventions to address them (Grigorenko, Klin, & Volkmar, 2003).

be change and there should be change, but it needs to be supported. If your students struggle with change, here are some ways to support their efforts.

CHANGE IN THE CLASSROOM

Routine in your classroom is not limited to the realm of schedule and activities. As discussed earlier, the need for predictability also prevails when it comes to students' physical space.

Walking into the classroom to find that the desks have been unexpectedly rearranged or work centers have been relocated can be disorienting and distressing to students on the spectrum. Seemingly small changes that you think won't matter may matter deeply.

For example, a fourth grader named Nikola refused to enter his classroom one morning. Despite the teacher's efforts to coax and cajole, Nikola's behavior escalated: he threw himself to the floor, kicking and flailing. With no other recourse, his teacher called the principal who was able to bring Nikola to her office where he calmed down quickly. Nikola spent the entire day working quietly in the principal's office, still unwilling to enter the classroom.

It wasn't until he got home that afternoon that Nikola was able to express what had triggered this outburst: Cut tennis balls had unexpectedly been placed over the bottoms of all of the classroom chair legs (to prevent the chairs from scratching the floors). This turn of events was unacceptable to Nikola. Not only was it an unexpected deviation from the classroom environment he had left the day before, but it violated a rule that was fixed and, to him, inviolable: that tennis balls are for playing tennis; they are *not* floor protectors and they do *not* belong on chair legs. Having been given no advance notice, no opportunity for discussion, adaptation, or participation, Nikola was unable to reconcile this new use of a familiar object with the rigidly preconceived notions he had in his head.

✳ **Heads Up:** Take the extra minute on Friday afternoon, for example, to notify students if, when they arrive on Monday morning, the desk groupings will be different or the computer will be against the opposite wall.

✳ **Teamwork:** Recruit students to help you do the rearranging. Having a hand in making change allows students to feel they have some control over the situation, and seeing the change unfold gradually before their eyes may make it less of a blow.

Chapter 3   The Simmering Pot: Keeping the Heat Down on Anxiety

CHANGE IN THE SCHEDULE

Try to be as specific as you can when creating the schedule and update it daily to reflect any changes that you can anticipate. For example, if you know there will be an assembly during reading workshop, put it on the schedule. If you know there will be a major deviation, such as a field trip, try to lay it out in detail, as follows.

Field Trips

Field trips can be very anxious times for students on the spectrum. All bets are off in terms of familiarity and routine.

✱ **Show:** Show photographs of your destination. Or, take the class on virtual field trips in advance of actual field trips. You may find a video tour on the location's Web site. If not, check YouTube for footage that other visitors have posted of their own visits there. This is a great way to show all of your students exactly what to expect, easing anxiety and, therefore, maximizing engagement.

✱ **Tell:** Talk through the details of an upcoming field trip with the class. (Remember to clarify whether or not you will be going to an actual *field.*) Describe as best you can what will happen on the trip: how long you will all be there, what time you plan to return, and what actions and behaviors you expect from your students. You might even want to show and bring along a basic schedule for the field trip.

✱ **Think:** Take a minute to think about each trip in terms of your students' specific anxiety triggers. Will there be loud noises? Will it be crowded? Will there be strong smells? Will it be muddy? Students on the spectrum may be better able to manage a field trip if they can prepare for such sensory and other challenges. Giving students the opportunity to bring ear plugs, wear boots, and so on, is an easy way to ease their adaptation to challenging environments.

Feeling Grounded

Some students on the spectrum are partial to wearing baseball-style hats with brims. It has been suggested that brimmed hats help students on the spectrum feel protected from overwhelming visual input, as the brims reduce their field of vision. Also, by eliminating upward views, brimmed hats help students on the spectrum feel more connected to the ground—literally more grounded. Consider allowing hats for outdoor activities and field trips.

✳ **Plan:** Consider asking your school administrator to boost your student-teacher ratio for field trips if you anticipate that any of your students may become overwhelmed by the deviation from their typical day.

At Exactly What Time Will We Be Spontaneous?

Even an activity you think will be a treat for your students, such as an extra outdoor recess on a beautiful day, might be received as an unwelcome violation by students on the spectrum. Any exceptions to the norm may cause them confusion, worry, and fixation: *What else is suddenly going to change? And when are we going to get back to what we are supposed to be doing?* Without warning, your "treat" could become another anxiety trigger.

✳ **Put Spontaneity on the Schedule:** Post planned surprises on the visual schedule in the form of a question mark or smiley face icon. Giving students the opportunity to *expect the unexpected* reduces some of the jolt caused by unscheduled events. Be sure, especially at first, that the "surprise" activity is an adequate payoff for the extra effort the student had to expend in not-knowing. Make it surefire fun for your most vulnerable students. This is a great exercise in slowly introducing students on the spectrum to being flexible and beginning to allow deviations from their schedules.

Off-Roading: *Unplanned Deviations to the Schedule*

Sometimes changes in the classroom or routine happen quite unexpectedly, offering no opportunity for you to forewarn your students. The sink floods, the gerbil dies, the pencil sharpener breaks. These unscripted situations, which violate expectations and trusted systems, can prove very distressing to students on the spectrum. Respect that there is big meaning in a big reaction. If students become extremely upset over the sudden breakdown of something in the classroom, that item was likely a comfort anchor for them and had a vital role in their routine.

While you cannot prepare your students on the spectrum for truly unexpected events, you can prepare them for the *possibility* of unexpected surprises by mapping out plans for those random moments. What follows are some common surprises that may arise, as well as strategies to help you prepare your students for them.

ANCHOR'S AWAY

An absent teacher is one of the most threatening disruptions for students on the spectrum. The implication of having a substitute teacher is that everything will be new, different, and not okay. And many times, that is indeed the case. Sometimes you have the chance to prepare the class for this event, and sometimes not. When you do know ahead of time that you are going to be absent, alert students (in as much detail as possible) about *what* and *whom* they might expect the next day.

But because you often won't know ahead of time when you're going to be absent, try to put these preventive strategies in place:

- Discuss early in the year with your principal why it might be important for your class to have the same substitute teacher whenever possible.

- Try to alert the substitute to your students' special needs or anxiety triggers, to whatever extent you feel necessary. Emphasize the importance of following the schedule and any other specific strategies you have found to be effective, such as using a quiet voice, allowing extra time, and so on.

- Get in the habit of always posting the next day's schedule before you leave each afternoon. This way, the schedule will be there in the morning, even if you are— unexpectedly—not.

- Periodically review a "just-in-case I am absent" protocol with the class: Reassure students about those elements of the day that will proceed in ways that are comforting and familiar, while giving them a heads-up about what could be different.

- Draw on the strengths of students on the spectrum by soliciting their help. Share that substitutes will try to follow the schedule, but may need help. Encourage your most vulnerable students to be special helpers.

Power to the People

Empower students on the spectrum who rely on the schedule by encouraging them to help you post the next day's schedule at the end of each day. Their participation in this activity will allow them to feel more in control and less reliant on your presence to maintain order.

FIRE!

Fire alarms can be overwhelmingly stressful to students on the spectrum for many reasons:

- Fire alarms require an instantaneous, pressured response with no advance notice.

- Many of students' rigid, internal rules must be broken, such as going outside without a coat and hat or without a backpack, or going out a different door.

- The sound of the alarm may be truly painful to your students who have sensory issues. It is very common to see students on the spectrum during a fire drill with hands over their ears and tears in their eyes, or even screaming, just to drown out the shrill noise.

✳ **Tip Them Off:** Usually the administrators in your school will know ahead of time when there is going to be a planned fire drill. Find out and tip off your most vulnerable students beforehand.

✳ **Know the Drill:** Use a Social Story (which is a prewritten guide for challenging situations) about fire drills to help acclimate students on the spectrum as to what to expect. (See more on Social Stories in Chapter 7.)

✳ **Schedules-to-Go:** For those times when the fire alarm surprises everyone, have a fire-alarm schedule in the attendance book that you take with you when the class has to evacuate the building. Hand copies of it to specific students as they walk out the door. This provides a script for this unexpected event as well as a transitional object onto which your students on the spectrum can redirect their focus, away from the chaos.

The Picture Communication Symbols ©1981–2010 by Mayer-Johnson LLC. All Rights Reserved Worldwide. Used with permission. Boardmaker™ is a trademark of Mayer-Johnson LLC.

Transitional Moments

Now you have provided students with a layout of the day so that they can predict what activity will be coming next, and what will happen after that. This will take you a long, long way toward smoothing out the bumps and keeping the heat down. But now let's look even a little more closely at another trouble spot: transitional moments. These are the moments that sneak in *between* structured activities. These moments are loose, undefined, disorganized, even chaotic, and frequent triggers to students on the spectrum. Transitions require students not only to complete what they were doing before, but also to ready themselves, physically and mentally, for what comes next. Even though transitions are often brief, they can be packed with provocation for students on the spectrum. If you have students who need more help shifting from one activity to the next, here are some common transitional challenges and strategies to help.

SHIFTING GEARS

During a transition, what may have been a quiet, organized activity abruptly explodes into action. Suddenly everyone is talking loudly. Chairs scrape against the floor as classmates get up to put away their materials or prepare for the next activity. Bodies are moving in every direction at once.

Even more challenging for students on the spectrum—who may have trouble regulating their moods—may be those moments when a transition requires a shift from loud, lively, and energetic, to quiet, organized, and still. Either way, suddenly nothing is as it was the moment before.

Transitional moments demand regulation, spontaneity, flexibility, organization, focus, sensory adaptation, language processing, motor planning, and much more—all at once. As you'll see in forthcoming chapters, none of these skills comes easily or automatically to students on the spectrum.

For example, your simple words, *Okay everybody, wrap it up*, at the end of a math project demand immediate response, yet are heavily loaded with implied meaning. On hearing those words, students are expected to perform several actions:

1. Heed your call to attention.

2. Decode your idiomatic language.

3. Adjust to the fact that what had become familiar and comfortable is now over; it's time again for something new.

4. Adapt to the sudden surge of noise and energy in the room.

5. Stop working immediately, regardless of whether their work is complete, even if their expectation had been to finish.

6. Clean up their work stations, sorting which materials should be put away and where (e.g., the linking cubes go back in the math bucket, the worksheet goes in the classwork bin, and the pencils remain at their desks).

7. Determine what they need to do to prepare for the next activity.

It's amazing that for most typical students all of this happens automatically and almost instantaneously. For students on the spectrum, just as they process all of those elements and begin to get in gear for this change of course—just as they begin to get a handle on all that was implied in your words—the moment has passed and it's on to the next activity. Now the class is lining up at the door or gathering on the rug or sitting back down with new materials. And chances are, your students on the spectrum are still sitting, math worksheets and linking cubes strewn about their desks, pencils in hand, brows furled, hands flapping, anxiety building.

But transitions don't have to go this way. By looking closely at the challenges presented, we can help smooth out those in-between times, too.

✷ **Warning, Warning:** Time prompts can be effective for the whole class. Alert students five minutes before an activity is going to end. This will give them time to finish up their work and prepare for the upcoming change.

An additional two-minute warning along the way will help students gauge their progress toward the transition. At the two-minute warning, have them stop working briefly to give you their attention. Explain specifically what you expect to happen during the transition: *When I say it's time to stop working, please gather up your linking cubes and put them in the math bucket. Put your papers in the class work bin. Then you may take out your lunch and line up at the door.*

Keep in mind that for some students on the spectrum that would be too many steps and too many words to process at once. If so, separate the instructions, and then reiterate them as needed, or list them in writing.

✴ **Follow Protocol:** Break down the expectations for a transition and put them on the schedule or on the board. Jed Baker (2001), an expert on social-skills training, suggests setting up 2- or 3-step mini-protocols for various transitions. For example, if you expect students to begin independent reading, have a rubric at the ready to show and display.

Getting Ready for Independent Reading

- *Quiet hands and feet*
- *Eyes on book*
- *Quiet mouth—read in your head*

✴ **Carrying Comfort:** Let students keep a small transitional object with them as a thread of continuity and comfort as they move from one activity to the next.

✴ **Straight Talk:** Be careful to avoid using idioms or slang when giving instructions. Students on the spectrum are very literal, so your instruction, *Okay everybody, wrap it up,* might ultimately get you a linking cube carefully wrapped in a math worksheet.

SEPARATION

One especially challenging transitional moment for students on the spectrum can be separation. Given their multifaceted anxiety and difficulty coping with change, many students will struggle with saying goodbye to everything that is home and family, as they move into a different environment. If this is an issue for your students, consider incorporating bits of home into their day.

✴ **My Life in Pictures:** Invite all students to bring in photographs of their families to post on their desks, to decorate notebooks or folders, or to create a family collage to post on a classroom wall.

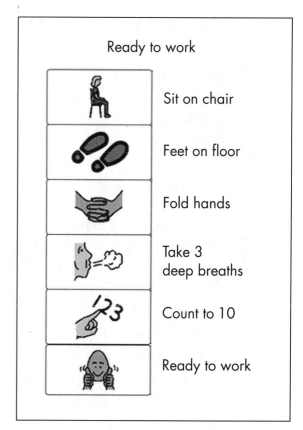

Ready to work

Sit on chair

Feet on floor

Fold hands

Take 3 deep breaths

Count to 10

Ready to work

The Picture Communication Symbols ©1981–2010 by Mayer-Johnson LLC. All Rights Reserved Worldwide. Used with permission. Boardmaker™ is a trademark of Mayer-Johnson LLC.

* **Smells Like Home:** Suggest that students wear something that belongs to a parent or other family member, such as a T-shirt or sweatshirt, which might be soothing to touch and might carry just enough scent of home to be a comfort. Or suggest a dab of mom's perfume or dad's cologne inside their shirt collar in the morning to provide reassurance through the day.

* **Getting in the Groove:** Allow students to ease into the new day by creating a routine warm-up activity that might provide them comfort. (See Chapter 4 for specific ideas.)

Behavioral Expectations

Maintaining routine refers to more than the organization of time and space. In your classroom, you create a set of routine rules for all students to know and respect. As discussed previously, students on the spectrum rigidly depend on rules not just to guide their actions but to manage their anxiety.

Rules Rule

When rules are well understood, students on the spectrum will likely be the first to remind you if you are not upholding them exactly as you have presented them. So when you find these students breaking the rules, there's probably a compelling reason. Here are some of those reasons.

RULE RIGIDITY

Like all other aspects of the social world, rule compliance requires nuanced abilities such as inference and generalization. Even rules you think are crystal clear may not be clear at all when interpreted by literal and inflexible thinkers.

Okay, Now What?

Sometimes students on the spectrum will follow a rule only to the extent that you have stated it and will not infer beyond that. When you see that students have stalled, consider that they might be awaiting further instructions. A classic example is when a teacher hands out a test and tells the students, *Do not begin the test until I tell you to . . . Okay, you may now pick up your pencils.* All the students begin working on the test, except for the student on the spectrum who is sitting still, holding her pencil.

Why? Because the instruction was for the students to pick up their pencils; no one said to *begin testing.* A more specific and productive instruction might have been: *Okay, now you may pick up your pencils and begin working on the test.*

Rules for Rules

Consider just how challenging it is for students on the spectrum to follow rules with rigid precision. Temple Grandin, a world-renowned professor of animal science who has high-functioning autism herself, still struggles to generalize rules and sort out their gradations. She works hard to make sense of the confusing (and un-rule-like) fact that rules themselves do not follow predictable rules. Some rules are inviolable, some can be manipulated within reason, and some rules are meaningless. Other rules seem to exist even though they were never stated as rules.

Grandin has created for herself some *rules for rules* by categorizing rules into four types along these lines:

1. *Rules for Illegal and Unacceptable Actions:* These are rules that can't ever be broken. Killing and stealing are against the law and are *never* okay to do.

2. *Rules for Illegal but Acceptable Actions:* These are rules that people break all the time even though doing so is against the law. Speeding and littering are rules that get broken and it's okay.

3. *Rules of Courtesy:* These rules are okay to break, but only sometimes. For example, sometimes it's okay to say, *Sure* instead of *Yes, please.* (Grandin has also struggled to recognize that courtesy violators do not necessarily need to be corrected by her.)

4. *Unspoken Rules:* These hidden rules address actions that should not be done, *even though no one has stated any rules against them.* These refer to behaviors that are considered "common sense," such as not pulling the arm of someone who is holding hot coffee, not banging a rock against a flagpole, not licking magic markers, and countless others. Have you actually ever stated rules prohibiting these kinds of actions? Did you ever think you'd need to? Probably not . . . until you needed to.

Caught in a Bind

Other times, students on the spectrum will stick to rules too rigidly, not understanding the nuance and inference often required of living in the social world. For example, a first grader named Jonah was unable to get his seatbelt buckled on the bus ride home one day. He was terrified that he was breaking a rule by not having his belt buckled, but he did not ask for help because another rule on the bus was *no talking.* He was in a total bind; whether he asked for help or he didn't, he'd be breaking a rule and he *can't ever* allow himself to break a rule. Jonah's solution was to clutch his seatbelt against the buckle, pressing them together as tightly as he could, in order to approximate being buckled in. Jonah rode white-knuckled and terrified all the way home. When he finally got off the bus, it was not the fear of having risked injury by being unbuckled that caused him to burst into tears; it was the intolerable wrongness of having broken a rule.

RULE CONTINUITY

Various adults in your students' lives are likely to have different sets of rules and expectations. Art, music, and physical education teachers, occupational therapists, school psychologists, cafeteria workers, recess aides, and bus drivers all have their own styles and expectations. This inconsistency can be confusing for students on the spectrum. Collaborate to develop continuity across the school day to whatever extent is possible. Listen and share experience as to what approaches seem effective.

THREE RULES FOR SETTING RULES

1. Be sure your rules are incontrovertibly clear to every student.
2. Be sure your rules are reasonable and enforceable.
3. Differentiate rules flexibly for specific students, as needed, but then uphold them with consistency.

Like the schedule, behavioral expectations should be posted in comprehensible terms, explained, clarified, and checked for understanding. To further your efforts for clarity, consider using a behavioral system, as described below, to support students who need concrete feedback as to their behavioral progress.

Token Economy Systems

The behavior of typical students may be reinforced simply by your smile or even by the self-satisfaction of doing something well. Such students may not need to participate in a token economy system to produce positive behavior. In fact, when we find students who are self-motivated, it's better not to diminish their positive predisposition by imposing unnecessary, external, token rewards.

However, students on the spectrum are usually unmoved by (or unaware of)

Hey! That's Not Fair!

Learning disabilities specialist Rick Lavoie suggests that when other students balk at individualized adaptations, explain to them that *fair* does not mean everyone gets the same. *Fair means giving each student what he or she needs* (2005).

unspoken or abstract reinforcements. They often benefit from concrete reinforcements of their effort and progress. Though intangible incentives, such as extra center time, extra reading time, or extra computer time may eventually motivate some students on the spectrum, for now start with the concrete incentives of a token economy system.

If you have students who need concrete incentives, set up a system whereby each student who needs the system has the opportunity and motivation to earn tokens by demonstrating differentiated target behaviors. When a student earns the necessary number of tokens (incentives), he may exchange them for a valued "treasure" (reinforcement).

Tokens can take the form of tickets, points, coins, stars, checkmarks, stickers, and so on. (If you would like to use more inventive incentives, please visit www. barbaraboroson.com.)

Using behavioral modification systems for only some students in your class can be tricky. Read about whole-class, team-building activities and incentives in Chapter 7.

✳ **Set Up Success:** Be sure the goal you set for each student is achievable. (Make it *easily* achievable at the beginning.) You can be sure that your system will backfire if you set up a highly motivating incentive that a student is incapable of attaining. Try to differentiate expectations for each student.

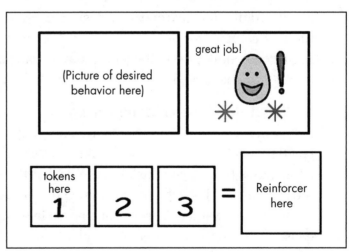

The Picture Communication Symbols ©1981–2010 by Mayer-Johnson LLC. All Rights Reserved Worldwide. Used with permission. Boardmaker™ is a trademark of Mayer-Johnson LLC.

✱ **So Far, So Good:** Place tokens in clear plastic bags or post stars or stickers on individual schedules so that students can monitor their progress. Or, let students see how many *more* tokens they need in order to earn the treasure. Create templates with delineated spaces into which students attach tokens as they earn them. This allows them to see clearly how many spaces they have yet to fill. (See sample template on p. 61.)

✱ **Follow Through:** Treat this system like a contract. If students uphold their end and earn the designated number of tokens, be sure to uphold your end and provide the contracted reinforcement. Be consistent; don't change the rules along the way or you will lose credibility and your system will lose its effectiveness.

✱ **Emphasize Effort:** Your short-term goal is to encourage positive effort. Be on the lookout for effort to comply, and respond promptly and positively to this emerging, adaptive behavior. True mastery may be a long time coming.

Avoid giving consequences if good effort has been applied. Students on the spectrum get more than their share of negative reinforcement every day. Practice noticing and acknowledging effort and progress: *André, since you raised your hand a few times today, here's a ticket for you. Tomorrow, let's see if you can raise your hand without calling out.* Remember, there will be no straight lines here; what was achieved yesterday may fall by the wayside tomorrow when André's shirt feels scratchy, or his bus arrives late, or he gets a paper cut on his finger.

✱ **Pair It With Praise:** Always tell students precisely what they are doing that earns them a token. This clarity serves two purposes: First, it reinforces the likelihood of students repeating desirable behaviors. And second, it helps teach them to connect the good feeling of getting a token with the more abstract reinforcement of praise. Someday, maybe, praise or pride alone—with no concrete token—will be enough.

✱ **You'll Get It Next Time:** When you feel that students on the spectrum have not put forth their best effort—*all* things considered—clarify for them exactly what action failed to meet your expectations. Explain that because of that action, they did not earn a token this time. If you don't tell them what they did wrong, they will not recognize the relationship between their action and your reaction.

But be forewarned: The loss of a possible token may be perceived as a very negative consequence by your system-dependent, rule-following, rigid students. So be gentle with your explanation, keep it positive, and check for understanding: *Now that you understand why you aren't getting a star today, I know you can do better tomorrow. What will you do differently tomorrow to get a star?*

ROUSING REINFORCEMENTS

Reinforcements can be of high value to students while still being of low cost to you. (See www.barbaraboroson.com for links to online stores that offer dozens of inexpensive products.) Here are some simple ideas to maximize the value of reinforcements available to students.

✸ **Offer Shoppertunity:** Let students who earn enough tokens shop for their treasure. Offer a wide variety of options from which they can choose. This also encourages students to set goals for what they would like to earn next week including "big-ticket" items that might require longer-term budgeting.

✸ **Make It Meaningful:** Individualize your choice of reinforcements. Since students on the spectrum may have a very narrow range of interests, reinforcements must be meaningful to each targeted student or they will not be effective. When selecting reinforcements, make personal motivation the priority, even if the treasure seems thematically disconnected from the activity.

✸ **Aim for Age Appropriateness:** By consulting with students and with parents or caregivers, try to choose a variety of reinforcements that are meaningful but also age appropriate. Even if your fifth grader on the spectrum would be motivated by Buzz Lightyear stickers, the spectacle of his shirt covered in these too-childish stickers would sabotage his efforts to socialize with peers. But if Buzz Lightyear is where he's at, maybe he could earn other space-themed items, such as moon-and-star decorated pencils or notepads, earth-inspired rubber balls, toy astronaut or alien figures, Styrofoam planets, or tickets toward a small toy rocketship or robot.

OPTIMIZING OPTIMISM

In many cases, you will find that your behavioral aspirations for students tend to be about correcting negative actions, such as *Stop kicking the chair legs* or *No grabbing scissors.* Challenge yourself to reframe these into positively-worded, outcome-oriented goals that convey what you want students *to do*, rather than what you want them not to do. Tell them: *Keep your feet still,* or *Wait your turn for scissors.*

By framing goals in the positive, you also cultivate a culture of optimism and are more likely to notice when students apply positive coping skills where they had previously struggled. *I like the way you wait your turn for the scissors now* is a more positive and productive reinforcement than *I see that you are doing less grabbing.* This kind of quiet progress may be easily overlooked, but is not easily achieved. Look for quiet improvements such as handling disappointment, good waiting, accepting *no*, stopping on time, and coping well with making mistakes (Baker, 2009).

Expressing positive goals in the form of rules will enhance clarity and boost students' motivation and ability to comply: *The rule in our class is: We wait our turns* or *The rule is: We keep our feet still.*

Reinforcing the Negatives of Negative Reinforcement

In most classrooms these days, the behavioral atmosphere is upbeat and optimistic, emphasizing incentives and positive reinforcements. Here are a few reminders about why negative reinforcements are negative, especially when working with students on the spectrum.

- Most negative reinforcements are more suppressive than instructive. Students on the spectrum cannot intuit why their behavior caused a consequence and then change their behavior spontaneously. These students require specific, proactive re-education in order to learn replacement behaviors, and in some cases environmental modification may be necessary as well.

- Negative reinforcements tend to be set as class-wide or school-wide policy, with consistency of enforcement as a primary goal (as is the case with a zero tolerance policy). But students on the spectrum have Individualized Education Programs because they cannot be held across the board to the same standards as typical students. Class-wide and school-wide systems fail to differentiate the special modifications or accommodations students on the spectrum need and deserve. When necessary, try to use natural consequences that emerge—by definition—*naturally*, in response to individual situations.

- Many negative reinforcements restrict learning opportunities. For example, suppose a student routinely tosses the game board when he realizes that he lost the game. If the response to this behavior is that he can no longer play games, he has lost all opportunity to learn game-playing skills. He needs to be re-educated about game playing and may need the game to be modified. If a negative reinforcement is necessary, a better choice might be requiring the student to clean up all the spilled pieces—a natural consequence, but not a restricting one.

- Often negative reinforcements are issued in the heat of an exasperated moment and without careful consideration. With students on the spectrum, this could mean inadvertently removing comfort anchors. Impulsively confiscating a beloved squeeze ball or an element of the regular schedule would only make an anxious student more anxious and thus more likely to erupt again.

Coaching Coping

Unfortunately, the incentives and reinforcements described in the section above will have little effect on students who have no internal control over their impulses. Not only are specific tasks difficult for students on the spectrum, but the skills required to cope and persevere with those difficulties may be inaccessible, due to regulatory challenges. When sensory overload kicks in or anxiety bubbles up, waving tickets or stickers before these students is only setting them up for frustration and disappointment, exacerbating an already overwhelming experience.

Rather than let unsettling situations escalate into crises, you can offer your students tools to support self-regulation. Here are some tools and strategies that may help students recognize their feelings and try to modulate their own responses.

✶ **Pack a Coolbox:** Don't just *expect* the unexpected—*prepare* for the unexpected. Create a relaxation folder or a small *coolbox* that a student who struggles with anxiety can use when she needs to calm down. Use the information you collected from parents, caregivers, and colleagues to fill the box with individualized affirmations, calming cues, and comfort objects.

Affirmations and cues might include statements like these:

> *The more you know about your emotions, the more you can control them instead of letting them control you.*
>
> —Tony Attwood, Ph.D. (2009)

- *I figure things out when I'm calm; I can't think as well when I'm not calm.*
- *Drawing a picture helps me calm down.*
- *Taking deep breaths helps me calm down.*
- *Counting to ten helps me calm down.*
- *I am a great swimmer!*
- *I can name every movie Bruce Lee has ever been in.*

Add comforting objects, specific to each student, to the coolbox. These might include items such as the following:

- representations of familiar topics or special interests, such as family photographs, a small stuffed animal, a motorcycle magazine
- a social story about staying calm (See more on social stories in Chapter 7.)

- sensorily supportive objects such as a squeeze ball, a koosh ball, or noise-canceling headphones, carefully differentiated according to each student's sensory needs

- an index card that lists ideas for calming down (You might want to work with the student, in a calm moment, to create it. Keep the card in the box.)

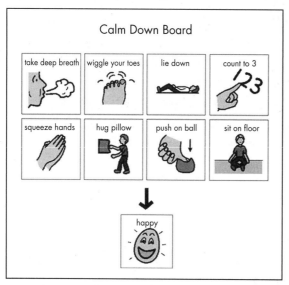

The Picture Communication Symbols ©1981–2010 by Mayer-Johnson LLC. All Rights Reserved Worldwide. Used with permission. Boardmaker™ is a trademark of Mayer-Johnson LLC.

Encourage students to browse through their coolboxes periodically even during calm moments, in order to practice and reinforce these self-regulatory skills and help prolong the current state of calm.

(Read about more ways to modify the sensory environment, including creating a sensory corner, in Chapter 4.)

✳ **Headed Toward Red:** Teach students to take their own emotional temperature, using a graphic of a thermometer with emotional gradations color-coded. Moods range from *cool, calm blue* to *hot, raging red.* Students can learn that when they recognize that their emotional temperature is headed toward red, it's time to take a break, take out the coolbox, or use whatever soothing strategy has been prearranged. (See the example of the Emotion Thermometer above; a color version is available at www.barbaraboroson.com.)

Chapter 3   The Simmering Pot: Keeping the Heat Down on Anxiety

✴ Coded Communication: Coordinate a signal that individual students can use to alert you when they feel they are beginning to heat up or lose control. Have a plan in place so that both you and the students know what will happen as a result of that signal, depending on the comfort needs of each student. A peek through the coolbox, a trip to the water fountain, a moment with you in the hall, or some other regulatory activity may be just enough to help students get back on track.

✴ Model Coping Strategies: When you find yourself struggling with something, vocalize your own process and coping strategies aloud. *I know that when I'm calm, I'll be able to figure this out. I'm going to take a deep breath to calm down so that I can solve this problem.* Show students how you persevere and don't give up, explaining, *Wow, this is hard, but I believe in myself: I'll persist. I know I can get it.*

Fading Structure

Put preventive strategies in place and keep them there. In time, you will likely see problematic behaviors abate significantly. That's a wonderful thing; that's success. Chances are, your students on the spectrum are probably doing well in large part *because* of your consistent strategies. If so, you are off to a great start together. Keep it up.

But watch yourself for signs of complacency. With successful preventive strategies in place, we can easily be lulled into believing that problem areas are no longer problem areas, and we can grow lax about maintaining these strategies.

For example, suppose you make a point of always notifying students ahead of time when you know you will be absent from school. So far, that system works well; your students on the spectrum seem to do fine with a substitute teacher. Certainly you might begin to think, *They are fine every time I have a substitute, so I don't need to prepare them anymore.*

Hold on. Give yourself some credit. Trust that your students on the spectrum are doing fine *because* of your careful preparation, and then stick with it. One brief hiatus can allow an otherwise avoidable problem to develop and set off the downward spiral you've worked so hard to avoid.

Instead, let nature take its course. There will be plenty of times when circumstances will result in an unavoidable deviation from the schedule (such as when you are unexpectedly absent from school, when there is an unplanned fire alarm, and so on). If, on the basis of reactions to such unavoidable events, you believe you can scale back some modifications, do so very slowly—one element at a time—per individual student. Do not risk triggering more anxiety. Make a small change only when you are sure your student is ready for it and then watch carefully for any ramifications.

✳ ✳ ✳

Here's what *you* can expect: No matter how much you work to prevent them, there will be occasional situations that get red hot. And there may be times when someone gets burned. In Chapter 9 strategies are offered to help guide you through the moments when the pot really gets boiling. But please read through the chapters between here and there first, because they will help deepen your understanding of students on the spectrum and all the challenges they face, so that you will become a master chef, expert at maintaining just the right temperature under your busily simmering pots so that they very rarely boil over.

Body and Soul

Regulation and Sensation

Imagine walking into the school cafeteria at lunchtime. Imagine that your <u>hearing is so sensitive</u> that common sounds are truly painful to you. The clatter of every fork stabs into your ears, the scratchy screech of every Styrofoam tray makes you shudder, and the cacophony of voices roars like a lawn mower in your ears. Your ears and eyes are sensitive to fluorescent light, so the glaring overhead bulbs buzz relentlessly, while their incessant flickering makes the room spin. Your <u>senses of smell and taste</u> are so acute that the combined aroma of turkey tetrazzini, boiled hot dogs, reheated green beans, and commercial coleslaw, overlaid with the caustic odor of cleansers and ammonia, makes you gag. Your body awareness is so precarious that the chaos of people moving in all directions makes you dizzy and disoriented, and now you can't find where you are supposed to sit.

You close your eyes and cover your ears to shut it all out, but you can still feel the press of the crowds while the smells linger in your nose and throat. Someone taps your shoulder to ask if you're okay, and your sensitivity to touch perceives it as a slap. Your fleeting impulse control has now vanished completely, and you whirl around and strike the offending arm away.

Now you hear voices yelling at you, your coping and problem-solving skills are maxed out, and all you know is that you can't be here. You begin to rock back and forth in a soothing rhythm but cannot block out the pressure pulsing in your temples. You spot the door and bolt out onto the empty playground. You sink to the ground under a tree, gulping in the fresh air, soaking in the silence around you and the stability of the tree behind you and the ground beneath you, and now the lunch monitor is hollering for you to get back inside.

Enjoy your lunch!

Overwhelming situations like these are common for students on the spectrum because their sensory and regulatory systems do not function in typical or self-protective ways. Often, their behaviors are mistaken as aggressive, oppositional, or antisocial. But in fact, these students may be at the mercy of intense sensory input and may possess limited ability to regulate their responses. This means they may overreact, underreact, or react impulsively, indiscriminately, and inexplicably. Difficulties with regulation manifest in areas of behavior, organization, socialization, focus, and more, and can forcefully derail students' physical and psychological well-being. This chapter will explain two major factors that affect self-regulation—executive function and sensory processing—and will show you how to recognize and address these challenges.

Executive Function

Executive function is the ability of the brain to think through situations and, when necessary, override impulsive or automatic responses. For example, executive function enables some of us to eat only one piece of birthday cake after lunch, even as the whole cake beckons. We have the capacity to think it through by examining various options and outcomes: We reflect on whether or not we are still hungry. We recall that the last time we binged on cake, we felt sick for hours. We recognize the possibility that others at the table might want some cake, too. We remember that we decided to cut back on sweets for health reasons. We speculate that too much cake now will ruin our appetite for the dinner celebration that is planned for later in the day. We use self-talk to mull over the decision: *I really shouldn't. But it's my birthday! But still. It's so good though! No—I'll be glad later if I don't have any more now.*

For those of us with adequate executive functioning, the frontal and prefrontal lobes in our brains operate as Chief Executive Officer, micromanaging every choice we make and everything we do. Executive function effectively orchestrates or regulates our actions and reactions in the context of conscious consideration and learned experience. When this system operates properly, we have access to useful planning skills such as objective thinking, prediction, reflection, flexibility, impulse control, and empathy, as well as critical coping skills such as waiting, tolerating frustration, staying calm, and shifting gears.

Students with executive function challenges struggle with many skills:

- considering the perspective of others
- interpreting and understanding the motivation of others
- modulating their own demeanor to fit a certain context
- planning ahead (foresight)
- learning from their mistakes (hindsight)
- focusing
- coping with frustration
- putting a thought or action "on hold"
- thinking objectively (reframing)
- thinking flexibly
- staying calm
- managing time and pace
- shifting gears or attention
- navigating transitions
- maintaining organization
- following instructions or directions
- adding new information to existing knowledge (working memory)

The absence of these skills can cause students to appear inconsiderate, rude, impulsive, rigid, manic, careless, stubborn, inattentive, highly reactive, thoughtless, impatient, disorganized, or disoriented.

Acting and Reacting

When the executive function system is not operating smoothly, nothing inhibits impulsive, distracted, or otherwise dysfunctional behavior. In other words, students with executive dysfunction simply act and react. That cake is a goner. Students may give no thought to how an action will affect them or others in the future or to what the consequences of that same action were in the past.

BRAKELESS BEHAVIOR

Martin Kutscher, a pediatric neurologist, explains that students with executive dysfunction live in the moment. For them, there is only this moment. And this moment. And this moment. The future and the past don't exist. These students get swept away by whatever is happening to them in any instant, uninhibited by any kind of self-regulatory controls. Kutscher calls this disinhibition "brakeless behavior," a term which vividly conveys not only the impulsivity of some behaviors, but also their unstoppableness (2004, p. 7). This may contribute to the tendency of students on the spectrum to repeat the same words or behaviors and may explain why those behaviors can be so intractable: there is no effective intrinsic system in place that signals *enough is enough* and then shuts the behavior off. (See more on repetitive words and behaviors, also known as *perseveration*, in Chapter 5.)

WHY ARE YOU LAUGHING?

Limited self-regulation may also cause students to respond to emotional or other situations in ways that seem inappropriate. They may laugh at or underreact to serious situations, and they frequently overreact to seemingly minor situations. They tend to go too far in any one direction, getting too wild or too silly, struggling to shift their moods efficiently from one register to another.

Executive Function Strategies

Since the minds of students with executive function challenges dart so quickly from one moment to the next, it is very difficult to insert a lesson on self-regulation *between* those impulsive moments. So a better approach is to weave the use of general skills that support regulation across the curriculum. If you have students who struggle with executive function issues, here are some strategies to help them practice skills that encourage reflection, prediction, impulse control, and other components of regulation. These strategies will not apply to every student. Try only those that resonate with your students and your class and feel doable to you. Pick and choose. You can always come back for more if you need them. (You can access additional information on this topic and more strategies at www.barbaraboroson.com.)

Teaching Reflection and Prediction

Students on the spectrum benefit greatly from learning to reflect and predict because the skills introduce the new *idea* of thinking before acting. Once this concept becomes familiar, you can begin prompting students to apply reflection and prediction skills *between* impulsive moments.

✷ **Cause and Effect:** To support foresight and hindsight, practice connecting cause and effect using concrete examples in the natural context: *We left the papers near the open window and the breeze caused something to happen. What was the effect of the breeze on the papers?*

✷ **Looking Forward:** Have students make predictions about stories or classroom events: *The workbooks are stacked very high. Does the pile of workbooks look stable? Why not? What do you predict will happen if we leave them piled so high? Why?* Support students' efforts as they try to apply these skills to social and other more abstract situations.

✷ **Looking Back:** Debrief both successful and unsuccessful situations with students on the spectrum. If a situation was stressful, you may need to provide time for students to calm down and regroup before you debrief. But as soon as possible, and without criticism, make conscious for your students whatever positive efforts and missteps they made. Remember that these are challenging new ways of thinking for students on the spectrum, so take your questioning slowly and allow plenty of time for language and thought processing. If you do not overtly connect the cause to the effect, these students will not learn from their mistakes; they will not spontaneously make the connection between their actions and the outcome of the situation.

For example, since Kenji does not think through what will happen if he keeps poking Anya's shoulder, talk him through the learning process:

- reflection: *What happened last time you poked someone?*

- empathy: *How would you feel if someone were poking your shoulder?*

- prediction: *So, then, how do you think Anya feels when you poke her shoulder?*

You may be surprised to note that this very basic line of reasoning may seem to yield a new epiphany every time. Keep at it because these kinds of connections are not happening automatically. Your words are sinking in, albeit slowly. Encourage students to plan how they might handle the same situation even better the next time.

Teaching Impulse Control

Impulsive students are unable to make conscious choices about their behaviors because they are unable to stop and think before doing. But *some* students on the spectrum may be able to understand that they can make choices about the ways they handle situations. Try to explain, to those you think might understand, that they can learn to choose whether to raise their hands or call out. They can learn to choose whether to get on the back of the line or cut in front. They can learn to choose whether to kick an adversary or walk away. This section will guide you to help some students locate that elusive moment of choice and use it to apply their new reflection and prediction skills. Again, these strategies will not work for everyone.

✳ **Look Behind the Scenes:** Students' impulse control can be affected by an overwhelming sensory environment (as shown in the lunchroom example on page 69). Modifying the sensory environment to meet the needs of sensitive students can go a long way toward facilitating impulse control. (See "Sensational Strategies" on page 89.)

✳ **Stop and Think:** Bolster students' efforts to control impulses by providing clear, related incentives and positive reinforcements: *Since you're interrupting, I cannot listen to you. If you stay quiet and raise your hand, I will listen to you.* The goal is to help students capture that instant, just before impulses take over, in which they can independently access that prompt: *Oh! If I raise my hand instead of calling out, I will get a turn to answer. So I will stay quiet and raise my hand.* Be patient; this is a lofty goal.

✳ **Don't Miss a Beat:** Be sure to notice the amazing progress evident when students verbalize their efforts to stop, such as when a student interrupts by calling out, *I'm not going to call out my answer! I'm going to raise my hand!* This kind of statement indicates that this student has been able to wedge a beat into that instant; he is thinking before doing. Acknowledge this powerful intermediate step that is well on the way to impulse control: *Good job not calling out your answer!*

Along these lines, I worked with a kindergartner who would get very angry with me whenever our time together came to an end. Every time I got ready to leave, Julian would glower and yell at me and accuse me of being a bad person for leaving. To ease the transition, I showed him a schedule of what he would be doing right after I left. To acknowledge his feelings, I told him I understood that he was sad to see me go and I reminded him of when I'd be back. I reflected to him that when he called me a bad person, it hurt my feelings. And I suggested that, if he feels sad at the end of our visits, he might say, *I'm sad that you have to go.*

Julian and I replayed this entire scenario regularly for weeks with no change in his behavior. Finally one day, as I was getting ready to leave, he muttered glumly, *I'm going to call you a bad person . . . tomorrow.* There it was; there was the beat. There was the moment in which he stopped and thought. He couldn't entirely not-say-it yet, but he had caught himself before the words burst forth. We were on our way.

Teaching Advance Planning

Students with executive function challenges may struggle to plan ahead. This may cause them to be chronically unprepared for certain tasks or activities, always showing up without the necessary tools or gear. Others may struggle with planning ahead in terms of pacing themselves. Impulsivity may drive them to finish their work as quickly as possible just to get it done. Others meander dreamily through their work with no awareness of expiring time. You can support planning and pacing by implementing some of the following strategies.

✴ **Count It Down:** Try using countdowns for time remaining in an activity. But be aware that while countdowns can help some students pace themselves, your frequent interruptions (*five minutes left . . . four minutes left . . .* and so on) may be overly distracting and disorienting to others.

✴ **Time Time:** For students who are easily derailed or are visual learners, use Time Timers, which are clock-face timers that graphically represent elapsed and remaining time. With these timers students can see exactly how much longer they will need to wait, comply, or attend to the task at hand, and they can pace themselves accordingly.

✴ **Chunk It:** Break assignments into small chunks, so that students can feel gratified and energized by mini-accomplishments, rather than having to sustain their attention and effort along the way toward a larger goal. For example, if you expect students to solve a page of addition problems and then use the sums to complete a color-by-number activity, try assigning the two activities as separate tasks. (You might try listing them on the schedule using separate icons: one for adding and another for coloring.) This way, students can feel they have successfully completed their adding before moving on to the next challenge.

✳ **Finish Later:** Students on the spectrum often have an urgent need for closure, a rigid, intrinsic pressure to complete whatever they've started. No matter how appealing the next activity may be, they may be unable to stop whatever they're doing until it's finished. The suggestion that they might "go back to it later" is too amorphous to offer any comfort. Try overtly scheduling an opportunity to tie up loose ends by putting a *Finish Work* icon on their schedule for later in the day. Or give students a folder called, *Work to Finish Later.* These strategies offer a kind of semi-closure, providing visual substance to your words and a tangible means of "putting a project where it belongs," even if just temporarily.

Teaching Waiting

Waiting means deferring want, which is especially difficult for impulsive students with limited executive function. Worse, when students on the spectrum are told to wait, they often do nothing but that. There is no notion of finding something else to amuse themselves *in the meantime* or occupying themselves *while* they wait. They just wait, and focus single-mindedly on what they are not getting. And that makes waiting interminable.

Offer alternatives to just waiting: *While you are waiting, please pick up five scraps of paper from the floor and put them in the recycling bin,* or *While you are waiting, go through your coolbox. I'll come get you when I'm ready.* Give students opportunities to practice deferring want for increasing increments of time and offer incentives for good waiting (Baker, 2009).

Despite these strategies for helping students on the spectrum develop regulatory skills, powerful sensory triggers may severely undermine their efforts to stay calm and consider or modulate their reactions to stimuli. The next section describes the overwhelming obstacles that can be presented by sensory challenges and offers many simple but critical ways to adapt the environment so that these sensitive students can cope.

Sensory Integration

Sensory information is processed in the brain through a system called *sensory integration*. When the sensory integration system works well, sensory input is efficiently and productively received by the brain where it is organized and responded

Chapter 4   Body and Soul: Regulation and Sensation

to in predictable ways. However, when the system is not adequately integrated, sensory input is processed in a way that does not yield an organized or predictable response. Disruptions to sensory integration can affect any or all types of sensation, and can sabotage students' efforts to learn, socialize, and stay calm. The sensory system can be so brittle that even one sensory offense can derail a whole day.

Sensory Processing Disorder

Significant disruption to the sensory integration process is called sensory processing disorder. Though sensory processing disorder is not an official diagnosis in DSM-IV, it is a discretely defined condition.

Sensory processing issues can cause a classroom decorated with brightly colored posters and artwork covering every inch of wall space to be visually overstimulating to students on the spectrum: they don't know where to look; colors swim before their eyes or give them headaches. The cluster-seating arrangement, which places your socially inept and distractible students in the midst of the other students, may be disorienting: the social environment feels incomprehensibly disorganized; faces are everywhere. The flashing lights that indicate the ending of an activity can be blinding and frightening. The sound of the clapping-rhythm response system you use to bring the students to attention may actually be painful to their ears.

Indeed, at school, the sensory assault of noise, movement, transitions, personalities, and more constantly swirls around, whipping up a menacingly stormy sea for these students. They may have an entirely different experience of your classroom than you might guess.

> *Be aware that even though [you] may have created a uniform experience for [your] class, this child's understanding of the experience, his interpretation of it, may be different than what we assume it would be.*
>
> —S. Jay Kuder (2003)

DID YOU KNOW . . .

While sensory processing disorder can occur in the absence of an autism spectrum diagnosis, more than 75% of individuals on the autism spectrum are believed to meet the criteria for sensory processing disorder. And among the approximately 25% of students on the spectrum who do *not* meet the criteria, most are likely to manifest at least some components of sensory processing challenge.

Since sensory assaults often spring up without warning, students are often on guard against them. Living with that relentless tension contributes significantly to the anxiety that is so common among students on the spectrum. But many aspects of the sensory environment can be mitigated and student responses can be modified. The next section describes what kinds of sensory triggers students face, followed by a long list of simple strategies to help settle those senses.

THE PROCESS OF SENSORY PROCESSING

Effective sensory processing is a multi-step system that depends on three separate areas of sensory function: *sensory modulation, sensory discrimination,* and *sensory-motor integration.* Challenges can occur in any or all of these areas.

Sensory Modulation

Sensory modulation is the ability to regulate responses to sensory input. Students with modulation challenges commonly respond in any or all of these three ways:

1. **Sensory Avoiders:** Students with high-responsivity to sensory stimuli are known as *sensory avoiders.* Seemingly innocuous or mild sensory input can be so painful to them that they hide from it or seek to defend themselves against it. These sensorily defensive efforts lead them to be fearful and cautious, or defiant—always

True to Their Experience

When students exhibit large and loud reactions, they are perceived as being *overly* responsive, making a big deal out of nothing. They tend to be dismissed as melodramatic. Instead, respect that these students react on the basis of what they feel. Sure, they seem extremely reactive, but if so, their intense response is perfectly suited to the degree of sensation they are receiving. What they are feeling, they are feeling big. Try to think of them as *highly* responsive; not *overly* responsive.

Similarly, when students seem oblivious to what's going on around them, they tend to be viewed as *under*-responsive, dull, or out of it. Sure, they seem tuned out, but if so, respect that their low-key response is perfectly suited to the degree of sensation they are receiving. What they are feeling, they scarcely notice. Try to think of these students as exhibiting *low*-responsivity, rather than as being *under*-responsive.

Chapter 4 Body and Soul: Regulation and Sensation

braced against sensory input and ready to react with a fight or flight response. Sometimes the use of more than one sense at a time can be entirely overwhelming.

2. **Sensory Disregarders:** Students with minimal responsivity to stimuli seem oblivious to sensory input. Known as *sensory disregarders,* they may seem sluggish, experiencing limited perception of pain, and requiring intense sensory input to get in gear. Students whose senses are minimally responsive can appear inattentive, self-absorbed, and disengaged.

3. **Sensory Seekers:** Students who are in need of intense sensory stimulation seek input constantly. Known as *sensory seekers* or *sensory cravers,* these students are on a constant quest for more, more, more. They are hyper-alert, always into everything. These are your bumpers and crashers, your risk takers. They hum, bite, sniff, touch, climb, jump, and spin, craving sensory input all the time (Kranowitz, 2005).

Sensory Discrimination

Sensory discrimination is the ability to perceive differences among various sensations. Some students may have such keen discrimination abilities that they can detect or focus on input so subtle that others may overlook it completely. But more often students with sensory discrimination issues are *sensory jumblers.* They may struggle to differentiate sounds (such as musical tones or rhyming words), pictures (such as same versus different, or foreground versus background), or smells and tastes.

Others who struggle with sensory discrimination may not realize when they are dizzy, hungry, or nauseous, for example. They may not recognize the difference between a gentle tap on the shoulder and a sharp poke in the arm—a confusion that has important social implications. They may have trouble determining the distance

Can You Hear Me Now?

When students seem to exhibit inadequate seeing or hearing abilities, parents or caregivers may wisely seek an evaluation with an ophthalmologist or audiologist to rule out a physiological problem. But if the root of the issue is, in fact, sensory processing, students may score just fine on seeing and hearing tests. In these cases, the disconnect is happening in the way visual and auditory input are being *processed* by the sensory system.

and speed of a moving vehicle when crossing the street, or may have figure-ground recognition challenges that make it difficult for them to interpret or sequence pictures.

For example, while consulting in a first-grade class, I worked on jigsaw puzzles with a student named Mateo. I noticed quickly that Mateo was unable to sort straight-edge pieces from middle pieces. Though I showed him the difference again and again and taught him how to run his finger across the straight edge, he did not seem to get it.

Finally I asked him to show me the straight edges on his incorrectly chosen pieces. To my surprise, he pointed out not the edges, but the straight lines drawn *on the pieces* as part of the picture. Even after I explained to him the difference between straight lines and straight edges, Mateo still could not differentiate the shape of a piece from the picture on it. He could not shift from looking at the image to looking at the shape.

It was only when I turned every single piece over to conceal the images—making all of the pieces uniformly gray—that Mateo was able to notice the shapes of the pieces and solve the puzzle quite efficiently—without the so-called "benefit" of the pictures.

Sensory-Motor Integration

Sensory-motor integration is the ability to plan and execute physical responses to various situations or stimuli. Students who struggle with sensory-motor integration have difficulty with coordination and movement. They may exhibit weak muscle tone and body control, slumping in their chairs, sprawling out on the rug, appearing generally floppy and clumsy.

Coping With Sensory Processing Challenges: Stims

When sensory input is troubling to those of us with typical sensory processing, we can often regulate the intensity of the input by altering our relationship with the external environment. When necessary, we cover our ears, close our eyes, hold our noses, and so on. But for students with sensory processing challenges, that same input may be overwhelming, causing them to seek comfort any which way they can. This section will describe one way students on the spectrum commonly seek to regulate the amount of sensation they absorb.

Many students on the spectrum exhibit repetitive behaviors at times, such as spinning, gritting their teeth, making noises, flapping their hands, flicking their fingers before their eyes, and more. Most of these seemingly inexplicable actions are examples of stereotypies, which are repetitive or ritualized movements, including tics. But when stereotypies occur in conjunction with autism spectrum disorders, they are usually known as *self-stimulatory behaviors* (and more casually referred to as *stims*) because they regulate the stimulation of sensory systems. Stims are distinguishable

Chapter 4   Body and Soul: Regulation and Sensation

from tics in that stims serve a regulatory purpose and relieve sensory stress, whereas tics are the result of firing neurons, and tend to serve no other purpose than to relieve the compulsion to express them.

Self-stimulatory behaviors are often interpreted as meaningless or dysfunctional but may in fact be vital to a student's ability to function. Stims are not deliberate actions; students do not do them *on purpose.* But understand that stims are most likely purpose*ful*: they occur for the purpose of modulating students' sensory experiences and anxiety. Stims help students in one or more of the following ways:

- stimulating their sensory input
- blocking out overwhelming sensory input
- releasing excess energy or excitement

Flapping, On the One Hand

Students who are minimally responsive to sensory stimuli may use stims to jumpstart their senses, like flipping the *on* switch in an otherwise sluggish sensory system. For these students, stimming can be pleasurable and helpful in activating their focus and engagement.

Flapping, On the Other Hand

Paradoxically, students who are highly responsive to sensory stimuli seem to stim more often when overstimulated by the external world. They lose themselves in the comfort of these repetitive behaviors in order to block out overwhelming input or release excess stimulation. For these students, stimming tends to increase when they are under stress or overexcited, and can serve a soothing purpose.

COMMON STIMS

You may notice students on the spectrum exhibiting any of the following stimming behaviors:

- grunting, chirping, or snapping fingers to remind them to tune in and listen up
- humming or repeating words or sounds to help them tune out the overwhelming noise of the classroom
- blinking at lights or wiggling fingers in front of eyes to stimulate the eyes to focus
- lining up objects or looking out of the corners of the eyes to help structure or limit an otherwise chaotic visual field
- scratching, hair twirling, or tapping to provide tactile input
- sniffing objects or other people to provide olfactory input

- licking or tasting inedible objects to provide oral input
- spinning, rocking, hand flapping, toe walking, jumping, or bouncing to help reestablish body position relative to the earth
- crashing, stomping, leaning, head banging, biting, chewing, or teeth grinding to stimulate muscles and joints

STEMMING STIMMING

Stims may help students sensorily but do them no favors socially. Still, when sensory reactions are disturbing to your class or to anyone in it, don't simply try to extinguish the behaviors. Instead, use the following section to help you understand the wide range of sensory disruptions that can affect the equilibrium of students on the spectrum. Then, at the end of this chapter, you'll find strategies to help you *adapt the sensory environment* to mitigate the impact these sensitivities have on your students and their ability to function in your classroom.

Types of Sensory Processing Challenges

Sensory processing challenges can affect any area of sensation, including not only the senses we are cognitively aware of, but also other body-centered senses we may not consciously perceive. If you teach students who seem to fit the descriptions above, the following section will describe how their challenges may manifest in your classroom, sense by sense.

The Basic Five

The senses that we are most readily in touch with, so to speak, are these basic five: hearing, seeing, touching, smelling, and tasting. Here is an overview of how students may respond to each of the five basic senses.

SOUND

1. *Sound Avoiders:* Students who struggle with auditory high-responsivity often hear sounds others cannot hear at all or are affected by sounds in intense ways. A variety of basic classroom sounds can be irritating or downright painful. Common auditory triggers include the buzzing of fluorescent lights, the scraping of chair legs against the floor, the peal of the lunch and dismissal bell, the squeaking of dry-erase markers on the whiteboard, the crackling of Styrofoam, as well as tapping feet, crinkling paper, and so on.

Auditory sensitivity is very common among students on the spectrum. Students with high auditory sensitivity can often be found trying to avoid input by covering their ears, tuning out, or acting out. Some resort to flapping or other self-stimulating behavior in an effort refocus their energy away from the unbearable input.

Paradoxically, some students actually scream when they hear an intolerable sound, seeking to drown out the offending noise with a more controllable sound of their own making.

2. *Sound Disregarders:* Students with auditory low-responsivity, like those with auditory processing challenges, may seem oblivious to ordinary sounds, and respond very slowly or only to exaggerated or very loud sounds. When the classroom marble jar crashes to the floor, shattering into pieces and sending marbles careening about the room, sensory disregarders don't even look up from their books. (See more about central auditory processing on page 162.)

3. *Sound Seekers:* Students who crave auditory input seek or create loud noise, prefer the volume on the radio or television to be turned way up, enjoy crowds and noisy places, and tend to speak very loudly.

SIGHT

1. *Sight Avoiders:* Students with visual high-responsivity may be overwhelmed by bright colors, busy visual fields, and certain kinds of lights. (See Lights Out box on page 84.) They may cover their eyes or make poor eye contact and appear inattentive or hypervigilant.

2. *Sight Disregarders:* Students with visual low-responsivity may react slowly to approaching objects or people, fail to notice obstacles in their path, have limited visual-spatial recognition, stare at the sun or other bright lights, and may seem to look right through you.

3. *Sight Seekers:* Students who crave visual input seek lots of screen time, gravitate toward shiny or spinning objects, flick their fingers in front of their eyes.

Layout Logic

Despite the many proven benefits of seating students in clusters, old-school classrooms with desks organized in neat rows are actually easier for students on the spectrum to manage. Freestanding desks in straight lines create a less distracting, less interactive environment and a clearer, visually more structured space. If you have students who are overstimulated or distracted by sitting face-to-face with other students, consider setting up a semi-enclosed carrel for them by placing backwards bookshelves or blank bulletin boards between your student and the broader visual field.

Lights Out

Fluorescent lights are ever-present in schools and pose a distinct problem for students on the spectrum. The incessant buzzing and flickering and harsh glare of these lights may be unbearable. Even the new compact fluorescent light bulbs (CFLs) flicker. Though the flicker may be imperceptible to you, it can be painful and provocative to someone who is visually highly responsive.

The best way to support a student who struggles with this is to keep those overhead lights off. Often natural sunlight will be enough to light the classroom. When the sun won't shine, consider using incandescent lamps; these create a warmer, cozier setting and eliminate the buzzing and flickering.

If you are unable to function without the overhead lights, try using only some of them, or changing the seats of affected students—perhaps the glare is diminished in certain locations or positions. Some students benefit from wearing light-colored sunglasses or a baseball-type cap with a brim to shade their eyes from the glare. If light poses an ongoing problem, suggest to parents or caregivers that they consult with a developmental optometrist, who may be able to provide Irlen glasses or similar custom lenses that are specially developed to filter out offensive elements of light.

Note that all desktop computer screens flicker as well. Students with visual sensitivity may be unable to tolerate looking at desktop screens. Laptop computers are the only kind that have no flicker.

TOUCH

1. *Touch Avoiders:* Students with tactile high-responsivity may flinch when others approach, find a light touch to be painful, and react angrily to innocuous physical contact. These students tend to avoid messy activities such as those involving paint or glue and be intolerant of getting wet. They are likely to find certain fabrics, seams, or clothing labels to be painful or unbearably irritating. Or they may prefer to wear long sleeves and long pants even in summer to protect themselves from bruises and scratches.

2. *Touch Disregarders:* Students with tactile low-responsivity have poor body awareness. These students are not likely to notice that their shoes are on the wrong feet, that their face is dirty, or that their nose is running. They may not notice that they have bumped into someone or not realize when they are being too physical with others.

3. *Touch Seekers:* Students who crave tactile input seek or create messy activities and tend to touch everything and everyone, often at inappropriate times or in socially unacceptable ways. They may also rub or bite their own skin, twirl their hair, chew on their fingernails, collars, or pencils, and prefer being barefoot.

Don't Disregard Disregarders

Touch Disregarders seem unaware of touch unless it is intense, and therefore they may have a diminished perception of pain. They may not realize it when they are significantly hurt, so watch them carefully.

By the same token, these students may not be affected by extremes of temperature, feeling perfectly comfortable in situations that are extremely hot or cold to others. They must be monitored in this regard as well, as they can fall victim to heat exhaustion or hypothermia.

SMELL

1. *Smell Avoiders:* Students with olfactory high-responsivity can be powerfully affected by smells that may be undetectable to others. They may get physically overwhelmed by individual smells or by combinations of smells. The lunchroom,

the bathroom, the gym, markers, pencil shavings, fresh photocopies, hand lotion, and others are all potential offenders at school.

2. *Smell Disregarders:* Students with olfactory low-responsivity seem oblivious to smells. They may not be affected by the various body emissions that their peers react to with loud objection, and, more importantly, may not detect the smell of smoke or leaking gas.

3. *Smell Seekers:* Students who crave olfactory input may seek to learn about their environment by smelling it. They may sniff at new objects to differentiate them from others, or may find certain smells soothing or exciting.

TASTE

1. *Taste Avoiders:* Students who have a high-responsivity to taste are often very picky eaters, avoiding strong flavors and certain textures of food.

2. *Taste Disregarders:* Students who have a low-responsivity to taste tend to be indifferent to the flavor of food or types of cuisine.

3. *Taste Seekers:* Student who crave taste stimulation may seek out spicy foods, crunchy foods, or seek to learn about their environment through taste, which may lead them to bite or lick inedible items.

Plus Two: The Interoceptive Senses

The interoceptive senses relate to our awareness of our own internal states, including balance and position, as well as hunger, thirst, fatigue, illness, and other physical discomfort. Generally speaking, students who have high-responsivity to internal input may seem hypochondriacal. But in fact they are feeling every internal irregularity quite acutely.

Students who have low-responsivity to internal input, on the other hand, may not know when they are sick, uncomfortable, or off-balance, and may miss the signal when it is time to use the bathroom. (Be careful not to blame students for persistent toileting problems. Offer support to the parents or caregivers, who are surely exasperated, by explaining that this stubborn situation could have a sensory explanation. Consult with the occupational therapist for strategies.)

Two specific areas of interoception are *proprioception* and *vestibulation*.

PROPRIOCEPTION

The proprioceptive sense relates to perceiving where our bodies are in space, based on input or pressure received by muscles and joints. Proprioception tells us what our body parts are doing or should be doing in any situation. When working effectively, this sense would, for example, guide our muscles to clench when someone puts a heavy book in our hands. Students who struggle with proprioception may not be able to regulate the force of their high-five or the pressure of their pencil.

1. *Pressure Avoiders:* Students who have high-responsivity to joint and muscle input tend to be physically rigid, avoid hugs, and steer clear of activities like jumping, running, or rolling.

2. *Pressure Disregarders:* Students with low-responsivity to joint and muscle input may trip and fall frequently and be unaware of their position.

3. *Pressure Seekers:* Students who seek joint and muscle input are bumpers and crashers: running full tilt into walls, sitting with their chairs tipped back, pratfalling over obstacles. They tend to run their hand along the wall in the hallway, may lean or press against objects, stomp their feet when walking, crack their knuckles, or use proprioceptively stimulating behaviors such as head banging, toe walking, or hand flapping.

> **DID YOU KNOW . . .**
>
> The words *proprioception* and *kinesthesia* are often used interchangeably. In fact, *kinesthesia* refers more to actual movement, whereas *proprioception* refers to the perception of movement.

VESTIBULATION

The vestibular sense tells us which end is up, based on the position of our heads in relation to the earth. Movement and balance activities such as spinning, turning upside-down, and jumping are regulated by the vestibular system. Depending on the functioning of the vestibular sense in each student, these kinds of activities may be either unbearable or unstoppable.

1. *Movement Avoiders:* Students who have a high-responsivity to movement struggle to maintain their sense of balance and physical equilibrium. They may have low muscle tone, slumping in their chairs or resting their heads on the table, and they

may struggle with bilateral coordination when required to use both hands at the same time. These students are commonly disoriented by movement activities such as biking, running, sledding, swinging, sliding, or spinning. They tend to be cautious and afraid of falling; they clutch your arm as they walk in the hall or cling tightly to banisters when on stairs. They may appear uncooperative—for example, refusing to get up on the chorus risers—but in fact, they are afraid.

2. *Movement Disregarders:* Students with a low-responsivity to movement can spin for a long time without getting dizzy, be unaware when they are off-balance, and fail to protect or remove themselves from precarious situations.

Four Is Shy and Quiet: Synesthesia

Heightened responsivity to sound allows some individuals with auditory sensitivity to make extraordinary connections to music because they can perceive elements others do not hear. Similarly, individuals with heightened sensitivities to any kind of sensory input, can demonstrate remarkable multisensory relationships with activities such as painting, sculpting, cooking, dancing, and more.

On rare occasions, individuals with unusual sensory perception experience synesthesia. *Synesthesia* is the perceptual joining together of sensations that are typically perceived separately. People who experience synaesthesia may see sounds, hear colors, taste shapes, smell textures, feel music, and more.

In his memoir, *Born on a Blue Day* (2007), Daniel Tammet, an adult with Asperger's Syndrome, describes his extraordinary capacity with numbers. Tammet associates every number with a specific shape, color, texture, and personality. By intuitively visualizing numbers in a vivid pictorial landscape, Tammet has memorized and can recite the value of *pi* up to 22,500 digits.

3. *Movement Seekers:* Students who seek movement are constantly in motion. They are thrill-seekers and daredevils. In school, they tend to fidget and wiggle, swivel in chairs, leap down multiple steps, and hang upside down.

Sensational Strategies

In the context of the sensory environment, sensory reactions are involuntary and stimming behaviors are vital comfort anchors. Instead of trying to extinguish them, consider what purpose disruptive behaviors serve. The connection between a behavior and its purpose is not always apparent. See if you can recognize your student in the sections above on sensory modulation: Is he a sensory avoider or a sensory seeker? Is she seeking less stimulation or more stimulation? Which sense or senses is he trying to modulate with a particular behavior?

Occupational Therapy

Occupational therapy is the go-to place for students who have sensory processing issues. Occupational therapists are qualified to use specific sensory integration therapy techniques during sessions with students. These techniques can be highly successful in helping to integrate the mind-body connection needed to regulate sensory input.

Occupational therapy interventions may include desensitization or stimulation through brushing, joint compression, deep pressure, therapeutic swinging, and many other techniques. These kinds of activities can help organize the sensory systems to calm students down and set them up for learning. Occupational therapists can teach parents and caregivers how to carry through some of these therapeutic techniques outside of school as well.

In addition to improving self-regulation, sensory processing, and adaptive responses, occupational therapy can also address the following related motor challenges that students on the spectrum may face:

- *Praxis* is our ability to plan a motor activity and then actually execute it. Dyspraxic students struggle to figure out how to cross midline, use both hands together (bilateral coordination), and organize body movements.

- *Fine-motor coordination* is our ability to use small muscles with strength, dexterity, and control. Students with fine-motor challenges struggle with handwriting, cutting with scissors, and more.

- *Hand-eye coordination* is our ability to synchronize the use of our hands with visual input. Students with hand-eye coordination challenges struggle with skills such as fastening buttons, stringing beads, and keeping their place while counting objects.

- *Oral-motor coordination* is our ability to use the muscles in and around our mouths with strength and control. Oral motor challenges can include chewing, drinking, and blowing bubbles.

- *Visual-motor coordination* is our ability to use the muscles in our eyes with strength and control. Students with visual motor challenges struggle to track left to right while reading, use both eyes together, and more.

- *Activities of daily living (ADLs)* are the necessary basic tasks of everyday life. Success with ADLs depends upon capacity with many of the fundamental skills listed above. Challenging activities of daily living may include personal hygiene, getting dressed, and eating with utensils.

Creating a Sensory-Friendly Classroom

If you have students who may be under sensory stress, this section will offer you an assortment of simple strategies you can use to make your classroom sensory-friendly.

Many of these strategies are easily implemented using supplies you already have in your classroom. Others require specialized sensory tools that can be provided by occupational therapists or ordered online. You can find links to sites that sell these kinds of tools as well as many additional sensory strategies at www.barbaraboroson.com.

SENSORY OPTIONS

The key to creating a sensory environment that supports all kinds of sensory processors is offering options. Since some students in your class may be sensory avoiders, some sensory disregarders, and some sensory seekers—while most are probably sensory *thrivers*—there is no one-size-fits-all solution. Instead, provide opportunities for students to regulate their own degree of exposure to sensory stimulation. This means maintaining flexible and differentiated expectations, such as the following examples:

- Even though most students in your class may enjoy painting with their fingers using shaving cream or pudding, students who cannot tolerate those textures should have access to a brush or a sponge.

- Some students don't exert enough pressure to color with colored pencils or even crayons; they need access to markers.

- If glue happens to produces anxiety, offer glue sticks, paste, rubber cement, tape, paper clips, or staples.

- If students are willing to touch clay but not immerse their fingers in it, offer gloves or even ice-cream sticks as alternative ways to manipulate the clay. Offer differently textured clay products such as Theraputty, Silly Putty, Play Dough, and so on.

- Some students welcome noise-canceling headphones to block out all background sound while doing quiet work. Others focus better with rhythmic music pulsing through those same headphones. And others won't be able to tolerate even the feeling of headphones against their ears.

SENSORY CORNERS

All students welcome opportunities to retreat and regroup. For everyone's benefit, consider setting up a sensory corner in your classroom. Find an available corner of your room and partially wall it off (using shelves, bookcases, or bulletin boards) to minimize visual and auditory stimulation and to allow some privacy. Make it cozy with a soft rug, along with cushions, pillows, or beanbag chairs, and perhaps a soft-light lamp.

Keep here a collection of sensory tools that students can choose from whenever they need to calm down or rev up. Tools can include squeeze balls, textured or weighted balls, bubble wrap, therapeutic putty, linking cubes, pull tubes, Slinkys, scraps of textured fabrics, beads, picture books, music with earphones, noise-canceling headphones, and more. Some students will busily push, pull, touch, and so on. Others may stretch out across the rug and close their eyes.

Students who struggle to keep their composure in the classroom may fare even better when they have access to a soothing space outside of the classroom. In an ideal world, your school might be one of those that already has a separate sensory room, outfitted with many of the tools and comforts used in a sensory corner, along with thick mats, weighted blankets, a swing, a mini-trampoline, and a soothing sound machine. But if not, and if you have students who might benefit from this kind of special space, see if the occupational therapist can justify the need for a sensory room and present the idea to school administrators. The one-time set-up costs will be more than compensated by the high-intensity crises it will help avert for many years to come.

SOOTHING THE SENSES

Sensory avoiders are the most vulnerable to becoming overwhelmed because of their high-responsivity to stimuli. It is best to modify the overall environment to meet their needs first, adding in optional stimulation for your sensory-disregarding and sensory-seeking students.

Sensory input in the classroom can be diminished in any or all of the following ways. Choose strategies that are not only useful for sensorily challenged students but also comfortable to you and reasonable in the context of your entire class. Remember to alert students on the spectrum before you make changes to the room, even if you are making the changes for their benefit.

Don't try to implement all of these strategies. Consider the specific needs of your students and try any of these strategies that sound promising and manageable to you:

✳ Place rugs in the room. No need to cover the whole floor; scattered rugs will help absorb sound and keep the room quieter. (Small area rugs also serve the important function of helping to visually define the boundaries of work and play areas.)

✳ Try to keep spaces well organized, free of clutter, and clearly delineated.

✳ Allow students to keep a small soothing sensory object—whether it's a scrap of silky fabric, a smooth pebble, a tiny stuffed animal, or something else—with them throughout the day. This can provide comfort on demand, serving as a touchstone in their pocket.

✳ Face students away from the glare of sunlight (which can change over the course of the day) and turn off the overhead lights.

✳ Seat students away from open windows and the hallway, away from the dripping faucet, the dehumidifier, and any other source of auditory distraction.

✳ Limit decorations on your walls, at least at the beginning of the year. Add elements gradually, watching for signs of distraction or disorganization.

✳ Minimize the amount of work on any one page. Use reading guide strips that highlight only one line of text at a time. Or create a cardboard cut-out template students can use to frame small amounts of work, effectively hiding everything else on the page.

✷ Seat students away from the gerbil cage, the bathroom, painting supplies, open windows, and any other source of potential odors.

✷ Alert physical education teachers and recess monitors of balance and equilibrium issues so that these students are never required to engage in activities that feel threatening.

STIMULATING THE SENSES

Students who are sensory disregarders and sensory seekers need access to sensory stimulation on their own terms. Offer lots of *optional* stimulating supports and activities to jumpstart or satiate their sensorily needy systems. Meanwhile, be sure to attend to the safety of these students on stairs and when using classroom and playground equipment.

Try some of these suggestions if they suit the needs of students in your class:

✷ Allow the use of worry beads, squeeze balls, or other fidget toys.

✷ Offer an extra snack break during the day to stimulate the senses when focus is flagging.

✷ Provide wiggle cushions that offer vestibular input to reduce fidgeting while sitting.

✷ Check that chair height is appropriate so that students' feet rest squarely on the floor, to support balance and security. Seat cushions and foot rests can be used to make minor adjustments.

✷ Offer plenty of movement breaks during which all students have the opportunity to get physical input. Try whole-class jumping jacks or yoga moments. Just one minute spent in the "downward-facing dog" position can reboot engagement and focus for students who need the vestibular input. For students who cannot tolerate going upside down, suggest still, upright poses such as the "mountain pose." (Display photographs of these yoga positions on the SMART Board or projection screen.)

✷ Try doing a moment of whole-class meditation several times a day. The expenditure of a few meditative minutes across the day could pay off with hours of calmer, more focused learners.

Chapter 4   Body and Soul: Regulation and Sensation

✳ Offer natural opportunities for weight-bearing or input-stimulating activities, such as stacking chairs, distributing text books, rubber-stamping papers, using a hole-punch, and so on.

✳ Provide pencil grippers for poor pencil grasp or vibrating pens to increase grip awareness.

✳ Alert physical education teachers and recess monitors of balance and equilibrium issues so that these students are closely monitored for risk-taking behaviors

As you have seen in this chapter, most students on the spectrum face an unrelenting onslaught of sensory challenges from all directions and lack the skills to regulate their responses. As long as they are out and about amid the social world, unpredictable input swirls around menacingly. Really, the safest place is *in*. The next chapter will lead you on a tour of that remote inner sanctum and show you how to bridge the gap.

The Inner Sanctum

Crossing the Bridge to a Remote Student

Challenges in the areas of socialization, communication, regulation, and sensation comprise a heavy burden that students on the spectrum bring to every encounter. If that's not enough to carry, pile on the anxiety that results from facing the world with so many challenges, and we can understand why every encounter feels overwhelming.

Does anxiety force these students to retreat into their predictable inner worlds as protection from the onslaught of external stimuli? Or is their remoteness the *cause* of their difficulties with the external world? There may be no simple answer, but there is no doubt that the *interplay* of remoteness and anxiety is powerful and self-sustaining. It produces fearful, socially separate students who are frequently lost in their own heads, not tuned in to what is happening around them, and seemingly unavailable to others.

Some students seem content to stay inwardly focused and do not welcome interlopers into their private inner world. They may not have the natural motivation to make contact with you, to establish a connection, to keep open the lines of communication. Others clearly want to engage but don't know how to do so in pro-social ways. They may have the motivation but be unable to demonstrate it in a way that is meaningful to you. Still others may come and go—one moment, totally engaged; and the next, nobody's home.

While remoteness may serve as a protective barrier for students, it also insulates them from important stimuli that actually must break through: like education and socialization. Surely you have many tricks up your sleeve to engage students; your lively demeanor and creative curriculum are designed to excite and draw students toward you and toward the learning opportunities you offer. But unfortunately, students on the spectrum will not simply come to you. So even while you're busy tending to the needs of the rest of your class, you'll have to take the time to go and get them. This chapter describes why students on the spectrum seem lost within themselves and offers strategies you can use to facilitate engagement.

Life on the Island

It is almost as though each student on the autism spectrum is on a remote island—alone. The waves wash in and out, the sun rises and sets, and there is a soothing, predictable rhythm to the day. The island may be beautiful and peaceful, but it is also solitary and stagnant. There is no learning, no growth on the island; just more of the same, day after day. If that is all your students on the spectrum know, they are missing out on the richness that life on the mainland has to offer. They do have the capacity to be vital participants—they just need lots of help. They need the psychic push to step up onto the bridge, the skills and stamina to make the journey across, and the ongoing support to manage the chaos, demands, and stimulation of life off the island.

This will be quite a journey—one students cannot make by themselves. You will need to help them cross the bridge. And even if you have numerous students on the spectrum in your class, you can be sure that they do not all inhabit the same island. Each dwells on a solitary island with its own culture and values. Each student will need to cross his own bridge, at his own pace, and only to the extent that he is able.

Early in your relationship, you may need to travel almost all the way across the bridge to reach a student. Take some time there to get to know the island, look around, listen to the sounds, check out the sights, get a feel for the culture there. What's it all about? What's the buzz on the island?

Then slowly begin to use what you know to draw the student toward you, coaxing a few steps at a time, helping draw her across the bridge toward the social world.

The View From the Bridge: Looking at Eye Contact

Eye contact is one of the most profound and obvious challenges for students on the spectrum. The absence of eye contact contributes to your perception that students are disengaged. Students who do not make eye contact are also deprived of the benefits of *joint attention*, which is the sharing of experience with others (more on this on page 102) and *social referencing*, which is the use of our eyes to confirm what we hear and to verify that we are being heard. A lack of eye contact can lead to serious miscommunications and social missteps.

Eye contact may be limited for several reasons:

1. *Sensory avoidance:* Students on the spectrum often avoid eye contact for sensory reasons. For some, direct eye contact may feel too intense and may cause anxiety, sensory overload, even pain. Other students may find looking at the eyes of others to be overwhelmingly distracting and disconcerting: Eyes are constantly shifting and darting around, while the up and down movement of lashes makes eyes seem to flash and flicker.

2. *Motor control:* Some students do not have the visual motor control necessary to stabilize their own eyes. They may be unable to focus on and track objects in motion or follow an object that moves across the center of their field of vision. Consult your school's occupational therapist to see if your students' difficulties with eye contact are a product of visual-motor issues such as crossing midline or visual tracking. If so, the occupational therapist may be able to offer visual training and muscle strengthening strategies.

3. *Social communication:* Some students on the spectrum may not perceive that making eye contact is a component of communication. To them, communication happens through speaking, listening, and writing; eye contact does not seem a relevant or necessary part, and so they do not look for messages you may be sending with your eyes. Check with the speech and language specialist to see if eye contact can be addressed in sessions as a component of social language.

In the natural classroom setting, baseline anxiety among students on the spectrum is likely to be fairly high. They are already very busy with their significant efforts to sit still, listen, process, make relevant associations, while also refraining from calling out, flapping their hands, grunting, and thinking about batteries. That may be about all they can handle at one time. Making eye contact could be one task too many. In fact, some students may be better able to engage in your lesson *without* the added anxiety or strain of making eye contact.

But in some circumstances, it is essential that students learn to focus their eyes on their tasks. For example, if they are crossing a street or cutting with a knife, they must be taught to look. The next section will describe some strategies you can use to encourage eye contact in the classroom.

Learning to Look: Eye Contact Strategies

For students on the spectrum, eye contact is usually a learned skill—not a natural reflex. Just as a stuttering student struggles to get words out, your student on the spectrum struggles to make eye contact. As is the case for stuttering, the more pressure there is to make eye contact, the more anxiety gets in the way, and the more difficult it is for students to comply. So eye contact should never be required and a lack of it should never be punished. But if you have students who struggle with eye contact, here are some gentle ways to encourage it.

PRACTICING EYE CONTACT

Lessons on making direct eye contact are best left for one-on-one, low-key moments. Assess a student's anxiety levels carefully before encouraging eye contact. Use your knowledge of individual anxiety triggers to help you judge when a student might be able to handle adding eye contact.

Try some of these strategies for supporting eye contact:

✳ **Seize the Moment:** Ask for eye contact when a student wants something from you. In these moments, since he has initiated the conversation, he is engaged and highly motivated.

✳ **The Eyes Have It:** Teach students that extra information can be found by looking at people's eyes. Offer verbal and/or visual prompts as needed to support eye contact. The spoken reminder *Look at me* may be all a student needs to remember to turn his eyes toward you. If it helps, you may want to point to your eyes or hold up a *Look at teacher* icon.

✳ **Take What You Get:** Clarify that you do not expect constant eye contact. Be specific that you would like him to look at your eyes *some* of the time, to show you that he is paying attention. Fleeting focus may be as much as these students can give you, but it may be enough.

✳ **Reinforce It:** Explain to him that when he looks at your eyes you can see that he is making a connection with you: *I can tell you're paying attention because you are looking at me.*

✳ **Generalize It:** Give your student specific suggestions as to how to generalize the new skill: *Now you may offer Cindy the glue stick. Try to give her the same great eye contact you just gave me.*

EYE CONTACT ALTERNATIVES

With training and reinforcement, many students can internalize eye contact as a learned response and use it habitually, but it may never evolve to the level of meaningful nonverbal communication. Coerced eye contact can result in a quite empty success. Some students who have been taught to make eye contact ultimately seem to look *at* and even *through* others rather than to *connect with* them. Be open to the possibility that making eye contact may not be the only way students can show you they are paying attention.

✳ **A Little to the Side:** Allow students to give partial eye contact by looking out of the sides of their eyes rather than looking at you face to face.

Don't Look Now

My own son's most thoughtful and reciprocal conversations happen while he is pacing around the dining room table. Without the burden of eye contact, and with the added proprioceptive input of rhythmic pacing, his sensory system is regulated to its most open, engageable setting.

✳ **As If:** Encourage students to "pretend" to make eye contact by looking at your nose, ears, or forehead, which are much more static than your eyes. While this strategy does not avail students of social referencing cues, it does create the more socially agreeable appearance that they are attending.

✳ **Cue Ready Position:** Use the phrase *Get ready* or *Show me Ready Position* with your students, which would imply a set of pre-explained expectations such as the following:

Ready Position

1. *Book on desk.*

2. *Pencil in hand.*

3. *Feet in front.*

4. *Mouth quiet.*

Place a *Ready Position* rubric on the desks of students who need it, listing the components of Ready Position. When you see your students in position, you have a roomful of attentive listeners, even if some of them are looking down or elsewhere.

✳ **Look at That:** There are times during lessons when you will need your students to look—but not necessarily at your eyes. If you are demonstrating an activity, tell them specifically to look at what you are doing: *Look at what my hands are doing* or *Watch what happens to this water.*

LOOKING TO LEARN

An indirect strategy for encouraging use of eye contact is to use nonverbal prompts instead of spoken words when possible. If a student on the spectrum asks you how many crayons she is allowed to take, hold up three fingers. If she asks you when the next full moon will be, look at her and shrug. But implement this strategy gradually. If you notice that she is not seeing your nonverbal signals, get her attention verbally first: *Look at me, Suki. I am going to show you my answer.*

And always check for understanding. If necessary, explain specifically what your nonverbal signals mean. Teach her that your three raised fingers indicate three crayons, that your shrug means you don't know the answer. Over time, this strategy can help a student develop the habit of *looking to learn* and will enhance engagement in general.

"Elsewhere" on the Island: Exploring Distant Shores

To begin engaging these remote students, you need to connect with them first on their terms. This may be no easy feat. Students on the spectrum may be mired in challenges to engagement that severely limit their availability to participate in learning, socializing, or anything outside the preoccupying inner workings of their minds.

A desire to share experience with others, known as *joint attention,* is often lacking among students on the spectrum. The absence of that social instinct serves to keep these students contentedly ensconced on their solitary island, and not necessarily motivated to get off. At the same time, students on the spectrum tend to get locked into repetitive patterns of behavior known as *perseveration,* which protects them from new and overwhelming experiences and satisfies their need for sameness. This next section describes the challenges of joint attention and perseveration, and then offers suggestions for what to do when you encounter these obstacles on your mutual journey toward engagement.

Joint Attention

Joint attention is the sharing of attention and experience with another person. An infant seeks joint attention by pointing out an airplane flying overhead because he wants to share the thrill of it with his mother. A toddler taking her first steps looks at her father to see if he noticed. A preschooler takes his teacher's hand and leads her to the easel to show what he colored. Even before they have words, most students seek to share experience.

But, even as babies, students on the spectrum are not likely to seek ways to connect or to compensate for undeveloped language in order to share experience. Even the common *pick me up* gesture, when a baby lifts her arms skyward, is seldom seen among children on the spectrum. This is because engaging another person to share in a discovery or an idea is a *social* instinct—as if to say, *Let's share this moment together.*

For these reasons, students may not be inclined to embark on any kind of journey with you. They may resist your efforts to join with them, and refuse your invitations to participate even in seemingly highly desirable activities. Joint attention does not tend to develop spontaneously among students on the spectrum due to challenges of ability in related areas. These include:

- *Mindblindness:* The inability to take someone else's perspective limits students' ability to share another's experience. (See more on mindblindness in Chapters 7 and 8.)

Chapter 5   The Inner Sanctum: Crossing the Bridge to a Remote Student

- *Nonverbal communication:* Students are often expected to infer meaning through visual cues. But when you point out an object to students on the spectrum, they are more likely to look, concretely, at your pointed finger than at what your finger is indicating. For them to follow the *implication* of your pointed finger requires them to assume your physical perspective: from *your* eye, down *your* arm, to an object in *your* field of vision. You are asking them to *join you* in your perspective. But they are just looking at your finger. (See more on nonverbal communication in Chapters 7 and 8.)

- *Inference:* Joint attention may require extrapolating from the concrete to the abstract. When you say, *Look at our soil pots today!* your students on the spectrum may obligingly look at the soil pots, but will not necessarily join you in inferring why the pots are cause for celebration, despite the emergence of green sprouts.

- *Flexibility:* Joint attention also requires flexibility. Even though the sink is overflowing right now, your student on the spectrum is preoccupied with something else. Executive dysfunction prohibits her ability to put reminiscences of *High School Musical* on a back burner until you have resolved your sink emergency. This kind of inflexibility, or rigidity, reflects the presence of another obstacle on the path toward engagement: perseveration.

Perseveration Station

Perseveration is a fixation or repetition of a word, phrase, gesture, activity, or thought, regardless of its relevance or irrelevance to context. Students on the spectrum rely on perseveration to provide themselves a cushion of familiarity and a locus of control over their environment. Perseverative behaviors and fixations help block out sensory threats or other challenging stimuli such as unstructured time, noisy activities, or difficult social or academic tasks, effectively insulating these students from the social world. Psychologist Tony Attwood (2009) suggests that one reason students, especially those with Asperger's Syndrome, perseverate is that they may be afraid of making mistakes. A rigid need to be *right* and a resultant fear of failure cause them to cling to sameness, to perseverate on what they know for sure.

You'll recognize perseveration as the seemingly endless examination of the same topic, over and over and over again. Perseveration can take any of the following forms:

- rigidly repetitive actions, such as lining up or stacking objects or exhibiting self-stimulatory behaviors (as described in Chapter 4)

- mental and conversational fixation on singular topics, such as air conditioners or the line of ascension to the British throne

- frequent repetition of certain words or phrases, such as *May the force be with you!* or *I'll get you, my pretty—and your little dog, too!*

Some students may use perseverative language or behavior as a way of trying to socialize, although their endless examinations of specific topics can instead quickly become conversation stoppers.

Others appear to zone out when the going gets tough, though they may, in fact, be zeroing in on a favored topic. Nine-year-old Tricia knows every stop of every train route in the metro area where she lives, along with what time each train is scheduled to arrive and depart each station. If you tell her your itinerary, she'll tell you which train line to board, what time the next train will leave, and what time it will arrive at your destination.

This kind of knowledge is appealing to Tricia because it is fixed and immutable—the facts are completely *knowable.* They represent long-standing consistency of system and schedule. Moreover, train times, like school bells, are reliably precise. When else in life can we count on something to happen at exactly 3:04 or 2:58?

Though spinning and chirping and reciting train schedules may ease certain discomforts inside students, such behaviors will only create and exacerbate other discomforts in the social world. Moreover, students' rigid adherence to repetitive ideas can interfere significantly with their coping skills. Perseveration comes with costs and benefits, as described below. Recognizing both sides of this equation can help you discern when to step in to try to interrupt the cycle, and when you might want to let it keep spinning.

The Costs of Perseveration: A One-Track Mind

Timothy Pychyl, a professor of psychology and expert on procrastination believes, "To *persevere* is a virtue . . . to *perseverate* is a problem" (2005, p. 1). Whereas perseverance is goal oriented, perseveration tends to be uncontrollable and boundless.

Indeed, psychologist Tony Attwood (2009) perceives *typical* students as traveling through life in an all-terrain vehicle on an open road. If they find they are headed in the wrong direction, they will say, *Oh! I must be on the wrong track!* and they readily change course. Students on the spectrum, however, ride a train along a single track. When they come upon an obstacle or a road block, or they find themselves on the wrong track, they get stuck. They insist, *This is the right track. Why isn't it working? Why am I not getting anywhere?* They cannot imagine a way around the road block or obstacle. These students may be proverbially—or literally—beating their

Chapter 5   The Inner Sanctum: Crossing the Bridge to a Remote Student

heads against a wall and be unable to stop. Students on the spectrum tend to be the last to know and the last to seek help when they are on the wrong track. This extreme rigidity can mean big problems when a student is really headed in the wrong direction.

The Benefits of Perseveration: X-treme Attending

On the other hand, at times this kind of singly focused, inflexible trajectory can have its benefits. Since students on the spectrum can't change tracks on their own, they may not give up trying until they reach their destination, no matter what. Sometimes getting stuck can be useful in terms of persisting and problem solving. These students may be inattentive to your agenda, but they are hyper-attentive to their own.

Some theories suggest that unawareness of or lack of interest in the social world allows individuals on the spectrum to go much deeper into their chosen topic than others can or do. Unfettered by social concerns such as *What will my friends think?*, or *Nobody else acts like this*, or *No one else seems interested in this so I should just drop it,* students on the spectrum have the social freedom to dig deeper and deeper and deeper.

Temple Grandin (2008) believes that the brains of individuals with autism spectrum disorders actually have fewer connections between various regions, which can make the learning of certain tasks very difficult but also allows for new and different connections to be made. She draws the analogy that when there are fewer connections between Los Angeles and New York, there may be more connections available between Los Angeles and Santa Fe.

Whatever the cause, incredible innovation, stunning artwork, and other astounding splinter skills can be manifested by individuals on the autism spectrum. Great thinkers such as Albert Einstein, Isaac Newton, Thomas Jefferson, Nikola Tesla, and Dian Fossey, and brilliant artists such as Andy Warhol, Wassily Kandinsky, and Hans Christian Andersen are all thought to have exhibited distinctly spectrum-like qualities throughout their lifetimes.

PERSEVERATION PRESERVATION

Stims and other perseverative behaviors can be especially difficult to manage in a classroom because they are by definition intractable and habit-forming. Since students on the spectrum can become locked into patterns of behavior, they may develop a physiological and psychological dependence on these behaviors. Even when stimming or perseveration appears disruptive and dysfunctional, it does serve an important, immediate, and discrete function for each student who exhibits it. Understanding that specific function can help you and your students *modify* the behavior into mutually meaningful forms of expression. Many professionals try to take an aggressive approach to quickly extinguish what they see as meaningless or disruptive behaviors. But behavior modification strategies are not indicated here; they are ineffective at best and would likely backfire because perseverative and stimming behaviors, like all other behaviors, are coping mechanisms. *Extinguishing a coping mechanism serves only to extinguish coping.*

Still Stimming

Later in this chapter, you'll find strategies to help you circumvent, rather than extinguish perseveration. But if you feel that a student's stimming or perseverative behavior is dangerous or interfering with social success, then in those cases, of course you need to intervene to modify these behaviors. (See more on modifying behaviors in Chapter 10.)

In practical terms, whether your students on the spectrum are destined to discover a cure for cancer or are spinning in endless circles, they will need to join their attention with yours to engage in learning the primary curriculum. Indeed, even Isaac Newton needed to learn reading and computation skills. So here are some strategies for garnering joint attention, working with and around perseveration, while still honoring the special needs and interests of your students.

Getting Engaged on the Island

Since students on the spectrum tend to be fixated on their own thoughts, it will be difficult to get them to emerge suddenly and join attention with someone else about something else. It's a huge leap. But if you have students who seem far, far away, try some of these strategies to draw them toward you.

✳ **Keep It Real:** In order to capture engagement, create lessons that are personally relevant and meaningful. Making connections to topics that are of personal interest to students will help them feel more comfortable venturing into new conceptual territory.

For example, near the end of each school year, Gail, a fourth-grade teacher, instructs her students on how to write persuasively. She has them hone their skills by writing a persuasive letter to her on a highly motivating topic: *What would be a better way to organize our classroom and why?* Gail reads each completed letter aloud to the class, and they discuss which elements are more well reasoned, respectfully presented, and compelling than others. Together they select the letter that is most persuasive and then Gail, while reserving some veto power, rearranges the classroom space according to the specifications in the winning letter.

✳ **Trade Places:** Switch roles with students, giving them opportunities to teach a tiny area of their own expertise. This, too, shifts the energy in the room, and also allows every student to shine.

✳ **Step Out of the Curriculum:** Go ahead and indulge interesting experiential and incidental learning opportunities. When you allow class discussions to veer off into enthusiastic, relevant tangents, lots of practical learning can happen. Because of their personal relevance, these moments can be much more effective than planned didactic lessons that may feel random and abstract to students.

But when you go off topic, explain clearly what association led you there. Remember that sudden directional shifts can also be confusing to students on the spectrum because these students are probably not making the same mental

A Pensieve Moment

In J.K. Rowling's *Harry Potter and the Goblet of Fire* (2000), fictional headmaster Albus Dumbledore introduces Harry to a "pensieve." A pensieve is a stone basin into which Dumbledore deposits his own memories or thoughts when his mind gets too cluttered or when he needs his mind clear to focus on something else. He retrieves his thoughts and memories from the pensieve only when he is ready to address and immerse himself in them.

Have your entire class create pensieves from coffee cans. Each student can decorate his or her own. Cut a slit in the lids. As needed throughout the day, your students can jot a note or a quick sketch of their distracting thought and slip it into the pensieve, to be retrieved later with your permission. Keeping the topic literally close at hand yet out of sight should allow for a better balance of comfort and engagement.

Promise (and deliver) *pensieve time*, each day, preferably near the end of the day: a few minutes during which students are allowed to open their pensieves and ruminate on the precious thoughts inside. The knowledge that there will be time allocated for those thoughts will help students on the spectrum curb them at other times of the day. All students in the class will welcome the opportunity to think, write, draw, discuss, or otherwise expand on their own ideas.

associations that you and others are. So indulge tangents mindfully, and when veering off course, be sure to make the connection and the intention clear.

Signal visually when you are pursuing a tangent by putting on a special hat or by actually moving yourself to a different position or location, to literally *step out of the curriculum.* When you take the hat off or move back to a typical teaching position, this is a signal to your class that it's time to refocus on the main topic at hand.

✴ **Alert! Alert!** Students on the spectrum tend to be slow in shifting their attention. Alert students when you are going to tell them something important. Be sure that you have been heard, and then pause for a moment to allow them to shift gears.

The Hook

A *hook* is a metaphorical connection or link that reaches a student on the spectrum, grabs hold of his interest, and lures him forth. A hook can be anything familiar that he can glom onto that will help guide him toward new and expanding experiences. Every student's hooks will be different, depending upon his specific areas of interest or fixation. Your mission will be to find the most effective hooks to lure each student off his island.

FINDING THE HOOK

Let's say you have a student who repeats the same fast-food restaurant jingle over and over—it seems to be all he thinks about or focuses on. Ideally, using the ideas for behavior interpretation described in Chapter 3, you have explored what he may be communicating with this preoccupation: What tends to trigger it? What comforts him about it? Maybe it soothes him because it reminds him of his family. Maybe singing the jingle helps him stay alert.

And ideally, using the sensory adaptation ideas described in Chapter 4, you have tried to reduce his reliance on singing this jingle. Still, despite your efforts, what if the preoccupation persists? What do you do with it? How do you get around it? Here's a thought: *Use* it.

USING THE HOOK: GRASPING ENGAGEMENT FOR LEARNING

Suppose you determine that it is, in fact, the food itself—let's say, the French fries— that the student enjoys thinking about. If so, then French fries will be your hook. French fries will be the bridge to engagement in the curriculum.

(I have deliberately chosen this very arbitrary example in order to demonstrate that regardless of the peculiarity or idiosyncrasy of the student's fixation, there is always a hook that you can use to incorporate your student's interest into any aspect of class work, as needed.)

Adding Individual Flavor

Look for ways to incorporate a student's special interest into elements of his own work and classroom experience. Every time he comes across them, they will boost his comfort and feelings of security.

✳ **Behavior:** See if you can find French fry stickers to use on his behavior chart or create your own French fries from laminated paper. Reinforce—or ask his parents or caregivers to reinforce—certain behavioral goals at the end of the week or month with some actual French fries.

✳ **Spelling:** Put thematically relevant words on his spelling list, such as *peel, fry,* and *hungry,* or *potatoes, vegetable,* and *delicious.*

Adding Whole-Class Flavor

Try incorporating a student's special interest into whole-class curriculum, to the extent that it engages everyone. Be flexible. Even if you've always taught measurement using blocks, why not try it with French fries?

✳ **Math:** Use a student's special interest as a manipulative while teaching basic math skills:

- Measure the length of French fries in inches and centimeters.
- Compare the length of French fries to the lengths of pencils, crayons, and markers, and graph the results.
- Estimate and investigate how many French fries must be lined up end to end to stretch across the room.
- Count how many French fries are in a typical container and multiply how many would be needed to feed the whole class or the whole school.
- Practice dividing one package of French fries among the students in your class.

✳ **Science:** Integrate learning about the components of a student's special interest into your science unit:

- *Where do French fries come from?*

- *What food group do potatoes belong to?*
- *What are the different ways potatoes can be cooked?*
- *Which are more and less nutritious cooking styles?*
- Compare fat, calories, sodium among the different cooking styles.
- Prepare French fries from scratch as a class.
- Make a Venn diagram comparing and contrasting French fries to carrot sticks in terms of shape, length, texture, flavor, nutritional value.

✶ **Social Studies:** Examine the popularity of a student's special interest around the world.

- *Where did French fries originate?*
- *What kinds of climates do potatoes grow in?*
- *Where are French fries most commonly eaten?*

The message to this student is: French fries can be an interesting topic, but you cannot keep singing about them. Instead, we will talk about them as part of our learning. Incorporating your student's favored topic into your curriculum will vastly improve your ability to engage him in the lesson, while the entire class learns as well.

USING PERSONAL CONNECTIONS TO BROADEN AND EXPAND

Of course, you don't want your curriculum to be completely, shall we say, *saturated* by fried potatoes, so ultimately you will use this hook to broaden your student's horizons and his ability to engage beyond its narrow focus. Because familiarity is a crucial learning element for students on the spectrum, your goal is to help them make connections between their own lives and new experiences.

✶ **Segue:** Now that you have him engaged, use his favored topic as a segue to introduce other topics:

- Discuss what foods we eat with French fries.
- *Where does ketchup come from?*
- *Where does beef come from?*
- *What's a vegetarian?*

Your student can follow the thread of familiarity through your social studies

Chapter 5   The Inner Sanctum: Crossing the Bridge to a Remote Student

curriculum, as you expand into related topics such as farming, agriculture, famine, immigration, shipping, trade, economy, and more.

✳ **Activate:** And now that you have introduced very varied curricular skills via his favored topic, those curricular skill sets are now familiar to your students. Activate that prior knowledge. For example, tell your class: *Remember when we multiplied and divided French fries? Today we are going to use that same skill with nickels.* Or, *Remember when we made a Venn Diagram about French fries and carrot sticks? Today we are going to make a Venn Diagram about Mexico and the United States.*

✳ **Orient:** If your student has trouble using these expanded skills, don't be afraid to invoke his favored topic when necessary. Thinking about it will help him feel safe and oriented and ease his transition to substituted objects. Prompt him to remember and visualize the process of grouping French fries; now encourage him to visualize grouping nickels instead.

Squeeze, Please

In her book, *An Inside View of Autism* (1992), Temple Grandin urges teachers to "use fixations to motivate instead of trying to stamp them out." As a fourth-grade student on the autism spectrum in the 1950s, Grandin recalls being attracted to election posters because she liked the feeling of wearing the posters like a sandwich.

Solely because of her fixation on "sandwich boards," Grandin became interested in the election. In retrospect, she feels this was a missed opportunity to expand her horizons. She wishes her teachers had seized on and encouraged this oddly acquired, newfound interest and broadened it to facilitate her involvement with the social world. Grandin says, "My teachers should have taken advantage of my poster fixation to stimulate an interest in social studies. Calculating electoral college points would have motivated me to study math. Reading could have been motivated by having me read newspaper articles about the people on the posters. Even if a child is interested in vacuum cleaners, then use a vacuum-cleaner instruction book as a text!" (p. 115).

(Grandin's appreciation of wearing "sandwich boards" actually had a sensory basis. Modern-day occupational therapy recognizes the physiological value of weight-bearing and joint-compressing activities. Therapeutic tools have been created to simulate these effects and also reduce hyperactivity.)

But if your invocation of French fries leads him off into his own world again, remind him: *I mentioned French fries just to help you remember, but we are not talking about French fries now. Now we are talking about nickels.* (This might be a good time to have him draw a picture of some French fries and stuff it in his pensieve.)

READ ALL ABOUT IT

Read books aloud to your class that you can connect to your student's perseverative interest. Make creative connections. The connections you offer may feel like a stretch to you, but any association will help open up your student to engage in new material. For example, use potatoes as your hook into books such as *Cloudy With a Chance of Meatballs, Stone Soup,* or *Potato Chip Puzzles: The Puzzling World of Winston Breen.* Movies and television shows are often familiar and welcome associations for students on the spectrum. Connections can be found everywhere: Did you know that Miley Cyrus's favorite food is ketchup? Imagine the possibilities . . . .

Exponential Potential

By the same token, new independent reading books may be difficult to introduce because of their unfamiliarity. Of course, students on the spectrum will welcome books that pertain to their favored topic, but this narrow focus is limiting and allows them to remain isolated on their islands. A more broadening experience can be achieved by introducing a series of books. Choose one book from a series that you can connect to your students' special interests.

Chapter 5 The Inner Sanctum: Crossing the Bridge to a Remote Student

When my son's special interest was pirates, I introduced him to the book about pirates from the Magic Tree House series. The word *pirate* in the title and the picture of a pirate on the cover engaged him instantly. Once he had read that book, the main characters were now familiar. Suddenly he no longer needed pirates to help him engage in the other forty or so books in the series because now the series' protagonists, Jack and Annie, provided that thread of familiarity. Then, reading those other Magic Tree House books exposed him to everything from mummies to the moon, from King Arthur to Louis Pasteur, and much more.

Now all of those topics have become familiar and can be used as hooks to even more new experiences. Each book served as another link, connecting him to the rest of the world, just as every moment of engagement you capture with your students draws them one step closer across the bridge.

(If you would like more information and more strategies to support engagement, hook into www.barbaraboroson.com.)

Crossing the bridge toward engagement will be a lifelong journey for students on the spectrum. They will need to bring more than a backpack, a water bottle, and a handful of French fries along. They will need their families beside them every step of the way. As you work to engage your students on the spectrum, let's look at why making this journey depends on engaging the family as well.

Chapter 6

Meeting of the Minds

Collaborating With the Family

Collaboration is a buzzword of 21st-century pedagogy. But never is it more important than when it comes to working with students who have pervasive special needs and their families.

Collaboration: What's in It for You?

From the very beginning of your relationship with students on the spectrum, collaboration with parents and caregivers will help you gain access to years of historical data including trials and tribulations, failures and successes. This allows you to hit the ground running with tried and true strategies, or with your own creative ideas that are *based on* knowledge of students' past experiences. It also prevents you from falling into the same potholes into which those before you have sunk. Don't try to reinvent the wheel; not only would you be wasting time and energy, but the delicate vehicle you are trying to rebuild could very well crash and burn while you're putting on those last bolts.

Putting Students in Personal Contexts

The frequent but small efforts required of you to keep in close touch with families will make your life infinitely easier in the long run. For example, if caregivers have a reliable way to communicate to you that this morning was really tough because Marisa lost her folder or because Peter's toothbrush fell in the toilet, you'll know why Marisa has arrived at school screaming or why Peter won't get up off the floor. Moreover, because you have previously sought out historical information about these students, you'll know what comforts Marisa when she's screaming and how to get Peter off the floor. You'll know what tends to help and what tends to make things worse. In other words: You'll be glad you did.

Keep in touch in a reliable, ongoing way about what's happening at home and elsewhere. Let your emerging understanding of your students on the spectrum, in the context of their pasts and presents, guide your interactions, interventions, and expectations from day to day and across the whole year. And as your relationship with your students deepens, you can offer parents a view of their child from the school context. Seamless continuity between the school environment and the home environment will show students that all adults in their lives are on the same page and uphold the same expectations.

CONTEXT CLUES FOR YOU

Consider each student in the context of his or her own history. Parents or caregivers of students on the spectrum may make special requests, such as meeting Cory at the bus or calling the nurse if you see Kai blinking her eyes quickly. Try not to disdain or dismiss these requests as the hovering worries of "helicopter parents." You can be sure that families of students on the spectrum have a history of struggles, littered with crises and traumatic events. Ask questions. You may learn that up until last year, Cory was a runner, and would head for the hills every morning when he got off the bus. Or that when Kai blinks her eyes a lot, she could be on the verge of having a seizure.

For example, Danny was doing fine during the first few days of fourth grade. But then his grandparents approached his teacher, Amir, and asked that Danny be given bathroom reminders every thirty minutes, just as he had been given last year. Amir resisted, perceiving the grandparents as anxious and overprotective: *Bathroom reminders? In fourth grade?*

But when Amir asked why, he learned that Danny had had daily toileting accidents in school right up until his third-grade teacher began reminding him regularly. Now the grandparents' thinking made more sense. Amir regrouped and worked with Danny's grandparents to create a system by which Danny would be supported, but would also begin to take responsibility for his emerging skill. Instead of giving Danny verbal reminders, Amir and Danny created a system whereby Amir would place plain yellow icons at numerous points on Danny's visual schedule, designed to prompt Danny to *assess* his need for the bathroom. With the support of this visual prompting, Danny became the independent arbiter of his bathroom needs.

Collaboration: What's in It for Parents and Caregivers?

Parents and caregivers of students on the spectrum often have very little access to information about their children's day, yet they have a real need to receive *even more* information than parents of typical children do. Here's why.

What's New? *Nothing.*

Students on the spectrum are likely to be ineffective conveyors of school-to-home information. Compared to typical students, they may appear as follows:

- less organized—forgetting to record assignments in their planners or forgetting even to bring home their planners

- less engaged—tuning out when you present important information

- less intuitive—misinterpreting which of your words are important to relay to parents or caregivers
- less verbal—unable to put their experiences into words

For these reasons, parents and caregivers of students on the spectrum receive much less information about the day and about upcoming events than do parents and caregivers of typical students. Your frequent contact may be their only source of feedback.

What's New? A Lot!

Parents and caregivers of children on the spectrum receive scant information but have much to worry about. Their kids get confused and disoriented, bullied and teased, overstimulated and overwhelmed on a regular basis. They misunderstand and miscommunicate. They lose their stuff and lose control. Their parents and caregivers know, when they send their children off to school, that their kids are in for a struggle because there is no such thing as a typical day for these atypical children.

Further, keep in mind that students on the autism spectrum who are in mainstream classes are being stretched to capacity—and sometimes beyond. This is the least restrictive environment; many other settings would offer more support. Though this may in fact be a suitable setting, you can be sure that your students on the spectrum are struggling to maintain their equilibrium in this highly stimulating and challenging social and academic environment.

In order to communicate effectively with parents and caregivers, it helps to tune in a bit to their experience. Remember, their child, who is one of many in your mainstream classroom, is also a powerful force in their family—practically, emotionally, and in other very significant ways, too. The next section will show you that parents face their own host of challenges raising a child on the spectrum.

Parents and Caregivers: Where Have They Been?

As challenging as your journey is with these students, their parents' journey has been all that and more. In addition to coping with the myriad challenges of just getting their children through each day, parents bear a lifelong emotional investment and ultimate responsibility for them, 24/7. By the time they come to you, these families may have traveled a long road of high hopes and dashed dreams.

This section describes some of the practical and emotional challenges parents and caregivers face. These issues are neither your problem nor your responsibility, but they are going to manifest in your classroom, during parent–teacher conferences, during impromptu school–home communications, and through the students themselves. Being aware of these extracurricular challenges will help you understand the whole child in a family context and will make your own educational efforts more informed and effective across the board.

So stop for a minute and consider the moment in which these parents were told or came to the realization that their *perfect* little child, born with ten fingers, ten toes, and infinite possibility, actually has a pervasive, permanent, neuro-developmental disability. For many parents of children with significant, pervasive special needs, coming to terms with a lifelong disability is akin to a death: it is the sudden shattering of hopes, dreams, and legacy. Often parents go through a lengthy and agonizing grief process that includes intense periods of denial, anger, self-blame, depression, and more, before they can begin to accept what is and what may never be.

Amid those feelings of desperation, parents had to kick into high gear, rallying on behalf of their child who is on a different trajectory from the rest. Just living with and raising a child on the spectrum day after day can be a physically and emotionally debilitating experience. But despite that, parents must quickly educate themselves about this exclusive society to which they have been appointed but never wanted to join. They must organize a support squad and round up services, squashing any vestiges of parental pride to shout their child's needs out to the universe in search of help. Obtaining services is time consuming and costly and most often not covered by medical insurance, so a heavy financial burden weighs on the family as well. All of this is in addition to attending to the everyday needs of a typical family, including those of the child's siblings who often get lost in the shuffle.

Given these overwhelming and unrelenting circumstances, it should be no surprise to you when you come across parents or caregivers who seem highly anxious or depressed. These parents have good reason to hover and worry or be sad, stoic, or angry.

Depending on where parents are in their personal journey, some may get teary every time you introduce a new issue of concern while others may flatly deny or reject your interpretations. Some ask that special allowances be made for their children beyond mandated modifications, while others insist that their child be held to the exact same standards as the rest. Just as you do with your students, be mindful of where the parents have been and meet them where they are, as you work together to support their child.

Living on the Edge

Just like their special kids, these parents or caregivers may be marginalized among their peers or feel like hangers-on in the school community. They have watched other people's children having play dates, excelling in sports, and getting invited to birthday parties, and they themselves feel the hurt of being left out of those opportunities for social camaraderie.

Plus, parents and caregivers of students on the spectrum may worry about their child standing out or acting up during school events. A school concert is all stress for these parents as they spend the evening gripping the arms of their chairs, braced against hearing the words *To infinity, and beyond!* soar out across the crowded auditorium in the middle of "Ode to Joy."

As you work to create an inclusive community in your class, you are modeling the acceptance of diversity for your students. Ideally, the school administration will follow your lead, taking proactive steps to share general information about autism spectrum disorders with the entire school community. The distribution of generalized, factual information can allay common fears and misconceptions and raise consciousness about the benefits that inclusive programs offer the entire community. An overall atmosphere of acceptance will help all families feel welcome, just the way they are. (See more on creating a supportive community in Chapter 7.)

Two Different Worlds

The only way school-home collaboration is successful is when it is built on mutual respect, which means acknowledging and accepting the various perspectives and experiences of all parties. Only when teachers and parents accept those differences can we see what we all have in common: namely, the best interest of the child we share.

When you first consult with parents or caregivers of students on the spectrum, you may feel they are describing an entirely different child than the one you see—and it's possible they are. If these differences are not addressed openly and productively from the beginning, you and the parents or caregivers will be pushing against each other all year. But there are often simple explanations for a student's variable functioning across multiple environments, and it will be helpful for both you and the parents or caregivers to explore them together. Sharing this understanding will set the tone for a year of productive collaboration and mutual support.

CHALLENGES AT HOME: THAT *NEVER* HAPPENS AT SCHOOL!

Some students hold themselves together fairly well at school and fall apart when they get home. It's not uncommon even for parents or caregivers of typical children to describe difficult behaviors that teachers rarely or never see at school. You may be surprised to hear parents or caregivers tell you, *She is a terror as soon as she gets home.* There can be a number of reasons for this kind of disparity.

Best Foot Forward

Many students, whether typically functioning or on the spectrum, arrive home from school worn down by the demands of the day. Students on the spectrum, especially, may be firing on all engines just to stay on track at school, and may be doing a pretty good job of it. But by the time they get home, they have nothing left; the pressures of the day have left them depleted and irritable, and their already compromised coping strategies are used up.

Reframe this troubling experience for parents or caregivers by pointing out that these students actually have their priorities in order: School is where they *should* put their best foot forward—this is where they need to stretch themselves to meet the expectations of the social world. These students recognize that home is a loving and accepting place in which they can vent their stress and slow their motors. That's a good thing. We all need a few minutes to kick back and recover from the stress of the day; but students on the spectrum, after struggling at school to stay engaged and socialize, likely need even more decompression time. Encourage parents and caregivers to allow their children to regroup and retreat for a while after school in ways they find relaxing (doing somersaults, lining up toy cars, watching a movie, and so on), before having to step up to more demands.

> **DID YOU KNOW . . .**
>
> For every hour of engagement, students on the spectrum need at least another hour of alone time to fully regroup and recover from the stress and stimulation of the social world (Attwood, 2009).

Something's Up

On the other hand, there may be specific problems at school or on the bus, or at home that these students are reacting to at home. Keep an eye out for signs of situations that might jeopardize students' safety or well-being. Remind parents and caregivers to keep in close touch with you regarding any changes in their child's after-school behavior. Since students on the spectrum are often ineffective communicators, they could be at the mercy of a bad situation and unable to report it.

What Now?

Another reason students on the spectrum may demonstrate lower functioning at home than at school is that they crave the structure of the school day. Maybe you have put in place many of the elements of a structured classroom as described in this book—you use pictorial schedules, verbal prompts with visual cues, organizational systems, transitional protocols, and a consistent behavioral plan—and these students are comforted by these predictable elements of the day.

However, the flexible, low-key atmosphere at home that works so well for other family members may be inscrutable and overwhelming for these rigid, anxious students. At home, rules may change depending on context; every afternoon may present a new commotion of comings and goings, and the dinner menu has not likely been posted a month in advance.

Validate the parents' and caregivers' best intentions in trying to maintain a relaxed environment for their child. But meanwhile, point out that this particular child may actually feel *more* relaxed in the context of clear and consistent rules, enforced quiet times, and a lot of detailed planning. Many families with children on the spectrum find it helpful or necessary—even if not exactly fun or spontaneous—to run their household on consistent visual schedules. If your families have not considered creating schedules for their children, share with them Chapter 3 of this book, which describes the need for structure and various types of basic schedules. Parents or caregivers can create visual schedules to delineate the more stressful aspects of the day such as the morning routine, the homework routine, and the bedtime routine. Whole weeks or months can be mapped out on schedules. Even vacation periods, when all semblance of routine tends to break apart, can be held together smoothly using visual schedules.

The Picture Communication Symbols ©1981–2010 by Mayer-Johnson LLC. All Rights Reserved Worldwide. Used with permission. Boardmaker™ is a trademark of Mayer-Johnson LLC.

CHALLENGES AT SCHOOL: THAT *NEVER* HAPPENS AT HOME!

On the other hand, some parents or caregivers may get defensive and reject your description of their child's challenging behaviors in your class: *No, Ricky would never do anything like that. He's never done that at home.* Sure, in some cases parents may be in denial about the significant issues their child faces, but more likely, they really are seeing a differently functioning child at home than you see at school.

Parents and caregivers may share with you that at home their child does his work independently, shifts gears easily, and plays beautifully with siblings. You're skeptical: you find that at school this same student cannot get through one problem on a worksheet without losing focus, bangs his head against the wall whenever there is a change to the schedule, and is provocative and rigid in social situations. But in truth, many students function much better at home than they do at school. Here's why.

In the Mix

If you are working with parents who have this experience, try to frame the discrepant behavior in terms of context. At school, the pressures are immense: there are engagement expectations, social stressors, academic challenges, linguistic demands, multiple transitions, and so much more, all amid relentless sensory stimulation and the chaos of twenty-some unique and unpredictable personalities swirling around in one room. Despite your efforts to structure and modify the environment, these factors can interfere with the functional efforts of a student on the spectrum.

At home, on the other hand, Ricky may do his homework in a quiet, solitary space with soft, ambient lighting. He may shift gears "easily" only because the family has learned to give him a 30-minute countdown before they need to leave the house. Siblings may have come to terms with the fact that Ricky needs to be the one who decides what they are all going to build, or that he needs to lick each Lego piece before he adds it to the building.

Reiterate that your mutual goal is to support students' ability to function in *all kinds of contexts*. If Ricky is indeed capable of more than you are seeing in class, try to adjust the modifications and accommodations you have made to his school program and environment. But also acknowledge to parents or caregivers that as wonderful as it is that Ricky can zip through his multiplication at home, unfortunately it's just not happening independently in the always stimulating and distracting school environment. Remind them also that school is more reflective of the big, wide world, in which Ricky cannot make up all the rules and in which licking toys is socially unacceptable.

Teacher/Parent Communication

To reap the benefits of these varied perspectives, create an ongoing communication system. Share with parents and caregivers your own philosophy about keeping in touch. How much can they expect to hear from you? What kinds of things do you want to hear from them?

Keeping in Touch

✳ **Respect Your Boundaries:** Many teachers, in an effort to demonstrate their commitment, give parents or caregivers their personal cell phone numbers. Although generous in spirit, this is, as a rule, unnecessary and inadvisable. Parents and caregivers can and should be expected to limit their contact with you to school hours. If your cell phone is ringing while you are spending time with your own family, working out at the gym, or sitting at a movie—when you need to be off the clock—you will grow resentful. Taking good care of yourself after hours will make you a better teacher between the bells.

✳ **Respect Their Boundaries:** Find out from parents and caregivers where and when they would prefer to be contacted by phone. Is it okay to call them at work? Is the work number or the cell phone number a better choice during the day? What kinds of information can you share with the babysitter?

✳ **Play It Safe:** Electronic communication with parents and caregivers may be most efficient, but runs the risk of violating student confidentiality. Electronic communications can be easily intercepted by third parties who could go on to change your words and/or send private information out into cyberspace *in your name.* Stick to the old-fashioned routes of telephone contacts and handwritten communication whenever possible.

Creating a Written Communication Log

Here are some suggestions for putting a low-maintenance system into place to ensure that effective school–home communication is seamlessly integrated into every day.

✳ **Check Yourself:** Consider how much feedback is realistic for you to provide: Will you be able to write in the log every day? Once a week? Be honest with yourself and be honest with parents and caregivers; don't set yourself up for a burdensome commitment that you later resent and cannot maintain. Meet with parents or caregivers early in the year to establish a format that feels manageable to you and valuable for everyone.

✴ **Use a Template:** To minimize daily effort, use a template that lists categories of functioning across a week and allows space for comments. Categories can include socialization, behavior, attention, engagement, and others. Or list specific targeted behaviors in each relevant area, such as listening, staying calm, staying in seat, taking turns, or whatever behaviors you and the parents are concerned about. Paste or staple the chart into a notebook and use a checkmark system or other simple notation to indicate how the student performed in each area each day. Update categories and areas to target each week.

_____'s Success Chart

Week of ___/___ - ___/___

	Mon.	Tues.	Weds.	Thurs.	Fri.
Goal #1:	AM ___	AM ___	AM ___	AM ___	AM ___
Comments:	PM ___	PM ___	PM ___	PM ___	PM ___
Goal #2:	AM ___	AM ___	AM ___	AM ___	AM ___
Comments:	PM ___	PM ___	PM ___	PM ___	PM ___
Goal #3:	AM ___	AM ___	AM ___	AM ___	AM ___
Comments:	PM ___	PM ___	PM ___	PM ___	PM ___

✓ = Good Job!   ✗ = Keep Trying

For reproducible versions of these forms, please visit www.barbaraboroson.com.

✴ **Elaborate:** When you do indicate a problem on the chart, take a minute to elaborate on it so parents or caregivers know how to address it at home. Or use stickers to show gradations of problems. For example, a green sticker means *no problem in this area today;* yellow means *minor problem;* and red means *major problem.* A red sticker could be designated to always warrant elaboration, whether in writing or by phone. Clarify terms that work best for you and work together with the parents or caregivers to develop a system with which they will feel comfortable as well.

✴ **And Your Point Is . . .?** When you write in the log, try to be very clear about your intentions. Indicate whether you are sharing an anecdote for the purposes of keeping parents or caregivers in the loop or in the hopes that they will actually do something in response.

Let them know if you have already debriefed the behavior and/or implemented a consequence at school.

Be specific about whether you are asking parents and caregivers to debrief further, enforce a consequence at home, or whether you are sharing this for informational purposes only.

Although in most cases, consequences for school behaviors will have been meted out at school, sometimes you may feel that a certain behavior should be reinforced at home. Your intention may change from incident to incident, so clarify your intentions every time you communicate in writing or verbally.

✳ **Watch Your Tone!!** ☺ So often, in this era of written communication, tone is lost to efficiency, as frequently happens in e-mails, text messages, and tweets. In the case of teacher–parent communication, the information you are sharing is highly loaded. Consider your words from the perspective of the recipient who is not a neutral reader, but the parent of a child with a disability. Regardless of the nature of the issue, personal buttons are being pushed for the parents every time you contact them with a concern. Your simple comment may inadvertently touch on very raw, underlying feelings of shame, guilt, defensiveness, denial, embarrassment, responsibility, frustration, disappointment, exhaustion, anger, and other powerful responses that undermine their fundamental desire to be supportive.

✳ **Weigh Your Words:** Be careful to use non-judgmental language and include supportive words and phrases. Suppose you write, *Randall used a racial insult against another student today and lost ten minutes of computer time. Please teach him about respectful language.* Reading that communication, a parent will likely feel chastised and defensive about your unwitting implication that they condone racism or have never tried to teach Randall to be respectful.

Instead, take the extra moment to smooth it out a bit: *Randall used a racial insult against another student today and lost ten minutes of computer time. We discussed how bad it feels to be insulted, and Randall did a great job apologizing to his classmate. I'm sure you've been over it with him before, but please remind him again about respectful language. Thanks! I'll keep you posted.*

✳ **Throw a Crumb:** Always try to intersperse good news and optimism amid your concerns.

✳ **Be "In the Know":** Urge parents and caregivers to share with you any concerns they have or events that may have been out of the ordinary or upsetting to the student on any given day. Be sure to check the communication log when it arrives every morning. Information there may well give you important opportunities to turn down the heat on simmering situations quickly and act preemptively. You won't stand a chance of teaching this student today if you don't know about the broken-shoelace debacle of last night. Seriously.

✳ **Follow Up:** Encourage parents and caregivers to write back to you about what transpired at home as a result of your report. And, by the same token, try to let them know of any news or developments related to what they wrote to you in the morning.

Medication in the Equation

Even when the lines of communication are open, medication can be a touchy topic between teachers and parents or caregivers. Many students on the spectrum are treated with prescription medications that help them modulate reactions, sustain attention, sleep, and so on. You may also come across students who are on specific strict diets or natural supplement regimens to support their engagement or flexibility. While some parents and guardians swear by their chosen diets, supplements, or pharmaceutical interventions, others are offended, personally or philosophically, by the very idea of psychiatric medication.

As a teacher, you have the opportunity to see your students on the spectrum function in varied dynamic situations for many hours every day. You are well-positioned to offer your observations, data, and impressions. But not being a medical doctor, you are not in a position to recommend that a student try medication. If you believe that your preventive and responsive behavioral interventions are insufficient, you can certainly describe your efforts and observations to parents or guardians. The school psychologist may broach the topic of evaluation with parents or guardians. But *recommending* medication is a hot button that is not yours to press. In fact, most states bar teachers and other school professionals from recommending psychiatric medication.

The Medication Decision

Understanding and respecting that parents and guardians may have powerful personal perspectives about administering psychiatric medication to their children may help you to feel more accepting of their choices, even while those choices impact you and your class every day. Many parents have compelling concerns about the short- and long-term systemic side effects that can accompany medication. And often parents fear they will be judged as inadequate parents for "resorting" to medication. Frequently the harshest judges they confront are themselves, as they may feel like failures for not being able to coax their children toward better functioning without the help of pharmaceutical intervention.

The decision to administer psychiatric medication to one's child reflects a personal, deeply emotional, and stressful process. Under no circumstances should a family feel pressured into providing psychiatric medication for their children. In fact, federal law prohibits schools from making medication compliance a requisite for attending school. Parents or guardians retain the absolute right by law to choose whether or not to medicate their children, and they have varied opinions on this topic.

Your best bet is to maintain an overall non-judgmental, confidential, and open relationship with parents and guardians, so that they will feel comfortable sharing information with you as needed.

Regardless of your personal convictions and despite the repercussions of parental choices in your classroom, try to demonstrate respect for whichever medication or dietary decisions parents make for their children. A prevailing belief that parents and caregivers want what's best for their children will guide you to accept different choices and understand that they are made on the basis of different histories, cultures, and personal experiences. (If you would like to learn more about parent perspectives regarding medication and other issues, please visit www.barbaraboroson.com.)

As you develop reciprocal and accepting relationships with parents and caregivers, the effort to accept differences continues among the students in your class. You have students who learn and function in ways that may be radically different from others. The next chapter describes the social challenges involved for *all* students in your class, and guides you to coax a cohesive classroom community from a collection of very diverse participants.

That's What Friends Are For

Socialization and Self-Esteem

The most compelling reason students on the autism spectrum are placed in mainstream classrooms is so they can benefit from the social examples of typical peers. The presumption is that by immersing them in a typical social environment, they will absorb social savvy and emerge, well, *socialized*. However, social skill instruction is not typically part of classroom curriculum. Instead, this hypothetical social awakening is often expected to happen by osmosis.

But students on the autism spectrum do not learn by osmosis. Instead, they may carry years of hurt and rejection, vestiges of failed social interactions from which they have learned nothing. These painful experiences chip away at students' self-esteem, leaving them less and less likely to venture into the social world. The more they turn inward to avoid social rejection, the less practice they get interacting. And soon, what were already compromised social instincts have turned into rusty, clumsy efforts to be part of the social world. Some students stop trying altogether.

Where is the No Child Left Behind Act when it comes to socialization? Nowhere. In terms of socialization, students on the spectrum are routinely left behind and, worse, left out.

Your creation and maintenance of a differentiated, supportive social environment in your classroom can break the painful cycle of rejection and withdrawal. Before your students on the spectrum will be able or even willing to risk social participation, they will need to know that you believe in them. They'll need to know that you *get* them, that you will help them through difficult moments with patience and understanding. They'll need you to model optimism, acceptance, and forgiveness. The safer the environment feels and the more positive experiences you create, the more motivated your students will be to risk social encounters.

CIRCUIT SAFETY

In *Look Me in the Eye* (2007), his memoir about growing up with Asperger's Syndrome, John Elder Robison describes the strain of socialization as compared to the safety of his favored private world: electrical circuitry. He recounts, "I got along well with my circuits, and they never ridiculed me. They presented me with tough problems to solve, but they were never mean. [Interacting with people forced me to move] farther away from the world of machines and circuits—a comfortable world of muted colors, soft light, and mechanical perfection—and closer to the anxiety-filled, bright, and disorderly world of people" (p. 210).

This chapter will show you how to teach and reinforce rote social skills in order to bolster self-esteem and arm your students on the spectrum with tools to bring to the social scene. You'll learn to support social thinking, scaffolding all the way, in order to encourage social savvy. And you'll find strategies to create a caring and accepting classroom community that will spark all kinds of *social* circuits.

The Hidden Social Curriculum

The terms *social skills* and *social interaction* refer not only to casual chatting and socializing; they also refer to social behavior, which is behavior that meets with conventional approval. Social behaviors at school include the following:

- following the rules of the classroom and other environments
- respecting the rights, space, and belongings of others
- responding to varied situations with flexibility
- acting in consideration of the feelings of others

All of these skills are necessary parts of effective functioning in a social world.

The unspoken messages of social interaction have been described as a *hidden curriculum.* In every aspect of life, students are expected to know or intuit appropriate behaviors without being taught them. Every context has its own set of unspoken expectations. For example, the specific demeanor that students use with the principal is not necessary or appropriate to use with peers—and vice versa. *Good behavior* in the gym is completely different from *good behavior* in the library. What's right in one place can be very wrong in another.

Gaps in intuition often cause important chunks of information to be missed by students on the spectrum. Eight-year-old Max was taught the rules of the playground at his new school. He was told, *Take turns on the equipment, no pushing, and no kicking.* It didn't occur to anyone that Max needed to be *taught* that walking in front of a moving swing would be dangerous; or that when an out-of-bounds kickball rolls near him, he can't just pick it up and walk off with it. Those matters of inferred sensibility are part of the hidden curriculum.

Other aspects of hidden curriculum vary from moment to moment. Although five minutes ago you were available to listen attentively to Candace's detailed description of her favorite movie, now that the hamster has gotten out of its cage and is headed for the classroom door, you are no longer available to listen. This turn of events has not been scripted for Candace, so the changed expectation for her behavior is not apparent to her. She rigidly clings to her role as speaker and sees no reason to stop talking.

Absent are these students' abilities to read nonverbal social cues in others, such as facial expressions and body language, as well as gestures, tone, and emotion. And, accordingly, absent is a sense of how others will interpret *their* words or actions when they walk away in the middle of a conversation or laugh when someone gets hurt. (See more on interpreting nonverbal and paraverbal communication in Chapter 8.)

Given their challenges in the areas of engagement, emotional regulation, flexibility, and communication, the constantly changing social landscape is a minefield to students on the spectrum. Teachers often assume that students are being oppositional when they do not perform social or behavioral skills that seem age appropriate or that they have been taught before. But students on the spectrum need information specifically taught and retaught many times before it sinks in.

Teaching the Hidden Curriculum by Rote

At the beginning of the school year, you probably review rules with your class. You support compliance with these rules by discussing them with the class, exploring their implications and applications, and posting them for easy and frequent reference.

For students on the spectrum, social expectations must be taught much the same way. Social rules must be broken down into specific components for students on the spectrum, then prompted, rehearsed, and memorized.

✳ **Script It:** You might ask the school counselor, resource room teacher, or speech and language specialist to write a Social Story. Carol Gray's Social Stories are short, highly individualized fact-based stories that guide students through specific challenging social situations, such as waiting in line, doing homework, staying calm, taking turns, and many others. Gray has created a specific formula for writing these stories that includes starting with the student's perspective, expanding to include other perspectives, and leading to a positive outcome. Social Stories vary in style and content according to a student's age, functioning, and specific reaction to a given event, so they are most successful when written with a particular student in mind.

These stories can be written for—or with—students who need them. They can be posted in the classroom, stored in individuals' desks or in designated folders, copied and sent home, reviewed every day, or consulted as needed.

Going to an Assembly

When I go to an assembly, I always want to dance or sing along with the music.

Lots of kids like to dance and sing.

Some assemblies are noisy, and it's okay for kids to dance and sing along.

Some assemblies are quiet, and kids need to be quiet.

When the other kids in the audience are being quiet, I need to be quiet, too.

I will try to sit still and keep my mouth closed at quiet assemblies.

When the other kids start clapping, I can clap, too..

✳ **Lay It Out:** Before students on the spectrum enter a new situation, try to brief them as to what they should expect and what social behaviors you expect from them: *At this assembly, there will be music playing and dancers on the stage. But we, in the audience, must sit quietly. After the dancers are finished, we can clap and cheer.*

✳ **Break It Up:** Reduce social rules into the smallest parts necessary; discuss them with your students on the spectrum and check for understanding. Show them a photo of what "sitting quietly" *looks* like and explain, *Sitting quietly means mouths closed, hands and feet still. No clapping, stomping, talking, or any other noise until the show is over. Can you show me how you will sit quietly?*

✳ **Encourage Memorization:** Review social rules the way you might drill the multiplication tables. New behaviors can become learned responses, such that when you give the prompt, *Georgie, what will you do when you are at the assembly?* Georgie will learn to respond instantly, *Sit quietly.*

✳ **Social Contracts:** Make individualized contracts with students as needed, modifying or adding new goals as targeted skills become assimilated. Here's an example:

Dana's Friendship Contract

- *If someone drops a pencil near me, I will pick it up and return it to the person who dropped it.*

- *When someone near me is working, I will stay quiet.*

- *When people say hello to me, I will look at them and say hello.*

Ensure that each term used in the contract is understood by the student. Discuss how Dana can recognize what *someone working* looks like. Be sure she has learned specifically what *stay quiet* means. If not, those details should be broken down further in the contract. Alternatively, depending on each student's functioning level, you may choose to present these goals in tactile, photographic, or pictorial form, and reinforce them with verbal reminders.

Prompt students to review their social rules periodically or just before embarking on interactive tasks. Revisit them together often.

Social Thinking: Variations on a Theme

The strategies discussed so far in this chapter teach students rote responses in scripted situations. With adequate practice, these skills alone can give students quite a leg up. Rote memorization will help them through the precise situations you have scripted. So, the next time someone drops a pencil near her, there's a good chance Dana will pick it up.

But you will need to teach the generalization of these skills as well, because your concrete, rigid students on the spectrum will not generalize them spontaneously. When a pen instead of a pencil drops near Dana—forget it. When it's a paper clip—no chance.

Taking social know-how one step further means being able to generalize and apply those rote skills flexibly, across a variety of situations that may not have not been specifically scripted. That is social thinking, a much more complex skill that often requires taking the perspective of others.

A Theory of Relativity—Taking the Perspective of Others

Dana's teacher tried to facilitate rule generalization and empathic understanding by teaching Dana an axiom: *Dana, your classmates are your friends. Friends help each other out.* Dana listened, but then, after some consideration, responded, *Why?*

Difficulty taking someone else's perspective is likely the single greatest impediment to students' successful social interaction. Many of the same challenges that keep students disengaged are the ones that render them socially inept.

MINDBLINDNESS

The ability to understand that another person's internal experience is different from one's own is called *Theory of Mind*, or, more familiarly, mindreading. A deficit in this area is called *mindblindness*. Students with mindblindness are unable to decode how

Stay Where You Can See Me

When outside or on a field trip, teachers often tell students, *Stay where I can see you.* This is actually a very challenging instruction for students with mindblindness, as it requires them to adopt your personal and visual perspective. How can they know what *you* can see?

Much clearer for *all* students and more effective, too, is this directive: *Stay where you can see me.*

the actions or demeanor of other people reflect their respective states of mind (Baron-Cohen, 1995, 2001). This significant interpersonal gap restricts students' abilities to interpret another person's perspective and accounts for the inscrutable nature of the hidden curriculum.

For example, although Carolena is doubled over, having a coughing fit to the point that her eyes are watering, Wesley insistently repeats his question about whether she likes to play Frisbee: *Do you, Carolena? Do you?* **Do you?**

Can You Feel What I Feel?

In addition to mindblindness, students on the spectrum also struggle with joint attention (as described in Chapters 5 and 8) and executive function (as described in Chapter 4). Together, these challenges render students on the spectrum quite limited in their ability to understand others and respond in socially welcome ways.

In ideal circumstances, these skills all add up to a kind of theory of social relativity; that is, the recognition that every individual's actions and reactions are relative to his or her own experience. But students on the spectrum, who lack these skills, are often seen as rude, selfish, inconsiderate, or stupid.

Tony Attwood (2009) points out that students on the spectrum tend to notice and understand objects and facts more than they do thoughts, feelings, and intentions. They can be highly observant when it comes to certain aspects of their environment while simultaneously oblivious to others. For example, a student on the spectrum is likely to notice a single book out of place on the bookshelf. But that same student won't notice the cries of the classmate whose fingers she steps on while going to reshelve that book.

Honesty: Such a Lonely Word

Students on the autism spectrum very rarely lie or use manipulation or guile. With their rigid adherence to rules, limited capacity to take another's perspective, and minimal awareness of social pressure or expectation, they are likely to answer questions directly.

This unmitigated honesty does not tend to curry social favor with peers. When seven-year-old Simon is asked by a classmate if he likes her shirt, he quickly responds, *No. I hate green. It's gross.*

When nine year old Yi Chen is asked to walk Joel to the nurse to get a band-aid, she declines: *No. I didn't hurt him, and I'd rather go to recess.*

The nuanced skills of being polite, telling part of the truth, and being a friend require social thinking skills, mind-reading, and the flexibility to bend the rules of honesty a bit now and then. But by teaching rules and algorithms, social thinking can develop, and even the nuances of honesty can be taught.

Teaching Social Thinking

Given these profound gaps in social understanding, it is easy to see why students on the spectrum are commonly thought to lack empathy. Their apparent disregard for the feelings of others implies a lack of caring. But the little-known fact is that students on the spectrum often care very deeply for and about others. The problem is that *they cannot read the signals* of another person's distress. And they do not make the critical connection: *What does any of this have to do with me?*

A spontaneous recognition of the feelings of others may never happen organically for students on the spectrum. But they can learn to *think* their way through to what someone else might be feeling, using context clues and other cognitive strategies. If you want to encourage social thinking and the generalization of skills toward empathic behavior, here are some strategies to try.

✴ **Reach for Reciprocity:** When appropriate, try joining students where they are. If a student's preferred topic of interest is guitars, join him in a lively discussion of guitars. But throughout the discussion, prompt him to interact with you and respond to your contributions to the discussion. Prompt him to ask you questions about guitars and to listen and respond thoughtfully to your answers. Ask him questions that are related to guitars but that encourage him to stretch slightly off subject: *What other kinds of instruments are there? How are they similar to guitars? How* *are they different? What do you like better about guitars? What might be better about the others?*

✳ **Role Play:** Give students the opportunity to role-play problematic interactions by setting up groups of students to practice these skills together. Play out real situations that went badly and then try practicing them in better ways. Challenge students to try portraying each character in a scene and debrief every time: *How did you feel when you were the one who got left out? How did you feel when you were leaving someone else out?*

✳ **Study Facial Expressions:** Much of the hidden curriculum is encrypted in the facial expressions of others. Spend time studying facial expressions with students.

- Most educational supply catalogs, stores, and Web sites sell emotion posters that show photographic faces revealing various labeled expressions. These posters are perfect for students on the spectrum who cannot interpret facial cues and may not even realize that facial expressions carry meaning. Have a mirror on hand and challenge students to try to match their own facial expressions to those on the poster.

- Play feelings charades, in which students act out emotions and peers have to guess what they're feeling.

- Take photographs of students' facial expressions and create a matching game with the photos.

✳ **Practice Body Language:** In addition to facial expressions, consider the many signals that we use subconsciously throughout the day that pose challenges to students. Students can memorize nonverbal communications and attribute generalized meaning to them. Teach them what shrugged shoulders mean. Teach them the difference between a head shaking horizontally (*No*) and a head nodding vertically (*Yes*). Teach them what *thumbs-up* means, what breathlessness implies, what *busy* looks like. Numerous books are available that interpret these cues into concrete language. (See Chapter 8 for more about nonverbal and paraverbal communication.)

(If you would like more information about social skills or more social skill strategies and tools, please visit www.barbaraboroson.com.)

Debriefing

When a student on the spectrum is involved in a troublesome social situation, debrief it with the student. Since students on the spectrum will not spontaneously reflect upon

Chapter 7   That's What Friends Are For: Socialization and Self-Esteem

or learn from their mistakes and missteps, the effect of their behaviors on others needs to be made overt, and a replacement behavior or reaction must be developed.

Consider this example as a guide for debriefing challenging behavior with students on the spectrum:

> **Scenario:** Jamal was removed from the lunchroom by an aide for shoving his sandwich in Chandra's face.

1. **Listen:** Simply doling out consequences for their misdeeds will neither help students on the spectrum learn what they did wrong nor will it change their behavior in the future. Instead, ask neutral questions that show that your mind is open to your student's interpretation of what happened.

> Jamal's teacher, Oscar, recognizes that chastising Jamal for his misdeed will close the door on a teachable moment. So instead, Oscar asks Jamal a question neutrally and openly: *What happened in the lunchroom?*
>
> Jamal responds, *Chandra said she was still hungry. I was giving her some of my lunch.*

What had been seen as a hostile or aggressive act is now revealed to have been an extremely empathic and generous act, only poorly executed.

2. **Mirror:** By mirroring students' words back to them, you demonstrate that you are listening and that they have been heard.

> Oscar tells Jamal, *You wanted to give Chandra food because she said she was still hungry.*
>
> Jamal, who has no idea why he's gotten in trouble for his actions, now feels understood.

3. **Acknowledge Intentions:** The good intentions of students on the spectrum often lead to bad outcomes. Because they don't know how best to approach a situation, their good intentions may be unnoticed, misconstrued, or even negatively reinforced. Look for opportunities to positively reinforce good intentions.

> Oscar recognizes this as a golden opportunity to grab hold of a terrific social instinct gone awry and reframe it as a strength. He tells Jamal, *You wanted to be helpful because Chandra is your friend. Good idea.*

4. **Introduce Another Perspective:** Guide students on the spectrum to put themselves in the shoes of another person. (But don't use those exact words, or you

can bet they'll start untying their laces.) This kind of mind-reading will not happen spontaneously, but powerful epiphanies can be realized as you guide students to make the connection between their own feelings and the feelings of others.

> Oscar talks to Jamal without accusing him: *Let's see if we can figure out why Chandra got angry. How do you think you would feel if someone suddenly pushed food into your face?*
>
> Because Jamal is now feeling less defensive, he is more open to learning. Oscar helps Jamal understand that because he thrust the sandwich in Chandra's face and didn't use words, Chandra did not recognize that he was trying to be nice.
>
> Oscar goes on to confirm that Jamal understands what the other student might actually have felt in the situation: *Chandra thought you were being mean because you shoved the sandwich right in her face. That didn't feel to her like you were being a friend.*

5. **Reteach:** Once students on the spectrum begin to understand how their actions are perceived, they can begin to explore new approaches. State clearly the new skill that should be generalized from this experience.

> Oscar gives Jamal a rule to remember: *Putting food in other people's faces is rude and disrespectful.*
>
> Oscar asks, *How do you think you could do it better next time?* He and Jamal rehearse different ways Jamal could handle that situation in the future, such as holding his food out in a friendly way and accompanying his gesture with words.
>
> Oscar summarizes for Jamal, *So from now on, when you want to share your sandwich, you will hold it near you and ask the other person: "Would you like a piece of my sandwich?"*

6. **Expand:** Students on the spectrum will need to be taught exactly how much to generalize this new skill. Push the boundaries of their rigidity by exploring variations on the situation.

> Oscar guides Jamal to apply his new skill to other, slightly different situations: *I think it's great that you like to share with others, Jamal. That's being a good friend. How would you offer to share other things besides your sandwich? How would you offer to share some grapes? How would you share a cookie?*
>
> Over time, as different teachable moments arise, Oscar coaches Jamal to expand the application even more broadly:
>
> - *Would you use the same words if you wanted to share a book?*
> - *How would you offer to share a ball?*

Chapter 7   That's What Friends Are For: Socialization and Self-Esteem

- *What would you say if you wanted to share an idea?*
- *What will you do if someone does not want what you are offering to share?*

7. **Make It Meaningful:** Describe what's in it for your students to adopt these new behaviors.

> Oscar encourages Jamal: *Other kids will be happy when you offer to share with them, as long as you offer in a respectful way. Sharing respectfully is a great way to be a friend.*

8. **Practice:** Be prepared to practice and review this new way of thinking many times before it becomes assimilated into daily behavior. Prompt students ahead of time, coach in the moment, and look for opportunities for practice.

> Oscar keeps an eye on Jamal in class, watching for natural opportunities: *Jamal, I see that there are not enough markers at Table 4. Why don't you respectfully offer to share some of your markers, using the skills we talked about?*

In the context of your busy classroom, social learning will rarely proceed as systematically as it does in this example, but keep these elements in mind as a framework to guide and inform your social interventions. In this case, a situation that would have left Jamal reprimanded, confused, and patently rejected, instead has now provided him with praise, support, and a way to act on his empathic inclination to be a friend.

Simply Sympathize

Listen carefully and without judgment. A student's experience is his experience. You cannot begin to know what it feels like for him to be at the mercy of his impulses, sensory reactions, preoccupations, social ineptitude, speech limitations, and anxiety. So if he was devastated by the fact that the pizza was rectangular today instead of triangular, then so it is. Don't disparage his distress as nonsense, because it's not. It's unbearable to him and is therefore a real force affecting your classroom community.

You don't have to empathize—chances are, you won't feel his pain. But try to sympathize with the fact that a situation is deeply meaningful to him and move forward from there.

Alone Together

During the preschool and early elementary years, typical peer interaction is in the realm of parallel play; that is, students play alongside each other without necessarily communicating or collaborating. As typical students develop through the elementary grades, play becomes more reciprocal and sophisticated. Communication becomes layered with implication and innuendo.

While peer socialization becomes increasingly nuanced, students on the spectrum remain rigid. They find no way to neatly apply a rigid rubric to spontaneous socialization. Conversations among typical students veer off on inexplicable tangents. Tones shift from sincere to sarcastic to sardonic and back with no prompts, no visual cues, no graphic organizers. Peer relationships change from day to day, moment to moment. Interactive play meanders freely through the wild fields of peers' imaginations, allowing a block to become a boat, a castle, an alien, a bird. But for students on the spectrum, whose thinking is grounded in the concrete, a block is a block is a block. (See more on conversational challenges in Chapter 8.)

Socialization: A Two-Way Street

While students on the spectrum struggle to make sense of their peers, their peers struggle to make sense of them. Collaborative work and play require flexibility, spontaneity, sharing, turn taking, patience, inferential thinking, and more—each of which poses another challenge to students on the spectrum as they try to apply rules and systems to this frenetic, improvisational dance.

When rules fail, these students may dig in their heels, wander away in mid-conversation or mid-activity, refuse to take turns, misinterpret information, change topics abruptly, interrupt, fall behind, overreact, underreact, resort to aggression or destruction, or fade into perseverative behaviors such as repetitive phrases, rocking, chirping, or grunting.

Or they may try to insist that others conform to their own sets of rigid rules. The alternately inscrutable, unavailable, and exasperating social operating systems of students on the spectrum require more patience and forgiveness than typical peers may be prepared to give. It takes work to befriend these students. Typical peers need to go *much more than halfway* to make a connection, which many peers are unwilling or unable to do.

Meanwhile, for better and for worse, many high-functioning children on the

Chapter 7   That's What Friends Are For: Socialization and Self-Esteem

spectrum develop insight on their limitations. During the later elementary years and beyond, they may begin to notice that they do not fit in. They don't get invited to parties. They are not part of the *jockocracy* that rules the playground. They feel the sting of children laughing at them—even if they have no idea how to respond. They know they are missing cues, missing social rules, missing the joke, missing something. They just don't know what to do differently. And often their attempts to make a situation better only make it much worse.

For example, in his memoir, Robison recalls his efforts to make friends:

> *At recess, I walked over to Chuckie and patted her on the head. My mother had shown me how to pet my poodle on the head to make friends with him. And my mother petted me sometimes, too, especially when I couldn't sleep. So as far as I could tell, petting worked. All the dogs my mother had told me to pet had wagged their tails. They liked it. I figured Chuckie would like it, too . . . . It never occurred to me that Chuckie might not respond to petting in the same way a dog would. The difference between a small person and a medium-sized dog was not really clear to me.*
>
> Smack! *She hit me!*
>
> *Startled, I ran away.* That didn't work, *I said to myself.* Maybe I have to pet her a little longer to make friends. I can pet her with a stick so she can't smack me. *But the teacher intervened.*
>
> *The worst of it was, my teachers and most other people saw my behavior as bad when I was actually trying to be kind. My good intentions made the rejection by Chuckie all the more painful . . . I never interacted with Chuckie again. I stopped trying with any of the kids. The more I was rejected, the more I hurt inside and the more I retreated* (2007, p. 9).

The next section will show you how to bring all of your students closer together by drawing both ends toward the middle: bolstering skills and confidence at one end and raising consciousness at the other.

Building a Classroom Community

Typical students have enormous potential to influence the lives of their peers on the spectrum. They have the potential to be friends, supporters, and champions or bullies, provocateurs, and antagonizers. They learn, from lessons and by example, to celebrate differences and stand up for what's right or to smirk and look the other way. Harness the potential for peers to develop and practice new attitudes about kids who are different from themselves. Your example and your efforts can imbue their opened minds with generosity of spirit and empower them to become conscientious citizens throughout their lives.

Tapping Peer Potential

> *In elementary school, it's "cool" to be kind. In middle school, it's "cool" to be cruel.*
>
> —Tony Attwood (2009)

In younger elementary classes, students are likely to be kind to each other because you tell them to be, because being kind is *cool.* These are the rules of school and friendship and the platitude *In this class, we are all friends* still has some traction.

But in the upper elementary grades, students begin to notice differences more and gaps in development may become more glaring. Students begin to branch off into groups of friends with common interests and reject others.

By utilizing some of the affirming activities suggested below, you can ensure an *It's cool to be kind* dynamic in and beyond your classroom.

SETTING A TONE: CREATING A CLASSROOM WITH A CONSCIENCE

From day one, your open acknowledgment and acceptance of differences will help set the tone for the year. As you demonstrate the importance and relevance of acceptance, be sure to weave all kinds of diversity into your curriculum. This means expanding beyond differences of race, to include culture, class, religion, gender, sexual orientation, ability, and more. Being in an inclusive class provides all of your students lifelong lessons in understanding, empathy, and community consciousness.

Models of Courage

Back up your inclusive words by filling your classroom library with biographies of people who exemplify courage in the face of discrimination, such as Ruby Bridges, Jackie Robinson, Anne Frank, Billie Jean King. Include biographies about individuals who have triumphed over physical challenges, such as Helen Keller, Stevie Wonder, Jim Abbott, Susan B. Anthony, and Cesar Chavez. *Different Like Me: My Book of Autism*

Heroes (Elder, 2005) offers brief biographies of influential people who showed signs of autism spectrum disorders, including Albert Einstein, Thomas Edison, Lewis Carroll, Hans Christian Andersen, and many others.

Affirm Acceptance

Where does intolerance begin? Try to raise awareness of social injustice among your students. Is it right to treat people differently because of the way they look, act, or learn? Try to ground these concepts by encouraging students to look around themselves. Who is being treated unfairly because they are different? How do we feel about that?

Since the goal is to move beyond *tolerance* toward actual *acceptance*, we need to incorporate meaningful explorations of differentness into the general curriculum. Celebrate diversity at all grade levels:

✻ **Grades K–1:** Use basic lessons of *same and different* to expand into conceptual differences such as religion, race, and ability. For example: *Everyone has different abilities. What activities come easily to you? What do you find more difficult?*

✻ **Grades 2–3:** Connect conversations about differences to intolerance and bullying: *What is bullying all about? Why do some kids bully? Why do some kids get bullied?*

✻ **Grades 4–6:** Use the social studies curriculum to connect historical examples of persecution to discussions of diversity and discrimination, courage, and acceptance. *Have you ever felt you were being discriminated against? Have you ever judged anyone on the basis of what he or she looks like without knowing who the person is on the inside?*

If you would like to learn more about integrating diversity into the curriculum, and the names of many recommended age-appropriate, thought-provoking books on topics like these, go to www.barbaraboroson.com.

Encourage Goodmouthing

Since the spontaneous social efforts of students on the spectrum may be clumsy at best and disruptive, intrusive, provocative, or destructive at worst, all members of your classroom community may need incentives to work cooperatively and gently together.

✻ **Modified Marble Jar:** Try modifying the classic Marble Jar system. Instead of awarding marbles for following classroom rules, use them to reinforce acts of kindness and inclusiveness. Add a marble whenever you catch a student being a good

Rules of Comedy

Jed Baker (2009), an expert on social skills training, synthesizes the nuances of humor into clear rules. His list is a useful guide for all students, so you may want to post it in the classroom.

- It's never okay to make fun of the vulnerable: many jokes are put-downs. But putting down someone who is already struggling is not funny—it's just plain mean.

- Blurting out random thoughts is not funny. And those impulsive comments are often the ones that get you in trouble.

- Making fun of yourself is never okay.

friend and reward the class when the jar gets full. Prompt students about what *being a good friend* looks like; for example, offering to help someone clean up a mess, taking turns, using kind words, including others in their play, and so on.

✳ **Put Down Put-Downs:** Have a class discussion about what put-downs are and how they make us feel. Many times students do not realize that what they think they are saying only in fun really cuts to the quick. Let all students know that teasing is *never* funny and that saying, *I was just kidding* afterwards does not erase hurtful words. In an inclusive class, it is vitally important to make your classroom a *Put-Down-Free Zone.*

✳ **Put Up Put-Ups:** As opposed to put-downs, put-ups are comments that make people feel good about themselves. As a class, brainstorm some great put-ups, then put up a Put-Up Chart. Explore together how put-ups can also be communicated without words: through a smile, a thumbs up, a high-five, and so on. Feed the Marble Jar when you hear or see spontaneous put-ups.

Consider doing a whole-class keepsake holiday project in which your students make Put-Up Books for each other. A week or two before the holidays, give each student a small notebook with his or her name on it. Pass the books around the class so that every student can write a personalized, signed entry into every other student's Put-Up Book, such as: *You're so good at the times tables!* or *You have a nice smile!*

When all notebooks have made it around the whole classroom and back to their owners (and you've looked them over for propriety), have every student add a put-up about him or herself. As important as it is for us to bolster each other, it is equally or more important to affirm ourselves.

Chapter 7 That's What Friends Are For: Socialization and Self-Esteem

All-Inclusive Plans

Since students' experiences at school extend well beyond the walls of the classroom, supports must be in place to help them through those times when the structure and predictability you have tried to create within the classroom suddenly vanish and it's every kid for herself. What follows is a description of two of the most socially challenging times: lunch and recess. After that, you'll find suggestions for how your school might create a network of peer support around students who need it.

LOVE IT OR HATE IT: LUNCH AND RECESS

The time of day that is most anticipated by many students can be the most challenging for students on the spectrum. Nothing at school is as unstructured as recess. The very purpose of recess, for most students, is to grant them a reprieve from structure: *Here's some free time! Get up and go!*

But for students on the spectrum, a break from structure is no reprieve; it's sensory assault and social agony. Lunch and recess tend to be wildly unstructured. There are no assigned seats, no *inside voices*, no designated partners, no activity schedules, no clear or fixed rules. Carefully calibrated student-teacher ratios evaporate as all kinds of students are thrown together in large numbers. Supervision is usually inadequate. This is prime time for bullies, and your students on the spectrum, with their blatant idiosyncrasies and social naiveté, are especially vulnerable. In the environment where these students typically need the most support, the least support is provided. These periods are fraught with confusion, hurt feelings, and rejection. Lunch presents all kinds of sensory overload, as described in Chapter 4. And recess is a social free for all. It's no wonder that many times students on the spectrum can be found hovering around the periphery of recess, trying to keep away from the hub of noise and chaos, possibly feeling left out, or perhaps relishing the peacefulness of a quiet corner.

Anything Goes

Recess activities are often organized and mediated only by students. While a valuable exercise for some, this dynamic can create a multitude of challenging situations for others—especially for students on the spectrum.

At one school where I consulted, Four Square was a popular recess game with endless variations. At any given moment, Four Square might be played according to *Old-School Rules, New-School Rules, Regular Rules,* even *No Rules.* The rules of the game changed constantly—even mid-game. How could a student who relies on the stability of rules play a game in which the "rules" change abruptly or vanish without warning?

Kwan, a fourth grader on the autism spectrum, wanted to participate but struggled to make sense of the game. I created a system for him: If most of the kids in the game and in the line say he's out, he should get out of the game—even if he doesn't agree. But for Kwan, that rule was not specific enough. Since the number of students judging the game could vary, the word *most* was far too abstract: Exactly *how many is most?*

Fortunately, Kwan was able to understand the idea of majority rules. I explained to him that if *more than half* of the kids say he's out, he's out. If *less than half* of the kids say he's out, he should stand his ground and state that most of the kids agree with him. If equal numbers disagree, he should request a do-over.

This plan created a rubric of expectations for Kwan. He likes to play the game. He still does not understand the overall rules—who would?—and he doesn't have the flexibility to roll with the changes, but now he has his own set of functional rules that he can cling to and apply consistently to an otherwise incomprehensible situation.

LUNCH AND RECESS STRATEGIES

If lunch or recess seems to be a hot spot for your students on the spectrum, take a little time to put a plan like one of these in place during this period.

✳ **Aides on Alert:** Have a word with lunch and recess aides: Alert them that certain of your students may need some extra support and ask them to keep an eye out or intervene gently when necessary. If you think they might need some strategies, offer them the benefit of your experience or a copy of this chapter.

✳ **Push-In Support:** Ask speech and language therapists or occupational therapists if they can schedule push-in sessions with these students during lunchtime or recess. Therapists can set up systems, group games, or activities on the playground that lunch or recess aides can use on non-therapy days.

✳ **Get a Jump on the Lunch Crunch:** If the lunchtime crush is overwhelming, consider allowing your students on the spectrum to go to the lunchroom five minutes before the lunch-rush, to avoid the line and find seats in a calm environment.

✳ **Out of the Fray:** If lunchtime is overstimulating, look for quieter, calmer places for students on the spectrum to eat lunch. If indoor recess is over-crowded and noisy, look for indoor recess alternatives. On indoor recess days, my ten-year-old son had a permanent pass to be a kindergarten helper, where he always felt safe and welcome, and had the opportunity to demonstrate his relatively mature, big-kid skills.

Peer Support

Most elementary schools do not offer formal, facilitated social skill groups, but these can be enormously helpful. The school counselor and speech and language specialist might be able to organize a small social skill or social language group or support network around socially needy students. If you have students on the spectrum who are friend-deprived, here are some avenues you or the therapists in your school may pursue to recruit peers for support.

A CIRCLE OF FRIENDS

Ask the school counselor, speech and language specialist, or special education teacher to create a circle of support around students who are socially challenged. As described by special education teacher Mary Schlieder (2007), a Circle of Friends participates in supervised lunch and activity groups with the target student about once a month, playing games and practicing social skills, such as making conversation and taking turns.

With the consent of the parents or guardians of all students involved, Circles of Friends work like this:

- Socially savvy students who have interests in common with the target student are invited to be members.

- Circle members must be informed about the social needs of the target student. They are taught that it is their responsibility to respect this student's right to privacy and confidentiality by not confronting him with what they have learned about his specific challenges and by not ever sharing that very personal information with others.

These structured groups offer students safe opportunities to practice socializing and to feel like a part of something. Moreover, the skills developed and relationships formed during these structured activities tend to carry over beyond lunch time and recess, creating new circles of friends and supporters for all students involved.

Facilitated games can include the following:

- *Telephone*, which encourages listening, turn taking, and flexibility

- *20 Questions*, which encourages thinking in categories and reasoning

- *I Spy*, which encourages joint attention

- *Charades*, which encourages joint attention and nonverbal communication

A Circle of Friends can also serve as your eyes and ears in the hallway, on the bus, in the cafeteria, or during other times that your student is having a problem or is acting in a way that might get him or her into trouble.

A SMATTERING OF FRIENDS

If your school cannot set up a true Circle of Friends, you can try implementing elements of it, taking whatever proactive steps you can to ensure that all students feel safe and included, even during the less structured, more challenging times of the day.

✳ **Daily Double:** Appoint companions-of-the-day to partner up with specific students for small-group projects, walking in the hall, or any other suitable activities.

✳ **Lunch/Recess Buddies:** Designate student volunteers to seek out any students who are alone. Volunteers can offer to sit with them at lunch and engage or join them in activities on the playground. Give volunteers some strategies to engage reluctant peers, but remind them that not all students welcome company; companionship should not be forced upon anybody.

Something for Everyone

Consider the various incarnations of peer support networks:

- Students who may have the potential to be bullies should be considered as peer supporters if they are highly social. The lessons in empathy that develop within this supervised relationship can expand the value of the group in numerous directions.

- When possible, also invite students who struggle with learning or physical challenges but are socially capable to act as models of social behavior. Imagine the pride they will feel by being hand picked to be a helper and the mutual benefits that result from the positive interactions.

- What better put-up can you offer students on the spectrum than an opportunity for them to help or mentor others? Maybe students on the spectrum can turn the jump rope, play catch with the kindergartners during recess, or carry books for a peer with a broken arm. Perhaps they can quiz peers on their multiplication tables or help them locate books on the library shelves.

Look for ways for every student to demonstrate his or her strengths.

Chapter 7 That's What Friends Are For: Socialization and Self-Esteem

Defend Dignity

Be sure to remind peers that even though their identified classmate struggles with challenges, he is still an individual and, like everyone else, has feelings and opinions that must be respected. Despite peers' best efforts, this student may not always be receptive to social overtures. He may prefer to be alone or with someone else sometimes, just as we all do, at times. Teach them to respect his right to make his own choices, and to try again at other times.

Bullying

Students on the spectrum are prime targets for bullying. Their awkward or "clueless" social behaviors leave them vulnerable to teasing, aggression, and rejection. Plus, their limited self-regulation makes them likely to get upset in dramatic ways that are gratifying and encouraging to a bully. Given the many challenging issues in your classroom, it will be important for you to be especially attuned to and proactive about what's going on behind your back and behind the scenes.

Help all students understand exactly what bullying is. Since bullying can take many forms and be quite nuanced, keep these three facts in mind as you work to help students on the spectrum recognize what is and is not bullying:

- *Bullying is intentional.* True accidents do not count as examples of bullying. Bullying is done on purpose to be mean.

- *Bullying is repeated.* Bullying is a pattern of ongoing intimidating or hurtful behavior.

- *Bullying usually includes a power imbalance.* This means that one student is leveraging his or her age, height, strength, popularity, ability, or even racial, religious, or cultural majority status against someone else to gain an advantage. With students on the spectrum, it is frequently social savvy that is leveraged.

Remind students that bullying isn't just the mean things they do; it's also the nice things they never do, like inviting someone to join them instead of letting her sit alone at lunch, or being friendly even to people they are not friends with. Jodee Blanco calls these subtle rejections acts of "aggressive exclusion," and they can be among the most chronic and insidious examples of bullying (2008).

Battling Bullying

If your students on the spectrum are being bullied, offer them clear strategies they can access when necessary. Teach them the following:

✳ **Steer Clear:** *Steer clear of kids who bully.* Make this point specifically; students on the spectrum may not intuit that proximity increases the likelihood of negative interactions.

✳ **Stay in View:** *Stay where you can see an adult at lunch, recess, or wherever you feel at-risk. Or find a buddy to stick with during these times.* Support students in this effort by recruiting peer buddies, as described on page 147.

✳ **Look Brave:** *When you do have an interaction with a bully, try to look brave, even if you don't feel brave. Being brave looks like standing tall and staying calm. Save your upset feelings inside until later and then speak to an adult privately about them.*

✳ **Think Proud:** *Find ways to feel good about yourself. Focus on what is special and wonderful about you. What are you an expert at? Do not let a bully take away your pride and your confidence.*

✳ **It's Not You:** *Always remember that it is the bully who is misbehaving and doing the wrong thing—not you. You have not done anything wrong. Lots of kids get bullied, but no one deserves to be bullied* (Baker, 2009).

ENCOURAGE COURAGE

Often the best protection from other kids is other kids. Harness elementary students' innate drive to do good and their basic desire to please in order to cultivate conscientious objectors and model citizens.

Teach students that they all share a collective responsibility to combat bullying and that bystanders are expected to take a stand against bullying whenever they see it. Explain that *tattling* is something done for the sole purpose of getting someone *in trouble*, whereas *responsible reporting* is done to get someone *out of trouble*. Younger elementary age students typically do plenty of tattling, but as they move through the upper elementary years, tattling becomes unpopular and peer pressure drives that sense of righteous indignation underground. Students on the spectrum, however, who may be rigid followers and administrators of rules, need extra help and examples in order to understand the difference.

Perseveration Exasperation

Occasionally, the impulsive or perseverative behaviors of students on the spectrum may result in others feeling bullied. Eight-year-old Mark became focused on experimenting with peers' names. He arrived at school one day insistent on calling his peers by their full names: "Theodore," "Stephanie," "Jacob," "Vincent," and "Margaret." Needless to say, when Mark was told to stop but didn't, Teddy, Steffie, Jake, Vince, and Maggie felt exasperated and disrespected.

Rather than simply issuing consequences, Mark's teacher, Rochelle, took him aside and asked him why he was persisting in this behavior. Mark was able to explain that he was curious about nicknames since he did not have one himself, and wanted to *hear* how full names become nicknames.

Rochelle praised Mark for this spontaneous course of study, and pointed out the signals of displeasure that Mark had not recognized in his peers. She then taught Mark that every person gets to choose what he or she wants to be called and that we must honor those choices.

Rochelle helped Mark create a way to explore the nickname phenomenon using people who were not part of the class. Mark made a chart comparing nicknames, starting with famous *Johns*: John Adams, Jonathan Livingston Seagull, Johnny Depp, Jack Nicholson, and so on.

✳ **Classroom Concerns:** Offer all of your students a place to vent their frustrations by creating a *Classroom Concerns* depository. Hang a large envelope on the wall. Students can write down their frustrations or worries at any time and deposit them in the envelope. Retrieve them on a regular basis and discuss your students' feelings with them privately. Try to listen openly to students' reports of their own experience, which may be quite different from your own. Often these discussions will lead to simple solutions such as a change in seating arrangement or addressing a certain behavior with another student.

BEYOND RESTITUTION

The perseverative and impulsive nature of students on the spectrum may take quite a cumulative toll on classmates. Day after day, classmates may be subject to the same disruptive or destructive behaviors. Here are three steps to guide provocative students toward making things right.

1. **Apology:** Even if an apology is uttered by rote, the words *I'm sorry* are crucial to effective socialization. Over time, those words may become spontaneous and heartfelt, but for now, they are just compulsory and need to be stated whenever appropriate.

2. **Restitution:** If Dion knocked over Kelly's block castle by being impulsive, careless, or inconsiderate, he should provide restitution by helping Kelly rebuild,

thereby restoring her castle to its original glory. With your support, this can serve as a valuable opportunity for Dion to practice collaboration, flexibility, and empathy: Right now, he cannot build *his* way; he needs to build *her* way.

If, however, the castle was the casualty of an emotional or physical outburst by Dion, then now is not the time for restitution. Dion may be in no condition to "help" Kelly. And Kelly may not be especially receptive to "help" or anything else from Dion. If restitution feels unrealistic, consider reparation as an alternative.

3. **Reparation:** Even with mumbled apologies, and with or without restitution, it is unquestionably a strain on classmates to spend the day in an environment in which their block structures get demolished without warning or they get poked, interrupted, and cut in line all day long. Reparation goes beyond restitution. Reparation is a way of making up for anguish, pain, and suffering.

In this example, as reparation, Dion could be encouraged to find a way to do something *extra nice* for Kelly to make her happy again. Kelly deserves that.

Chances are, Dion will suggest something generous but egocentric, such as, *She can borrow my Dictionary of Aircraft Engines!* If Kelly declines Dion's proposal, guide Dion to consider Kelly's interests, so that he can offer something that would be meaningful to her. This is a good opportunity for Dion to practice taking another person's perspective: *What would Kelly like?* Maybe Dion could offer to give her his computer time today or take over her classroom job for the rest of the day or week.

Now Kelly has been more than compensated for her loss. And Dion has taken several steps closer to social understanding.

ADDRESSING THE CLASS

If you find that members of your class are struggling with the inclusive dynamic despite your efforts to foster an accepting community, you may consider asking the school counselor to facilitate a class discussion about a specific student who has exhibited provocative or otherwise confounding behaviors. (If you think this strategy might be helpful in your classroom, check out www.barbaraboroson.com for a detailed guide to facilitating this kind of conversation.)

Using these strategies, a supportive classroom community is within reach, but it is not a one-shot deal. Long-term maintenance will require your consistent modeling and positive, proactive energy. What an example you will be setting at the helm of a truly heterogeneous society, an inclusive environment in which all individuals are welcome and accepted. The next chapter will take this one step further, describing what can make communication so difficult and how to create a classroom that is responsive to the communication needs of all students.

Say What?

The Spectrum of Communication

Communication includes spoken and unspoken interaction. Among students on the spectrum, communication can be compromised by a wide variety of challenges, some readily apparent and others more subtle.

Students on the spectrum may have challenges with word production that manifest in every encounter. These students may be nonverbal or inconsistently able to produce conventionally meaningful sounds or words. For some, coherent thoughts or words may form in their minds but get tangled or garbled on the way out of their mouths.

Other students on the spectrum may exhibit challenges with the interactive or social elements of language. Some may deliver highly complex and well-articulated declamations but be robotic in their tone. Others may be articulate and animated, but repeat the same expressions over and over or only quote movies or television shows. Others may speak persuasively, but only on a topic of their choosing. Still others have memorized appropriate conversational fragments that they sprinkle handily into common dialogues but cannot deviate from.

This chapter describes the myriad challenges of both spoken and unspoken communication that students on the spectrum may face and offers strategies to help you create a classroom that is responsive to all kinds of communicators.

Challenges of Spoken Communication: Expressive Language

Many components of spoken communication may challenge students on the spectrum. Here is a brief summary of how each of these challenges may manifest in your classroom. As you read through, keep in mind that every single one of these challenges is exacerbated by anxiety. Read on to find out how a responsive classroom can reduce anxiety and open up new and effective lines of communication.

Expressive language is the cognitive process involved in formulating and transmitting information. Expressive language challenges may include articulation, fluency, pronoun reversal, semantics, and echolalia.

Articulation

With typical development, a student's speech, by age four, should be 100% intelligible, across contexts, even if there are still some articulation errors. For example, the sentence *I saw a wabbit on my birfday* contains two articulation errors, but is still intelligible. By age seven, however, a typical student should have mastered articulation of all speech sounds.

Significant or persistent errors in articulation could signal a variety of dysfunctions.

- *Dyspraxia,* which is a problem with motor planning, can cause students to be unable to figure out how to shape their mouths around the words that are clear in their heads.

- *Dysarthria* is a neuromuscular impairment that can account for poor muscle control and coordination and can cause students to be physiologically unable to manipulate their mouths to form the words that are in their head.

Speech and language specialists and occupational therapists should be consulted to assess the etiology of the difficulty and recommend intervention.

Fluency

The rhythm and flow of speech, known as fluency, is most commonly affected by stuttering or disruptions in speech. These can include inadvertent repetition or elongation of sounds or prolonged silences during speech production.

Stuttering can also be characterized by interjections, which are grammatically irrelevant interruptions to one's own speech. Sometimes we use interjections deliberately to decorate language, as in *poof!* or *bada-bing, bada-boom*. But frequent interjections such as *uh* and *um* can be indicative of a processing delay, in which the concepts are slow to develop in the student's mind or slow to form themselves into words.

Over time, dysfluencies can become intractable, so intervention by a speech and language specialist must be provided promptly in order for a student to benefit from new strategies. Stuttering can cause shame and stress for students, and also worsens under stress. You can help by being reassuring and by encouraging dysfluent students to take their time with speech. In this way, you are also modeling patience and acceptance for your other students.

Pronoun Reversal

The confusion of subjective pronouns is known as *pronoun reversal*. Most often, this manifests as the use of *you* to mean *me* and *me* to mean *you*. For example, when admiring someone's toys, a student might offer a convoluted compliment, such as *You like my toys*, when, in fact, she means to say *I like your toys*. Or, if someone asks a student, *Do you have any pets?* he might reply, *You do have pets! You have a dog and a bird!*

In some cases pronoun reversal can be an extension of echolalia, wherein a pronoun that is already in use gets repeated. (See more on echolalia on pages 158–159.)

But pronoun use is inherently complicated because pronouns are subjective; the words *I, me,* and *you* refer to different people within the same conversation, depending upon who is speaking. These are called *deictic forms*—their meaning changes depending upon the context of their use. These fluid early elements of language development are challenging to rigid, concrete learners.

Further, to understand that *I* means something different to each person who says it requires taking the perspective of others, or mind-reading, which is especially challenging to students on the spectrum.

Semantics

The rules that govern the meaning of words are known as semantics. The use of practical semantics is a particular trouble spot for students on the autism spectrum for several reasons.

How Sarcastic Can You Be?

One day, a group of fifth graders was being particularly loud and unruly. Their teacher, Arthur, used sarcastic words to chastise his class: *Can you be any louder?* Malik, a student on the spectrum, ever eager to please, promptly raised the volume of his voice. Arthur did not realize he had inadvertently invited this result because he was not even aware that he had used sarcasm. He sent Malik to the principal's office.

Consider carefully how you use language in your classroom. Subtle idiosyncrasies of speech, such as sarcasm and idioms, that you may use casually with your peers, are neither advisable nor appropriate in an inclusive classroom.

ABSTRACTION

Conceptual and abstract words such as *life* or *future* or *kindness* are hard for concrete or visual learners to grasp. Similes, metaphors, idioms, jokes, proverbs, and sarcasm are commonly lost on students on the spectrum as they struggle to understand even direct statements. This challenge extends well beyond the literal interpretation of basic proverbs such as *The early bird catches the worm.* It means that the allusions of poetry may be inscrutable. And practically speaking, being mired in the concrete world can have catastrophic social implications.

Embedded in Concrete

When students answer you in a surprising way, always consider whether they might have misunderstood your question. Students on the spectrum sometimes find abstract questions very amusing when they interpret them concretely. At the grocery store after school, Cindy and her mother ran into an old friend. The friend exclaimed, *Cindy, you've gotten so big! Are you in elementary school now?*

Puzzled and bemused, Cindy corrected the seemingly foolish woman: *No, I'm in the grocery store now . . . just like you.*

MULTIPLE MEANINGS

Another semantic challenge faced by students on the spectrum is fluidity of meaning. Fluidity is not a comfort zone for rigid students on the spectrum. When students first learn the meaning of the word *bark*, for example, they learn that it refers to the sound a dog makes. That definition becomes fixed in their heads, like a rule. So when they are told, *Please do not peel the bark off of that tree*, they are utterly muddled. They cannot automatically accommodate or generalize this new usage.

IDIOSYNCRASIES AND NEOLOGISMS

Other semantic challenges common among students on the spectrum include a tendency toward idiosyncratic language and neologisms.

- *Idiosyncratic language* is the use of common words or phrases in unusual ways, as in *The weather is blurry today.*

- *Neologisms* are invented words. In recent years, many neologisms, such as *blog* and *cyber* have been accepted into common parlance as we develop a new Internet vocabulary. However, when students on the spectrum create their own neologisms, though sometimes clever, they rarely carry shared meaning and serve mainly as further impediments to communication.

  If a student uses similar sounds or words consistently, you may come to recognize that *mim*, for example, always means something affirmative. In the context of your classroom, then, *mim* serves as language because it is communicative. Chances are, your student's family will have been conversant in *mim* for a long time. The family may have adapted to and adopted some of this student's words into their own family-speak, enabling *mim* to become a part of their agreed-upon language conventions.

Idiosyncratic language and neologisms reflect the gross approximateness of language use among students on the spectrum. As stated above, these students may not entirely grasp a specific concept or connect what they see before them to what they've already learned. They may not be able to access or retrieve the precise word for a concept, or they may not have heard or assimilated the pronunciation of the word correctly. They just try to come as close as they can.

Echolalia

The repetition of the speech of others is called *echolalia*. When you ask a student, *Are you finished?* and he responds, *You finished,* he is exhibiting echolalia. While

Chapter 8   Say What? The Spectrum of Communication

A Word Is a Word

Of course, a long-term goal is acquisition of conventional communication that can be understood out in the world. But it is important to consider that, depending on your students' histories and current levels of functioning, an incomprehensible grunt from one student may be a magnum opus from another. A student may have gone from being completely nonverbal for many years to using one sound consistently in a meaningful way. If they use any sound or word to convey a consistent meaning, they are using at least primitive language. Be sure to acknowledge their contextually successful effort to communicate, even as you prompt the use of conventional responses.

echolalia can occur to a small extent in any child's development, it is more common and persistent among students on the spectrum. Echolalia can be immediate, as in the repetition of words just heard; or delayed, as in the repetition of words heard long before, including those heard in movies or television commercials.

Though echolalia may seem uncommunicative or indicative of a lack of comprehension, it may in fact be an important communication tool for students on the spectrum. Sometimes students may use immediate echolalia as an intentional effort to maintain social interaction in the face of having no spontaneous response at their disposal.

Delayed echolalia may serve a more specific communicative purpose when used consistently. For example, a student who has read or seen *Diary of a Wimpy Kid* may have learned that the nonsensical phrase *Zooey Mama!* is a way of expressing humor or enthusiasm. Your student may adopt that phrase into his repertoire and use it every time something strikes him as funny. Another student may use the expression, *Lions and tigers and bears, oh my,* from *The Wizard of Oz,* to demonstrate that she is feeling anxious.

While these kinds of expressions may appear to be meaningless, it will be helpful to all when you make the effort to decipher their origin and their meaningfulness to the students who use them. If the students themselves cannot explain these expressions to you, their parents and caregivers are the next best resource for this kind of background information.

Because echolalia can serve different purposes for each student, your response to echolalia must be individualized. Consult with a speech and language specialist who can determine whether a student's echolalia is productive and how best to respond to it.

Creating a Responsive Classroom: Supporting Expressive Language

If you have students in your class who have mild-to-moderate expressive language challenges, this section offers some communication strategies to support them. Later in this chapter, we will look at tools that can be used to support the efforts of students who need a little more assistance.

✳ **Sending Up an SOS:** Create a system or signal that individual students can use to communicate with you without words. Whenever students' ever-present anxiety builds, their limited word retrieval skills may fail them altogether. They may become too anxious to organize the words to tell you they need to use the bathroom or that they don't know what page you're on. Work individually with these students to formulate some simple, private signals they can use to let you know they need help or need a break. They can pass you a card, hold up two fingers, and so on. Five minutes to regroup can buy many hours of engagement and expression.

✳ **Better Than Ever:** Students who struggle with expressive language may have fully formed thoughts in their heads but can't necessarily translate those thoughts into words. These students may be reluctant to participate in language-based activities, may raise their hands and then forget what they were going to say, be unprepared when called on, or use more immature language than their peers. But remember that perfect language production may be an elusive goal, and current functioning levels may reflect many years of hard work and progress. Try to acknowledge and celebrate even the tiniest steps forward.

✳ **Note to Self:** Allow students to jot down or quickly sketch their thoughts on a sticky note or index card during a lesson. They may have an easier time putting their idea into words if they can see it manifest before them.

✳ **Repeat Yourself:** Use classroom routines to encourage language use. Depending on your students' communication needs, create systems that require the use of routine language. Perhaps your daily morning meeting can require each student to greet a peer on either side using one of several possible greetings. The routine of this ritual will quickly become familiar to students and increase the likelihood that they will be able to participate.

✳ **Talking on the Job:** Create daily jobs in the classroom that encourage interactive language use: Perhaps your appointed attendance monitor can call the roll, or your designated lunch monitor can take a survey each morning to see who is planning to buy lunch that day. Prompt the use of social skills (such as not interrupting, addressing others by name, saying thank you) when performing these tasks.

✳ **To the Point:** Keep your questions very direct. Keep in mind the old joke in which one person asks a passerby, *Excuse me, do you know what time it is?* The passerby looks at his watch, answers *Yes,* and keeps walking. In that instance, the response does fit the question; the problem was that the question was not specific enough. With language-challenged students, consider the directness and specificity of your questions and statements. When you ask, *Who can tell me today's date?* your expectation is not as clear as it is when you say, *Manny, please tell us what today's date is.*

✳ **Break-Out Sessions:** Look for creative, structured opportunities to support language. Small collaborative groupings can help reinforce academic lessons as well as increase the likelihood that your anxious students will participate, since they may feel less intimidated sharing in a small group than with the whole class. Small groupings may also bolster a feeling of connectedness among students. Try these small-group strategies to support success:

- Assign roles within each group, such as reader, scribe, facilitator, timekeeper, materials manager. Carefully chosen roles are helpful in that they create boundaries on communication expectations, reinforce students' special strengths, and simultaneously stretch their skill and language base.

- Try setting up a group project by distributing materials in such a way that each group member has something the others need. One has the scissors, one has the glue, one has the papers, one has the crayons. Encourage the students to ask the others when they need something. If necessary, prepare students for this activity by practicing ways to ask for things (Kuder, 2003).

- Attach name tags to desks using Velcro instead of tape. This allows you to alter the seating arrangement easily, while still providing each student with a clearly designated space of her own. As long as you alert students to such seating changes beforehand, this system can promote socialization and collaboration, while at the same time supporting flexibility.

✳ **Sing It:** Musical processing is quite different from language processing. Many students who struggle to express a sentence can sing fluently and tune in better to music. Try putting some of your classroom routines to music (along the lines of the classic *Clean-Up Time* song) and see if expression and comprehension improve.

Challenges of Spoken Communication: Receptive Language

Receptive language is the cognitive process involved in the comprehension of language. Imagine being in a country where everyone speaks a language you don't understand. The words come quickly, and you have no time to translate or process the words before responding. Students with receptive language challenges may have that experience in their own classroom. If they cannot keep up with the language swirling around them, they tune out, and then tuning out becomes a learned behavior.

Central Auditory Processing

Difficulties with discrimination of sounds, filtering of sounds, or synthesizing auditory information could be due to central auditory processing challenges. Among other complications, central auditory processing difficulties can result in students doing the following:

- hearing and learning sounds incorrectly, impacting speech development

- missing critical information, which compromises comprehension and capability across all aspects of school and life

- overlooking meaningful auditory input while tuning in to background noise, or not being able to differentiate among stimuli. This confusion impedes focus and interaction. Sometimes students with central auditory processing difficulties may seem to be ignoring you, but in truth, their auditory focus is somewhere in the distance at that moment and they truly cannot hear you.

Creating a Responsive Classroom: Supporting Receptive Language

If you have students who have mild-to-moderate *receptive* language challenges, this section offers some communication strategies to support them. Later in this chapter, we will look at tools that can be used to support the efforts of students who need a little more.

162

Chapter 8   Say What? The Spectrum of Communication

✳ Less Is More: When students on the spectrum don't understand what's going on, more words can equal more overload. Their language and auditory processing systems can get overwhelmed or shut down completely. Explanations sometimes require the use of many words, but for these students, those words will run together as noise and be blocked out. So take it very slowly, and offer little bits of information, allowing plenty of time along the way for processing.

✳ A Work in Process: If possible, when you first want to ask a question, call the student's name or touch her desk to get her attention, and wait to be sure you have engaged her before proceeding. (Try to avoid tapping the shoulders of students on the spectrum, as unexpected touch may be jarring.) Once you're sure you have her attention, then ask the question. Patiently give her the time she needs to process the question and formulate an answer.

For example, you just asked Carla to name a local mountain range. Your question is greeted with silence. Though she appears to be ignoring you, she may be slowly processing your question. Try to give her the time she needs.

Often, in an effort to be helpful, a teacher will gently repeat the prompt: *Carla, did you hear me? I asked you to name a local mountain range.* Unfortunately, Carla— who had been working on tuning in to your request, then struggling to remember what the words *local* and *range* mean, and was beginning just now to consider what local mountain ranges she knows and retrieve and express the names of them—has been thrown completely off-course by this interruption to her process. Now she has to process your *new* question: *Carla, did you hear me?* Then she will have to start all the way back at the beginning of her effort to come up with a mountain range.

Try not to interrupt the process; just be patient. But if a student asks for help or seems truly lost, try reframing the question in a simpler way. Perhaps the wording of your question was challenging. This time, reword it: *Can you think of any groups of mountains near where we live?*

✳ Read and Repeat: Provide books that will be welcome and accessible because of their predictable, repetitive qualities. (See www.barbaraboroson.com for a list of books that feature catchy, repeating phrases or recurring themes.)

✳ Don't Do This: Since some students may miss the beginnings of your communications while they reorient their attention and process your words, try to frame instructions in the positive. Tell students what *to* do, rather than what *not* to do, so that they do not miss the critical word *don't* at the beginning. It is also helpful to call a student's name first, to give her a moment to tune in.

Instead of telling Rita: *Don't poke Fernando!*
Try this: *Rita?* (pause) *Please keep your hands to yourself.*

An added benefit of positive instructions is that embedded in the instructions are specific behavioral alternatives which might not otherwise be inferred. Now Rita knows exactly what to do with her hands when she stops poking Fernando.

✳ **Preteach:** Preview books and chapters with the class, outlining what to expect in the upcoming pages. This will support students on the spectrum by making new information predictable, which will bolster active listening and comprehension.

Creating a Responsive Classroom: Tools for Students Who Need More

If you have students on the autism spectrum who have little or no functional expressive language and very limited receptive language, consider these tools that can bolster their abilities to participate fully in classroom communication.

Picture Exchange Communication Systems

You can use Picture Exchange Communication Systems (PECS) to provide visual representations of common thoughts and objects to boost expressive and receptive language.

✳ **PECS for Expressive Language:** Using PECS, students can "speak" by showing picture-based communication cards. At any time, they can select one or several that convey the message they are trying to communicate. Some cards are photographic, some pictorial, and some offer only written words. Some support the expression of basic concepts such as *All done* or *More, please*; others convey whole sentences, such as, *I need a break*, *I don't understand*, and many more.

✳ **PECS for Receptive Language:** You can supplement the meaningfulness of your own spoken words by pairing your words with visual cues. You can use the cards to do the following:

- add visual cues to your curriculum by lining them up for storyboarding or for laying out the elements of a unit

- demonstrate concepts such as: *Same/Different*, *First/Then*, or *Cause/Effect*

- supplement your spoken instructions and facilitate transitions by using picture-based communication cards such as *Hands down*, *Eyes on me*, or *Line up*

164

Chapter 8   Say What? The Spectrum of Communication

First	Then
Put toys away.	Play on computer.

Picture-based communication cards can be as simple as words and pictures you draw on index cards, or photographs you take in the classroom or cut out of magazines. They can also be in the form of professionally developed software and hardware programs. At least twenty thousand pre-made downloadable icons cards are available through a variety of sources. (Links to sources of icons can be found at www. barbaraboroson.com.)

Picture-based communication cards can be organized by category and stored for easy viewing and access in a three-ring binder with plastic sleeves. Affix a Velcro strip across the front of the binder to display cards currently in use. Alternatively, the cards can be organized into a Velcro-lined flip book with a shoulder strap that you and your students on the spectrum can carry and access easily throughout your day.

Assistive Technology for Communication

Assistive technology, such as speech-generating devices and data processors, can help students whose communication needs significantly interfere with their ability to function in class. Such devices do not diminish students' efforts to use conventional communication. Instead, assistive technology devices help communication-challenged students begin to perceive themselves as communicators, which inspires them to continue working on developing their conventional communication skills.

SPEECH-GENERATING DEVICES

Assistive technology in the form of speech-generating devices can be used to support students with expressive or receptive speech or language difficulties. Nonverbal students or those with expressive challenges can type their communications into speech-generating devices, which then produce synthesized speech, giving voice to the typed communications. Students with slow auditory processing, attentional challenges, and other language reception issues can use this technology like a tape recorder to record your instructions or information and replay them as needed.

DATA PROCESSING DEVICES

Assistive technology can also help students express themselves via modified data processing devices. These feature the following supports:

- oversize keyboards, high-contrast screens, and combination keystrokes (that can be activated by pressing one key instead of holding two at once) to support fine-motor and sensory-motor challenges

- word retrieval and word prediction software to support expressive language challenges

- conversion software that reads students' words aloud for communication and/or to provide auditory feedback

- automatic, instant save features and on-screen templates to provide organizational support

If you think you have students who might benefit from assistive technology, ask your school administrator or the district's evaluative team for an Assistive Technology Evaluation to assess the students' needs in these areas.

Beyond Words: Challenges of Social Communication

Effective communication depends on more than the verbal elements of language. The subtext of social communication, also called *pragmatics*, poses an enormous challenge to students on the spectrum, leaving them mystified and quite inept. This section will work to demystify these challenging elements of communication and show you how to support more meaningful communication in your classroom. Pragmatic competence depends on facility with nonverbal and paraverbal communication, as described below.

NONVERBAL COMMUNICATION

Nonverbal communication, commonly known as body language, refers to gestures, facial expressions, body position, and body posture. Important implication lurks in

166

Chapter 8   Say What? The Spectrum of Communication

conspiratorial winks, meaningful kicks under the table, rolled eyes, and more. All of this information may be completely overlooked or misread by students on the spectrum. Casual banter is incomprehensible, and students on the spectrum are left lost and confused, teased and bullied.

For example, when nine-year-old Monique flubbed the ball in a kickball game, her teammates rolled their eyes and groaned, *Oh, great kick.* Monique's enthusiastic response—*Thanks!*—was as sincere as it was socially devastating.

PARAVERBAL COMMUNICATION

Paraverbal communication, commonly known as *prosody*, refers to the tone and inflection behind our spoken words. Prosody is *how* we say what we say. Elements of prosody include pitch, volume, intonation, rate, rhythm, and emphasis. These elements are essential to conveying a speaker's feelings and intentions and are critical components of social language. Most of us use prosody subconsciously to convey the mood of our words, indicating happiness, sadness, frustration, humor, politeness, wariness, anger, and so on. Typically, listeners construe meaning from our words on the basis of both what we say and how we say it. Without adequate prosody, many well-articulated verbalizations can be grossly misunderstood.

R U 4 Real? ☹

Words all by themselves are highly subject to interpretation. Communicating without the benefit of recognizing those unspoken clues is like trying to decipher the tone of a terse email, text message, or instant message. Words alone do not communicate the mood behind a typed message such as *Thanks a lot.*

Exclamation points and emoticons are the written equivalents of tone, facial expression, and other body language. All are used to ensure that our message is read in the way we intend: *Thanks a lot!!* ☺

Not coincidentally, the neologism *emoticon,* a word created specifically for e-communication, is formed by the two words: *emotion* and *icon.* As described above, actual pictorial icons help students on the autism spectrum understand and express facts, instructions, interests, needs, ideas, and, indeed, emotions. Pictorial icons have been helping students on the spectrum express and organize themselves for decades.

As typical students move through the elementary years, language becomes layered with unspoken innuendo such as sarcasm, impatience, kindness, disdain, anger, and more. Words are used in ways that don't match their definitions. Suddenly *Yeah, right* means *No way.*

Prosody is a profound area of challenge among students on the spectrum as they cannot interpret—and often aren't even tuned in to the existence of—unspoken messages. For this reason, they may overlook or misconstrue the inflections in others' speech. Combined with their mindblindness and limited joint attention, a lot of information gets lost in translation, and the interactive and social implications are devastating. Students on the spectrum often cannot tell the difference between a sincere comment and a sarcastic remark, a sad sentiment and a cheerful expression, or between a suggestion and a command.

Little Professors

Challenges with prosody can go both ways, in that students on the spectrum who have trouble interpreting typical prosody may also have trouble speaking with typical prosody. This gap is particularly striking among those who are higher functioning or have Asperger's Syndrome. These students tend to be highly articulate and verbal and had little or no delay in speech development. Yet in some cases, their speech develops with a monotonous, robotic quality. They are often known as *little professors.* While this nickname is largely due to their pedantic tendencies, it may also reflect the flatness of their affect and tone—devoid of emphasis and emotion.

Pragmatics

The ability to interpret nonverbal and paraverbal cues is called pragmatics. This composite skill is necessary for students to be able to use language in a natural context, to make conversation. No component of language is more dynamic than conversation because it is by definition interactive, and therefore dependent on the unpredictable, spontaneous input of others. This is why pragmatic language, also called social language, is one of the most challenging aspects of language for students on the spectrum, even when their speech skills are strong.

NONVERSATION

Communication challenges, in combination with social limitations, make conversation rather one-sided with students on the spectrum. Interactions are not exactly *inter*active, and conversations seem, well, more like *non*versations.

168

Chapter 8   Say What? The Spectrum of Communication

Pragmatic difficulties are especially apparent in students who have Asperger's Syndrome. These articulate students tend to possess a wealth of knowledge on a particular subject. What can first seem like a highly sophisticated level of conversation can quickly become peculiar, if not annoying, to listeners as students reveal their poor pragmatic know-how. A conversation devolves into a nonversation as these students doggedly pursue their own conversational agenda, oblivious to a listener's lack of interest and unaware of any expectation that they refocus their attention elsewhere.

In the later elementary years and beyond, conversation among peers becomes nuanced and loaded with social implication. The ability to interpret unspoken meaning is a litmus test for peer acceptance. Fitting in socially is all about reading between the lines, getting the joke, and so on. Social communication is more complex now, and students need to comprehend the words and implications coming at them as well as the receptivity of peers toward their own contributions.

Give It to Me Straight

Students on the autism spectrum often feel more comfortable interacting with adults than with peers for a variety of reasons:

- Familiar adults are more likely to be accepting of differences in conversational style, such as self-centeredness or lack of give and take.

- Familiar adults tend to be straightforward and friendly. Students can or should be able to trust that you will say exactly what you mean and that you are not being sarcastic or disdainful.

- Adults may be more patient awaiting word retrieval and will accept linguistic approximations in order to support a child's efforts.

- Conversational content with adults tends to be linear, whereas peer topics and responses can be wildly unpredictable and loosely connected.

What's That Supposed to Mean?

When talking with peers, on the other hand, students on the spectrum never know what to expect. For example, when eight-year-old Kameron steps off the bus at school, his peers ask him a seemingly simple question: *What's up?* Obligingly, Kameron looks quizzically at the sky and everyone laughs. What is so funny about that?

Without social intuition, students on the spectrum can't tell when to laugh along and when they are being laughed at; they don't know how to join a conversation and when to stop talking. Without the ability to read nonverbal and paraverbal cues, they struggle to make meaning out of words alone. Without flexibility, they get left behind when conversations meander inexplicably and take sharp unexpected turns. Without joint attention, they don't engage in the conversational topics of others. These pragmatic challenges compromise students' ability to use language in a natural, interactive context. Like so many other skills that many of us develop spontaneously, effective use of pragmatic language must be taught to students on the spectrum.

PRAGMATIC PITFALLS

Here are some common pragmatic challenges among students on the spectrum:

- joining into existing conversations
- modulating language according to context
- knowing when to stop talking
- taking turns speaking and listening
- considering the interests of others
- initiating socially appropriate topics
- reading between the lines
- interpreting non-literal language
- utilizing gestures and facial expression to support verbal communication

These challenges are very apparent to others and can be quite off-putting, especially to peers. They pose a dramatic impediment to socialization.

Creating a Responsive Classroom: Supporting Social Communication

Effective pragmatic language use takes practice. If you have students who struggle with social language, start by consulting the speech and language specialist in your school for support. Often speech and language specialists have specific curricula to support social language and pragmatic skills.

Speech and Language Specialists in the Classroom

In recent years, pragmatic language has become widely recognized as a critical element of social success, and so a greater emphasis is being placed on teaching pragmatics in

170

Chapter 8 Say What? The Spectrum of Communication

natural social contexts. Therefore, speech and language specialists are more frequently pushing into the classrooms than pulling students out for sessions, in order to provide support in the natural pragmatic environment.

Push-in pragmatic language support provides several holistic benefits:

- The speech and language specialist is available to troubleshoot real-life problematic interactions for the student, intervening and re-teaching in the moment.

- Students on the spectrum may not generalize the language skills they practice in the small therapy room, whereas learning the skill in the classroom encourages continuity of use across contexts.

- The classroom teacher can weave the specialist's cues and strategies into classroom routines, further increasing the likelihood of generalization.

- Pushing-in supports the whole-language view of learning, which frames language as an integrated system that involves cognition and socialization, as well as language skill development.

In spite of those strong reasons for push-in speech and language support, specialists often find that students on the spectrum feel more comfortable practicing language skills in the small-group setting of the therapy room. In most cases, a combination of pull-out and push-in service is most helpful, whereby students can practice in the safety of the small group, then try out their new skills, with support, on their classroom family.

Practicing Pragmatics

Beyond the help speech and language specialists can provide, here are some strategies you can use to facilitate conversational competence.

INITIATING CONVERSATION

Many students on the spectrum long to interact with peers but have no idea how to initiate, join in, maintain, or end conversations. Try laying out some guidelines.

Who Is Available for Conversation?

Encourage students to survey a situation before moving in. A good candidate for conversation would be the following:

- someone who is standing alone
- someone who has finished working
- someone who is not involved in another activity

Topics for Conversation

Review effective topic openers such as these, categorized by Jed Baker (2009):

- Past topics: *How was your* _____*?* (week, weekend, day, vacation); *Guess what! I* _____*!* (something you did)

- Present topics: *What are you* _____*?* (doing, reading, eating, playing)

- Future topics: *What are you going to do*_____*?* (after school, this weekend, over vacation)

- Interests: *How is* _____ *going?* (sports, projects, activity); *Do you like* _____*?* (sports, television show, music, movie, book)

Look for natural opportunities to practice identifying conversational topics during morning meeting, read-aloud time, assemblies, and so on.

Getting to Know New People

Give students strategies for branching out to make new friends.

- Name: *What's your name?* (pause and listen) *Mine is* _____.

- Age: *How old are you?* (pause and listen) *I am* _____.

- Fun: *What do you like to do for fun? Do you like to* _____*?* (television, movies, games, sports, places)

- School: *What school do you go to? What grade are you in?*

- Family: *Do you have any brothers or sisters? Do you have any pets?*

JOINING IN

Students on the spectrum often struggle to know when and how to join in with a conversation or play activity that is already in progress. Some may join simply by playing alongside the others without ever interacting; some may barge right in and take over; others may stand nearby and watch but never approach; and others will simply steer clear. Their rigidity and difficulties with impulse control make interaction especially challenging.

Jed Baker (2009) breaks the joining-in process into comprehensible steps that can be taught:

1. Watch and listen to what the other kids are doing. Decide whether you want to join them in what they are already doing.

172

Chapter 8   Say What? The Spectrum of Communication

2. If you want to join them, walk up and wait for a pause in the play.

3. Say something nice, such as, *You're good at that!* or *That's cool!* or *That looks like fun!*

4. Ask if you can join them: *Can I play?* or *Can I help?*

5. If they say *No,* move on and look for someone else to play with.

MAINTAINING CONVERSATION

Students on the spectrum often have difficulty knowing how to build on existing conversations. Here's where the waters get really murky. When they ask peers, *What are you playing?* or *Do you like the Jonas Brothers?* there's no telling what kind of response is going to come back at them. How can they plan what to say next when it's all unpredictable, it's moving so fast, and none of it seems to make any sense?

Listen Up

Often students on the spectrum are so preoccupied with what they want to say next, that they do not listen to or even hear the words of others.

✳ **Stop, Look, and Listen:** Remind students often to *stop, look, and listen.* Post that prompt on their desks in words or icon form.

If necessary, teach them a visual cuing system so you can convey this message, as needed, even from afar. For example, students can learn that when you call their name, they must look at you for a cue. If they see that your finger is up, that means they need to stop talking. If they see you touch your ear, that means they should be listening.

You can use this kind of signal system to support students whenever you notice them monopolizing conversations, intruding on others, or interrupting classroom lessons or activities. (This kind of system offers the added benefit of showing them that nonverbal cues are important vehicles of communication.)

✳ **Cross Fingers:** Gail, a fourth-grade teacher, encourages all of her students to cross two fingers when they have something to say but must wait their turn to speak. When their turn to speak finally comes, the tactile prompt of crossed fingers actually helps them remember what they were going to say. This simple strategy is especially helpful to students on the spectrum because once they learn to trust this technique, they may be better able to put their compelling comment on a back burner—temporarily—to focus on another speaker's words.

✳ **Active Listening:** Teach students to *show* that they are listening. Explain that even though they know that they are listening, others need to know it, too. This is an especially important strategy for students who have limited eye contact and may appear inattentive. Remind students on the spectrum specifically that it is not enough to ask a polite question; they must also listen to the answer. Encourage students to use verbal indicators such as, *Wow!, That's cool!,* or *Really?* when they hear something interesting, to give proof that they are engaged.

Staying on Topic

Even once students on the spectrum can recognize a topic of conversation and listen, more skill is required to respond. Due to difficulties with focus, impulse control, flexibility, organization, processing, perseveration and other issues, students may not recognize the conversational threads or unspoken associations that lead from one topic to another.

✳ **Look for Connections:** In his memoir, John Elder Robison recalls that as a child he was so used to living inside his own world, that he answered peers with whatever he had been thinking about. He writes, "If I was remembering riding a horse at the fair, it didn't matter if a kid came up to me and said, 'Look at my truck!' or 'My mom is in the hospital!' I was still going to answer, 'I rode a horse at the fair.' The other kid's words did not change the course of my thoughts" (2007, p. 20).

Encourage students to look for connections between what was just said and what they will say next. Introduce a card game such as Uno or Blink that illustrates visually that connections can be made in different ways. In these games, players add cards to a pile by matching them on the basis of color, number, suit, or picture. Teach students that words connect to other words on varied bases as well. Words can connect to others by being about a similar experience, seeking more information about a topic, offering an opinion about a topic, and more.

Teach stock connective phrases such as these:

- *That reminds me of . . .* or *Speaking of . . .*
- *What was your favorite part?*
- *That sounds fun! Can you tell me more about it?*
- Questions that begin with *who, what, when, where, why, how,* and *what else*

174

Chapter 8 Say What? The Spectrum of Communication

Constructing a Conversational Tower

Many students are able to relate to maintaining conversation in terms of building a Lego tower. In order for a conversation to keep going, the various pieces must connect and fit together tightly. If they don't, the tower will become unstable and fall down; the conversation will collapse.

For example, Erin begins a conversation by saying, *This science unit is confusing*. She has put out a Lego piece from her pile. Now, if Tanya wants to build a conversation with Erin, Tanya must choose a piece to add that will fit onto Erin's piece.

If Tanya puts out this piece: *I have a chocolate cupcake in my lunch today!*, then Tanya's Lego piece does not connect to Erin's Lego piece. The conversational tower will fall apart, and Erin may look for someone else to talk to.

Instead, Tanya might put out pieces like these:

- *What part do you think is confusing?*
- *Really? I think it's okay so far.*
- *Do you want me to help you?*
- *Yeah, I'm confused, too.*

Any of those pieces would attach neatly to Erin's.

Erin will then add more pieces to this sturdy tower and, lo and behold, a reciprocal conversation is now under construction.

---

are also useful "wildcards" for students to play as a way of demonstrating their interest in the speaker's topic.

In Uno and Blink, eventually the time comes when no one has a card in hand that can connect with the pile. At that point, game play pauses while each player selects a new card from the deck. In conversation, students on the spectrum can be taught that when they can't find anything to say that connects to the conversation, they can "draw a new card from the deck" with this handy question: *Do you mind if I change the subject?*

Taking Turns

Conversational skills also rely on the ability to take turns, including the subtle skills of knowing when to start and, often more important, when to stop. These skills are difficult to script because conversations vary in terms of topic, pace, expertise, formality, and more. But to some extent, students can practice turn-taking skills with instruction and guidance.

✳ **Learning to Listen:** If you have monopolizers in your class, incorporate structured conversational skill-building elements into class activities such as morning meeting or smaller group discussions.

- Provide a wand, empty paper towel roll, or a *My turn to talk* card that will delineate whose turn it is to talk. Explain that only the person holding the "microphone" may speak; everyone else must be a quiet listener. Practice this technique in dyads first, expanding into small and then whole-class groupings as skills develop.

- Challenge the speaker to make a connection between what he or she says and what was said just before. Dissect connections together and encourage students to name them. This will help students recognize that a topic is the thread that weaves and holds a conversation together. Redirect topics as needed.

- Offer strategies for recognizing when it's time to pass the microphone. Quantify time limits, as appropriate, such as a certain number of sentences or minutes. Use a gentle bell or chime, if necessary, to delineate the end of a speaker's turn.

- Acknowledge the patience and effort of the listeners. Curbing impulses to blurt out thoughts can be quite a challenge in itself. Some students fear they will forget what they want to say. Suggest that they cross their fingers or jot down a quick note to themselves to help them remember what they are waiting to say. Some students on the spectrum like to keep a tiny notebook in their pocket for moments like these.

QUITTING TIME

Outside of this kind of structured conversation, students on the spectrum may expound endlessly on their topic of interest. Ultimately, they'll need to learn to read the interpersonal signs of disinterest, without a wand or timer, and infer that it's time to stop.

✳ Remind students to look at faces and body language to get information about the listener's level of interest.

✳ Show them what faces look like when they have lost interest.

✳ Teach them to read the nonverbal cues from others that indicate that it's time to

176

Chapter 8 Say What? The Spectrum of Communication

"Close Talkers"

Personal space, also called *proxemics,* is another aspect of nonverbal communication that can be very loaded socially. Know any "close talkers"? Surely you've had students who barge right into your area of comfort when they speak to you or others who keep an impractical distance. We all have individual standards for our own personal space, and it can change from context to context.

But there is a generalized personal space rule that students should learn to respect. Try teaching them to keep an *arm's length distance* from anyone they interact with. This is an effective concrete strategy that students can apply to all situations, whether interacting with peers or with the principal.

Some students who come too close may be seeking sensory input. Ask the occupational therapist to explore this issue. A weighted vest or other input-providing device might help resolve this problem.

On the other hand, some students on the spectrum may require a greater personal space around themselves than you might expect. Grant that space in order to allow them to be at ease, especially when approaching students who are anxious, agitated, or sensorily defensive. Stand in a position that would not cause them to feel cornered or trapped. Turning slightly sideways and maintaining a generous personal space may feel less threatening to anxious students. Occupational therapists may also be able to use brushing and other strategies to help desensitize these students.

stop talking, such as someone looking at the clock, standing up, moving toward the door, and so on.

✳ Have them practice talking *a little bit* about a subject.

✳ Teach polite ways they can end a conversation:

- *Well, I have to get back to work now.*
- *I think the teacher wants us to be quiet now.*
- *I have to get my stuff. The bell is about to ring.*

✳ Remind them to follow those up with a *Bye* or a *See you later.*

If you feel your students need more conversational strategies, please visit www.barbaraboroson.com for more information on additional strategies.

✳ ✳ ✳

Regardless of the types of communication challenges you and your students face together, a truly responsive classroom can allow many different communication styles to be developed and accepted. Sometimes, however, students' efforts to communicate take the form of intense behavior. The next chapter will address behavioral communication, and ways to be responsive—and effective—when the going gets tough.

Boiling Up and Over

Turning Crisis Into Opportunity

You may be wondering why this chapter comes so late in this book when behavior is such a pivotal classroom issue. Here's why: If you have taken the time to understand all of the issues and challenges addressed in the preceding chapters, and if you have implemented some of the suggested preventive strategies, you have already warded off many crises. Many, many times you have kept the pot cool by avoiding triggers and respecting anchors, by creating a predictable classroom routine, establishing a smart sensory environment, maintaining positive, supportive relationships, and so much more. And many, many times, when the pot began to heat up, you read the signs and intervened quickly, confidently, and effectively, providing soothing sensory tools, social supports, comfort objects, and more. Congratulate yourself and your students because together you have kept things simmering along much more smoothly than they would have without your preventive and responsive efforts. Trust that this is true.

If you have not read the preceding chapters but just jumped to this chapter for a shortcut to help with challenging behaviors, the ideas here won't amount to much. They will get you through a tough moment, but they cannot sustain you or help you sustain your students on the spectrum. Please take the time to read through the other chapters; that's where you'll find most of the answers you need to head off crises and maintain equilibrium.

Still, in spite of all of your effort, the peace you have facilitated is admittedly a fragile one. You simply can't plan for everything. Potential anxiety triggers lurk everywhere for students on the spectrum. Comfort anchors that are critical to their functioning get lost or wet or broken. Their internal security systems are at Code Red at all times. Every interaction, every transition, poses the terrifying threat of unfamiliarity; every moment is fraught with the possibility that they will have to deviate from the comfort of their individually scripted guide to life. If it's off their script, they're not prepared for it, and feelings of panic and desperation can be instantaneous, inexpressible, and overwhelming.

Disruptive and destructive behaviors have the potential to escalate into crisis situations or trauma, or to transform into opportunities for growth. This chapter will show you how to help students grow from each experience so that when, on occasion the pot does boil over, no one will get burned.

Temperatures Rising

Given all the factors at play, it is no wonder that students on the spectrum sometimes lose control. They work at least twice as hard as typical students at everything they do. While your whole class is learning the rules of a new game, students on the spectrum are also trying to maintain focus and eye contact, comprehend instructions, wait their turns, keep their hands from flapping, and not talk about Super Mario Bros. While your whole class is taking a test, students on the spectrum are also trying to tolerate the glare on the paper, organize the sea of words swimming on the page, keep intrusive thoughts at bay, and avoid chewing their collars. This is hard work at best, and when all other things are not equal, the pot may boil over.

When circumstances feel overstimulating or overwhelming, students on the spectrum try to block out the offending input. Most often they either retreat into themselves to seek order internally, or they act out.

ALL IN A MINUTE

Consider this example: When Jelani puts on his coat at home before walking out the door every morning, he begins a tense transitional period between home and school. From that moment, his anxiety is elevated, and he takes comfort in repeatedly reminding himself that as soon as he gets to class, he will take off his coat, hang it up on his trusty third hook from the left—the one with the red knob—and then be able to settle into his day at school. Jelani relies on this daily routine of going directly to the coat closet to hang his coat on his hook. Even if it will be 85 degrees and sunny today, Jelani may need to wear his coat to school simply because he cannot begin his school day without seeing this routine through from start to finish.

But one day he arrives to find that something unthinkable has happened: his hook has fallen off the wall. Or the red knob is missing from his hook. Or Ava has accidentally hung her coat on his hook. Or the coat closet is closed altogether because someone just vomited in there. Or no one's hanging up their coats this morning because you're all leaving for a field trip in ten minutes.

Any of these scenarios violates Jelani's script. He can't possibly settle into a new day without hanging up his coat. Hanging his coat on his hook is one of the anchors that allows Jelani's day to proceed. It's part of his routine: He can't improvise around it, and he can't let it go.

He doesn't know if he is allowed to hang his coat on another empty hook—that information hasn't been specifically addressed in the rules. He doesn't have the language or social know-how to ask Ava appropriately why her coat is on his hook or if she might move it. He can't possibly keep his coat on until the field trip because that's just not how a day is *supposed* to begin. And worst of all, he doesn't know how to adapt internally to this unexpected change. His fragile balance is toppled.

Now that anxiety is brimming, what limited expressive language and impulse control Jelani may have had access to before is seriously compromised. He may fly into a rage, knocking his coat, or Ava's, or everyone's to the floor. He may yell at Ava. He may start growling. His hands may start flapping. He may curl up in a quiet corner of the closet and cry. He may keep his coat on—zipped up to his chin, hood on tight—and shut down completely by refusing to participate in the morning activities. Or he may come out of the closet and simply take his seat, looking as if everything is just fine, while inside he is reeling with anger, panic, and confusion. And most notably, he may not understand or be able to explain what is causing his breakdown.

By the time he comes out of the coat closet, he is in a dysfunctional state, unavailable for learning, and you may have no idea what's happened. You ask him, and he cannot respond. Your other students can only offer: *He was just sitting there crying!* or *Jelani just started screaming at me for no reason!*

Now Jelani's anxiety is way up, and his coping skills are way down. And it's only 8:01. When Jelani emerges from the closet, he may find that his desk has been moved. Or the book he set carefully on top of his desk yesterday is not there now. Or the classroom clock has stopped. Or the reading center is now in another corner of the room. Or, potentially worst of all, his teacher is absent. His anchors are floating away, and with them his self-control.

Whether he says it with words or by sitting down on the floor, by pulling his hat down over his face or by knocking his desk over, Jelani's unspoken message is this: *I am not joining Morning Meeting unless I can hang my coat on my hook first. That's how I always do it. That's the only way I know how to do it. The rule is: Morning Meeting always comes* after *I hang my coat on my hook, and that's how it has to be, because if it isn't like that, I have no idea what to do or what will happen next.*

Turning In and Tuning Out

Some students try to cope with anxiety by going deep into their world of lists and systems. They far prefer to confine themselves to the structure and predictability of rules than to face chaos or disorder. So they try to maintain sameness by insulating themselves from the unexpected and clinging to the familiar. You ask Jelani, after he emerges from the coat closet, *Why did you knock all the coats to the floor?* His anxiety is high now, and getting higher all the time: It's bad enough his hook fell down; now he is in trouble, too. This is a place of sheer panic. If he can answer at all, he may respond, *The longest dinosaur ever was the Seismosaurus, which measured more than 43 yards long. That's as long as two school buses in a row. The Seismosaurus was a relative of the Diplodocus, which . . . .* He is not showing off. He is not being provocative. He is not trying to be funny or a wise guy. He is giving you all he's got. He is operating straight from anxiety. The situation around him is out of control, so he retreats into his head to what he knows, what will not change (what, in this case, has been the same for millions of years).

Other students on the spectrum may be unavailable for conversation as they are putting all their energy into coping. They tune out their surroundings and tune in to a place of comfort in their minds. They scroll through the daily train schedule or visualize the disk drive operating inside their computer.

Acting Out

Still others have physical ways of modulating stress. They turn to behaviors that may soothe their senses and be comforting in their familiarity, even if they appear bizarre to others. They may find comfort by spinning, hand-flapping, rocking, making noises, toe-walking, head-banging, biting, grinding their teeth, and more. In so doing, they refocus their energies on something repetitive and physically distracting so they can let the

Chapter 9   Boiling Up and Over: Turning Crisis Into Opportunity offending stressor fade into the background. To the extent that you can, grant students time to regroup and restore, as you look for signs that they may be ready to rejoin the class activity. But sometimes physical reactions take the form of destructive behaviors which can be overwhelming to everyone involved.

Any of these coping styles can represent a crisis for students on the spectrum and/or the people around them. Take comfort in the knowledge that crisis and trauma are very different things. Whereas *trauma* connotes sustained injury or pain, *crisis* signifies a point at which change occurs, for better or for worse. A badly handled crisis can certainly result in trauma to the student and to others around him or her. But with some prior knowledge and strategies at hand, you can help a student through a crisis in a way that is transcendent. New learning and growth can emanate from a crisis that is gently supported, carefully considered, and thoughtfully debriefed.

Here is a quick guide for how to respond in the moment of a crisis. Then read on to see what comes after the crisis; that is, how to interpret the behavior and make the necessary modifications to head off recurrences.

Crisis Management Strategies

There is no one formula that fits every crisis, since every crisis is as individual as the student involved. Here are a variety of crisis interventions. Familiarize yourself with these approaches now so you'll be prepared for those sudden eruptions.

Crisis—Step 1: Safety First

Protect anyone who may be in danger, whether it is yourself, other students, your colleagues, or the student herself.

✴ **Find a Safe Space:** Keep a soothing space in mind, such as a sensory room, therapist's office, or other quiet place in which the student in crisis can calm down. If you have an aide in your room, have the aide try to escort the student to a safe space outside the classroom.

✴ **Call for Help:** If you do not have an aide, call for help from other adults to take the student to a place where she can regain composure. Prepare a roster for yourself, listing staff members who can be on call and *are known and trusted by the student*, such as the school counselor, resource room teacher, nurse, or librarian.

✳ **Clear the Room:** If the student in crisis cannot be safely removed from the classroom, find a staff member to remove your class to another space while you stay to support the struggling student in the classroom.

Also keep in mind that calming down amid a sea of gaping onlookers is humiliating and next to impossible. Even if it is not a dangerous situation, try to isolate the student in crisis so he can recover with dignity.

Crisis—Step 2: Defuse the Situation

If you do not know right away what the behavior is communicating (and you probably won't at this moment), that's okay; simply try to ease the situation in the moment. You'll analyze it later. (See "Interpreting Behavior" in the next section.)

Access information you have proactively obtained from this student's history regarding how best to help him calm down.

✳ **Restrain Yourself:** *Before* you face any crisis situation, find out what your school or district's policy is regarding the physical restraint of students. It can be tricky to protect yourself from liability while protecting your students from imminent danger. Alert school administrators that you may have volatile students in your class, and ask them what alternative strategies they endorse and recommend for those times when students are physically out of control.

✳ **Shush:** When trying to defuse a situation with a student, use as few words as possible:

- Since this student's sensory system is already overloaded, any excess verbiage will likely contribute to the crisis, so keep it soft and succinct.

- If you perceive that logic and rationality are gone, stop talking.

- Show the student the *Calming Down* card that you have placed in his coolbox, as described in Chapter 3. Silently offering this card to the student provides him not only a basic list of calming strategies that work for him, but also the familiarity and visual input he may need to help him break through the crisis.

✳ **Don't Engage:** If you think the student is able to listen and hear, demonstrate *supportive non-responsiveness* to the behavior:

- *When you use a calm voice, I will help you.*

- *I cannot understand you when you're yelling.*

- *When you stop kicking, I can come closer and help you.*

Exude Calm

When students lose control, they depend on the adults around them to maintain control and restore equilibrium efficiently. If your tone reflects that you are out of control and overwhelmed, your students are likely to become even more frightened and overwhelmed. Use the strategies in this section to help you regulate your own emotional temperature as you dig deep to discover the heat source. Calmness and confidence are great predictors of a smooth outcome and also serve as excellent modeling behaviors for all students.

✳ **Distract:** If you have a volatile student, get in the habit of keeping samples of your student's special interests on hand, such as a toy dinosaur, a sticker, a Bakugan card. Don't worry that this will reinforce the tantrum—these are comfort objects. As long as you don't present the very item a student is tantrumming about, you are not rewarding the tantrum. It's not okay to give in to what set students off; but it can be okay, periodically, to distract them with something they love. If, however, you find this is becoming a pattern, you'll need to develop a proactive plan (Baker, 2009). (See Functional Behavior Analysis on pages 196–197.)

✳ **Respect the Moment:** Do not confront a student with ramifications or threaten consequences in the moment. If you point out to him, *Do you see Morgan's papers all*

Taking Care of You

Acknowledge to yourself the toll this experience may have taken on you. Find your own trusted person with whom you feel comfortable venting whatever anxiety, fear, frustration, self-doubt, anger, resentment, or any other strong feelings you may experience as a result of this incident. Or find another outlet for your feelings. Get in touch with your own comfort anchors. Crises can be exhausting and demoralizing for anyone involved. Expressing your energy and venting your professionally pent-up true feelings will enable you to renew, regroup, and return to school tomorrow.

torn up on the floor? That's what you did. You are going to have so much to clean up, you will be increasing anxiety and fueling the continuation or exacerbation of the outburst. Now is not the time.

✳ **Give It Time:** Do not try to debrief the incident with the student right away. His sensory system will likely be raw from the offending event and the ensuing outburst. He is very likely frightened; it's terrifying to lose control of oneself. And depending on his social development, he may be embarrassed by his out-of-control behaviors.

Take time also before having the student rectify whatever may have gone awry as a result of this incident. If others were wronged by the student's behavior, apologies, restitution, and reparation may be called for, as discussed in Chapter 7.

✳ **Glad You're Back:** Once the student is calm, allow him time to regroup and gear up before rejoining the rest of the class. When he does, try to return to routine as quickly as possible. Returning to the class will be emotionally challenging, so try to make it as smooth as possible. Now is not the time for a big greeting or a round of applause; nor is it the time for chastising or consequences. Now is the time to let those raw nerves recover and let the student's system reset. Welcome the student back into the fold quietly, warmly, and without fanfare.

> *Yesterday ended last night. Every day is a new beginning. Learn the skill of forgetting. And move on.*
>
> —Norman Vincent Peale (1996)

Crisis—Step 3: What Happened?

Then, when you can, begin to work through what happened. This next section will help you look at behavior as communication so that both you and your student can learn from it. Without this next step, nothing will have been learned and crisis behaviors will continue unabated.

Understanding Behavior as Communication

Working to extinguish a student's negative behaviors will not get you to the root of the problem. At best, it's like offering only a cough drop to someone who has strep throat.

It may help for the moment, but it's missing the point and will allow things to get much worse. Instead, this section will show you how to dig a little deeper to address the origin of disruptive and destructive behaviors and work to prevent them.

The route to diminishing challenging behavior is recognizing and heading off or relieving the antecedent anxiety.

Anxiety as the Antecedent

When you see flagrant behaviors among students on the autism spectrum, they are rarely just actions; they are *re*actions. These moments are often the result of a powerful inner conflict. Sometimes one need arises in opposition to another that is equally compelling, and a student's capacity for rational thinking vanishes. For example, Galina is contentedly following instructions, eagerly coloring the squares on her worksheet. Suddenly her crayon breaks. This violation of crayon status quo may be an insurmountable, catastrophic turn of events for her. Galina may have her own internal set of rules about crayons: *Crayons must be whole.* Her rigid need to complete the worksheet as instructed is now in direct conflict with her rigid inability to color with a broken crayon. Panic crashes down from two directions: The integrity of her crayon has been literally broken and cannot be restored, *and* she sees no acceptable way to comply with the teacher's instructions. Both are unbearable outcomes to which she perceives no solution. Galina dives under her desk, curls up into a ball—moaning and rocking forward and back—and refuses to come out.

That example occurs in a few seconds. Now multiply the contents of those seconds across the day. Home and the bus, too, are part of the social world, so by the time students first arrive in your classroom in the morning, their day has already been going on for an hour or two. That's plenty of time for lots of their strict internal rules and expectations to have been violated.

Boiling Points

Again, for each student the triggers are different, but consider the possible anxiety triggers within a single morning. When Tomás wakes up, he finds that the shirt he had planned to wear is dirty, and this new shirt has a scratchy label. His sister urgently needs to use the toilet so he has to wait to brush his teeth. There are no more waffles. It's snowing, so he has to wear boots when he expected to wear shoes. The bus is late. The driver is different. The number on the bus is changed. His usual seat is unavailable. The driver takes an alternate route to school. Anxiety is creeping up and up and up.

Tomás's reliance on routine situations proceeding as expected may be critical anchors to his functioning, so all of these sensory challenges and deviations from routine have raised his anxiety or already sparked a meltdown, before he even gets to school.

Plus, there's no telling how the responsible adults in Tomás's life responded to his anxiety around these changes. How much do they understand about his needs? What skills and strategies do they have in place to help mitigate his reactions? How much time and patience do they have? How much patience do they have *left* after last night's three-hour meltdown when his favorite television show got pre-empted? For better or worse, the reactions of parents and other adults can also contribute to the degree of anxiety that spills into your classroom as your students on the spectrum cross the threshold each morning.

When Tomás arrives at school, he spends the morning yelling out: *Remember the Alamo!* over and over and over. You have absolutely no idea why. Your challenge (in addition to the mighty task of maintaining focus and patience among all of your other students) is to recognize that Tomás's disruptive behavior is his signal to you that something is wrong, and that it most likely has nothing to do with The Alamo. It's time to for you to go exploring—but not necessarily in Texas.

Clearly, a behavior and its triggers may have no apparent connection to each other. This section will show you how to understand difficult behaviors in a deeper way, putting them in the specific context of the whole child.

The Last Glass

When considering the accumulation of assaults a student on the spectrum may face, Lenore Gerould (1996) compares it to balancing a tray of water glasses on one hand. Each student seeks to keep his tray balanced, but every upsetting event is like another glass of water added to the tray. Some glasses are heavier than others, and the student must constantly try to adapt and cope as the tray wobbles. In the end, it takes only one more glass to topple the tray and send everything crashing down. That last glass may not have been the heaviest or the fullest, it was just the one that came right before the fall.

Every student on the spectrum needs someone who really knows him and his triggers to notice how heavy and unstable his tray is getting. For example, suppose you have a student who can't tolerate his clothes getting dirty. Even if he seemed composed when he returned from art class with paint on his shirt, that paint adds another glass to his tray and may contribute to his edginess this afternoon. Help keep every student's tray light and steady by maintaining a watchful eye, soliciting information from other adults in the building, and by maintaining the preventive strategies discussed in Chapter 3.

But when that tray tips, and it will, you'll need to know how to read what's going on and how to help.

Interpreting Behavior: Finding the Heat Source

Occasionally, after she's calmed down, a student on the spectrum will be able to tell you why she thinks she lost control, but more often than not, she will blame whatever event immediately preceded the crisis: *I couldn't get my shoe tied, so I threw it.* It's very unlikely that the student will be able to recognize that the uncooperative shoelace was only the last glass on the tray.

If your students on the spectrum exhibit disruptive or destructive behavior, take a look at these strategies to help you interpret the meaning of the behavior so you can turn the heat back down and keep it down.

Learning Together

When possible, as you come to understand what sparked a challenging behavior, collaborate about it with the student, if you feel she is capable of insight. For those students on the spectrum who are capable of this kind of metacognition, helping them to realize why they do what they do is a crucial first step in developing behavioral self-control. (But keep in mind: It's a first step on a very long journey.)

In a calm and quiet moment, help her to make the connection between an accumulation of small upsets and an out-of-control reaction or between a big trigger and a big reaction. Ask her what she thinks. Let her digest your suggestions and respond on her level. What is her interpretation? Does she agree with your analysis? Does she have any other suggestions to make it easier next time?

Most young students on the spectrum, however, are not able to engage in much self-reflection. Not only are they unlikely to make these connections themselves; they cannot be expected to apply an abstract cognitive-behavioral theory to their sensory-oriented, anxiety-fueled, impulse-driven systems.

But they can and must begin to make concrete connections between cause and effect, and they can learn to substitute certain behaviors for others in an environment that supports their needs. Chapter 4 offers strategies for modifying the sensory environment, and Chapter 7 offers strategies for debriefing behaviors and teaching social thinking. This next section will help you uncover those connections for yourself, using your own knowledge and experience, the feedback you get from parents or caregivers, and the input of students themselves to try to determine what triggered a problematic behavior.

Examine behavior from any or all of the following perspectives.

Interpreting Behavior: Significance

Before you go too far, consider the *significance* of a behavior, and assess whether or not it truly constitutes a problem. Take a moment here to look at this radical possibility: *Is the behavior objectively problematic or simply different?*

For example, sure, you don't expect students to stand up when they speak up in class, but is the fact that Karina always stands up when she participates really a problem? Is the fact that DeShaun needs to tap his foot while reciting the Pledge of Allegiance really disturbing anyone?

Stretch yourself to think outside the box whenever possible and be open to allowing differences to the extent that they are not disruptive or dangerous to others. If an unusual behavior is non-problematic, leave it alone. Students on the spectrum have enough to work on and you certainly have enough on your plate, too. Whenever possible, let it go.

Interpreting Behavior: Purpose

Consider the *purpose* of the behavior: What is the student trying to communicate with this behavior? Look for patterns of behavior. Consider how this incident connects to prior incidents and what may be the antecedent for these reactions.

It can be especially hard, in the heat of the moment, to remember that challenging behavior is often not directly related to anything that happened immediately before but may be the result of the accumulation of stress and struggle due to a series of unexpected changes or sensory affronts. Most students hold themselves together as best they can until one last stressor tips the tray.

Be sure you are familiar with the specific anxiety triggers and comfort anchors of students on the spectrum: only then will you be able to assess accurately what may have contributed to this reaction.

LOOK FOR PATTERNS

Using what you know about a student, work to put the problematic behavior in context by looking for patterns.

Who: Does this behavior tend to happen in the company of certain people?

- Might specific teachers or aides have different ways of interacting with the student or different expectations?

- Is everyone who works with this student educated about how best to support him?

- Do certain peers tend to be in the mix?

When: Is there any pattern or cycle related to the timing of the behavior?

- Does this behavior happen more during anxiety-provoking transitional times, such as first thing in the morning, just before or after lunch, or near the end of the day?

- Does this behavior arise more often on transitional days, such as Mondays, Fridays, or right before or after vacation?

- Does it tend to happen before lunch when he might be hungry? Is it usually after lunch? What does he eat and drink for lunch?

Where: Is there a consistent place or context where this behavior tends to occur?

- Does it usually happen in the classroom, in the lunchroom, in the hallway?

- Is it often during a certain subject?

What: What's happening right *before* the challenging behavior emerges? Are there any consistent warning signs or early indicators that she is escalating?

- Was she refusing to participate?

- Had the volume of her voice increased?

- Was she stimming (for example: flapping, pacing, humming)?

Also consider what occurs right *after* the challenging behavior emerges. Sometimes a student on the spectrum resorts to challenging behavior because it's the only way he knows to get the support he really needed sooner.

- Does the behavior always happen before a certain activity that feels overwhelming to him?

- Does the behavior happen *so that* he will get time in the cool-down room where he can have a much needed break from the classroom?

Why: As you examine possible triggers, try to figure out *why* those contexts are triggering challenging behaviors. Contexts that are often agitating include factors of the following:

- socialization and self-esteem
- regulation and sensation
- health or medication
- anxiety about what's missing
- anxiety about what's next

Fear is the main emotion in autism.

—Temple Grandin (2009)

If you're having trouble identifying contexts along these lines, many specific factors to consider are listed at www.barbaraboroson.com.

Modifying the Environment

Now that you understand what a student on the spectrum may be reacting to and why that trigger is causing a problematic behavior, you can begin to formulate some new preventive strategies for modifying the environment to reduce the student's need for the behavior.

Modifying the Physical Environment

In some cases intervention will be as simple as turning off the lights, putting a blue chair with a student's name on it in the lunchroom, asking parents or caregivers to send in more food for snack, or providing a student with a timer to help him wait. In these examples, you are resolving the antecedent by changing the physical environment and, if you've correctly identified the problem using the strategies in the preceding pages, the challenging behavior should fade naturally.

Modifying Routines and Expectations

Sometimes your intervention will also involve changing routines or expectations to support this student. Consider that a student may need the following:

- preventive time in the cool-down room built into his daily schedule

- an opportunity to take a walk down the hall every day mid-morning, or regular opportunities to deliver the attendance or collect papers

- a schedule to take with him to specials

- modifications to his work: fewer problems to do, less information on each page, extra time, and so on

- opportunities to do his work while sitting in a beanbag chair, standing up, or using assistive technology

A TOKEN EXAMPLE

Jorge, a second-grade teacher, used a token reward system to help his student, Kayla, stop biting other students. Jorge was very pleased to see that his system quickly extinguished this very disturbing behavior.

But within a few days, Jorge noticed that Kayla was exhibiting new repetitive behaviors. Now she was gnawing on her shirts and chewing on crayons. Trusting in the now-proven effectiveness of his token system, Jorge used the same system to extinguish the gnawing and chewing. Sure enough, within a week, Kayla was no longer chewing and gnawing.

Meanwhile, Kayla's classroom personality had begun to change dramatically. She had become restless and reckless, constantly bumping into objects and classmates, and repeatedly leaning her chair onto its back legs until she crashed to the floor. I was called in for a consult because Jorge was exasperated. He felt that he and Kayla were taking one step forward, two steps back.

We reviewed the chronology of events and invited the school's occupational therapist in to join us. Through our discussions, Jorge came to view Kayla's behaviors in a new light. The chewing and gnawing and bumping and crashing behaviors had all emerged to compensate for the loss of the *proprioceptive input* Kayla had been getting from biting. All of her seemingly disparate behaviors were actually communicating the very same message: Kayla's system needed that input and would obtain it, one way or another.

We worked together to address Kayla's behaviors from a brand new proprioceptive perspective, customizing a sensory diet just for her.

- We looked for patterns and noted that Kayla's challenging behaviors seemed to be less prevalent on days when she had physical education or occupational therapy because her joints and muscles were getting lots of good input from the physical activity. Therefore, the occupational therapist switched Kayla's session schedule to ensure that Kayla would have either physical education or occupational therapy on almost every day of the week.

- The occupational therapist provided a small squeeze ball for Kayla to keep in her pocket.

- Jorge incorporated a "Jumping Jacks Jam" into his class's daily morning meeting. He also agreed to give Kayla the option of doing some of her daily work standing and leaning against a wall, rather than sitting.

- Jorge encouraged Kayla's parents to send her crunchy and chewy snacks, such as raw carrots, hard pretzels, granola bars, and dried fruit. On difficult days, Jorge agreed to allow Kayla to chew gum.

These socially appropriate strategies gave Kayla ready access to the proprioceptive input she craved and the psychic comfort of feeling sensorily balanced and supported. That comfort provided the added benefit of reducing her anxiety and making her better able to go with the flow of the external world. She no longer needed to seek sensory input; sensory input was now built in. Her destructive and disruptive sensory-seeking behaviors faded away.

Give Me Five

Students with limited social skills and minimal or no language may use negative behaviors as inept attempts to interact with other students. By biting others, Kayla had indeed been making a connection of sorts. The same goes for students on the spectrum who hit, shove, poke, tap, bump, interrupt, and so on. If a student never interacts with others except to, say, bite, and you simply extinguish biting, now she is not interacting at all.

Be on the lookout for social effort. Teach students to greet peers in ways that are comfortable to them while being safe and welcomed by peers. Instead of alienating and hurting peers by biting them, Kayla was taught to greet peers with high-fives, which supported her efforts to socialize while simultaneously supplying her even more of that much needed proprioceptive input. (Small glitch: Kayla enjoyed this ritual so much that she began high-fiving students repeatedly throughout the day until Jorge set a clear limit of one high-five per peer, per day. Given all the other input that was now built into her schedule, twenty-four high-fives per day was enough, even for Kayla.)

Chapter 9 Boiling Up and Over: Turning Crisis Into Opportunity

Modifying Behavior

Even after you have identified the triggers and adapted the environment or expectations, remember that students on the spectrum may still be highly reactive. Limited executive function severely restricts their ability to stop and think before reacting. But modifying the environment as described above, and using incentives, reinforcements, and other behavior-modifying strategies described in Chapter 3 will help. This section will describe procedures to follow if challenging behaviors persist in spite of your preventive and responsive efforts.

Measuring Progress

When working to ameliorate persistent challenging behaviors, it's helpful to view them in terms of three basic, measurable elements: frequency, duration, and intensity. Gather data to help you compare these elements over time.

Frequency: How often does the behavior occur? Track how many times a particular behavior happens in a day, in a week, in a month.

Duration: How long does it last? Note how long the behavior persists each time it emerges.

Intensity: How bad does it get? Consider the behavior on a scale of 1 to 10, with 1 indicating a mildly disruptive behavior and 10 meaning a frightening, destructive or dangerous behavior.

I consulted at a school where Conor, a first grader, was having harrowing tantrums every day, lasting up to ten or fifteen minutes. Working together, his team, teacher, parents, and I were able to understand the function of his behavior, modify his environment, and implement a new behavioral plan. (See Functional Behavior Analysis on pages 196–197.) Conor's teacher, Carmen, began to track the frequency, duration, and intensity of the tantrums.

When I returned to the class a few days later, Carmen was discouraged. She said, "It didn't work: Conor is still melting down every day."

Carmen and I sat down together and compared the frequency, duration, and intensity of Conor's outbursts to what they had been before our intervention. We realized that although the frequency of outbursts had not diminished (yet), they were now lasting only about five minutes—less than half as long as before. And they were no longer escalating to the point that Carmen was concerned for Conor's safety or the safety of the other students. So our plan had made a significant positive impact on the duration and intensity of the tantrums. We had more work to do to reduce the frequency, but we were definitely on our way.

By breaking the plan into measurable components and comparing them over time, Carmen was able to note real progress in not-so-obvious places. This recognition gave Carmen something to celebrate with Conor and gave them both a reason to be hopeful. And hope, of course, is one of the best predictors of success.

Functional Behavior Analysis

When challenging behaviors persist for any student, call on school counselors or school behavioral specialists. They are specifically trained in managing difficult behaviors and can organize an action plan for assessment and intervention.

A Functional Behavior Analysis (FBA) is a systematic means of understanding ongoing challenging behavior in light of its context and function, and using that information to map out a plan for positive change. School counselors or behavioral specialists are directed (according to the Individuals with Disabilities Education Improvement Act) to utilize an FBA approach when addressing ongoing problematic behaviors.

An FBA is usually developed by a school psychologist or other behavioral specialist in collaboration with the interdisciplinary team members, parents, and, when feasible, the student. An effective FBA has three parts: a description of a challenging behavior, an interpretation of the behavior, and a behavioral intervention plan.

1. Description of Behavior: The school psychologist or behavioral specialist may ask you to track the frequency and details of a problematic behavior and record a brief description of what it looks like—before, during, and after. If you are asked to provide this kind of information, it may help to look at it from an "ABC" perspective:

A = Antecedents: Look for possible antecedents of the problematic behavior.

- How had the day been going overall for this student?
- What may have upset her before this behavior occurred?
- How was she acting before her behavior became problematic?
- Where was she? Who was she with?

B = Behavior: Describe the behavior itself.

- What happened? When and where did it happen? Who was present?
- How did staff respond? What helped? What made things worse?
- What were the duration and intensity of the behavior? How long did it last this time? How bad did it get?

C = Consequences: Examine what occurred as a result of the behavior.

- How did the situation resolve?
- How did the student react and recover?
- What were the effects of the behavior on others?"

2. Interpretation of the Behavior: The school psychologist or behavioral specialist will work to interpret patterns around this behavior. Since FBAs are designed to be broadly applicable and aren't specifically for students on the autism spectrum, your input will be especially valuable. Chime in with specific patterns you have observed and antecedents you have identified (as described earlier in this chapter). Be sure to contribute those all-important sensory components, because otherwise they could be easily overlooked during a standard FBA process.

3. Behavioral Intervention Plan (BIP): With the support of the interdisciplinary team, including you and the student's parents or caregivers, the school psychologist or behavioral specialist can craft a plan to prevent and respond to similarly challenging behaviors in the future. When appropriate, the student can collaborate and sign off on the plan as well. All members of the team should agree to support the plan's implementation and have a copy of it to refer to. Continuity across environments will maximize success.

To formulate a BIP, the school psychologist or behavioral specialist studies the descriptions and interpretations of the behaviors and uses them to recommend new environmental and behavioral modifications. An effective BIP relies on clearly delineated target behaviors and objective means for assessing change.

Be patient with your students as this process unfolds. Remember, some of these behaviors have been locked in for many years; it could take nearly as long to unlock and unlearn them. Note subtle signs of change and celebrate them.

By now you've read about establishing an optimistic environment, heading off anxiety, soothing the senses, collaborating with colleagues and family, capturing engagement, creating a responsive classroom, building a classroom community, and responding to challenging behaviors.

Now, at last, in the next chapter, you'll see that it's time to activate this knowledge and put it all together so that you can effectively engage your whole class in a dynamic curriculum.

Info In, Info Out

Making Curriculum Happen

Being the dedicated educator that you are, your most pressing question may be, *How do I teach curriculum to students on the autism spectrum?* After all, that's the bottom line, right? But guess what: Most of the answers to that question are in the chapters that come before this one. The fact is, if you have read the preceding chapters, then you have been laying the groundwork since page one. Ideally you have learned why you couldn't possibly have taught curriculum to students on the spectrum until you first implemented new strategies and new ways of thinking. Most likely, you've come to see that these students can't be available for curricular learning until you have addressed their anxieties, modified their sensory environment, hooked them into engagement, cultivated a classroom community, facilitated their communication, interpreted their behavior, and the rest. That's why this chapter on curriculum comes at the very end of the book.

And that's why this chapter all by itself would be woefully inadequate. If you haven't already read the chapters that come before this one, please go back and start at the beginning. I promise that you will find strategies to implement *right away* to help you break through to these students and create a productive learning environment for your entire class. Once anxieties are alleviated, senses soothed, and minds wide open (or at least, ajar), then please go ahead and use this chapter to help students on the spectrum learn and assimilate curriculum, and then demonstrate what they've learned.

Students on the spectrum who are in a mainstream class assimilate new knowledge differently and need to be taught the conventional curriculum in unconventional ways. They may have and need very different ways of engaging in the curriculum. Difficulty absorbing information can be due to varied areas of challenge:

- distinguishing main idea from detail requires sensory discrimination
- overall understanding requires engagement, focus, and joint attention
- understanding the organization of words or instructions on a page requires visual-perceptual skill
- filtering out irrelevant sounds and promptly synthesizing spoken words requires central auditory processing
- reading across a page requires visual tracking
- integrating all of these skills together requires comfort and composure

All of the learning challenges listed above are discussed in preceding chapters, along with strategies to address them. As you attend to those challenges, you are helping students on the spectrum become *available* for learning. But even once they are available, they face a critical obstacle as they try to assimilate new information. *What do they do with the information they acquire?* This section will look at the way information is commonly filed in the minds of students on the spectrum, and then give you strategies to help organize their thinking, working from the outside in.

Concrete Thinking

The majority of students on the autism spectrum are considered to be primarily visual learners, meaning that they interpret the world largely on the basis on what they see, and will understand lessons better with the supplementation of visual cues.

However, some students on the spectrum are primarily auditory learners, relying on sound and language to help compensate for their inability to attend to or interpret visual and other input. Others struggle mightily with auditory processing. They may be primarily kinesthetic learners, needing to interact physically with their environment in order to make sense of it. Still others may need to touch, taste, or smell to learn. And others need multisensory or vari-sensory approaches. (See more on vari-sensory input on pages 209–210.)

What Forest?

Most students on the spectrum tend to learn via a visual-perceptual system through which they see and process information in the smallest possible parts. Developmental psychologist Uta Frith (2003) calls this *weak central coherence,* meaning that students may be exceptionally detail oriented but overlook the *big picture.* These students are experts at storing and retrieving specific facts. They may note every tree, and may even be able to describe the differences among leaves from tree to tree, but they do not notice or recognize the forest. *What forest?* A cluster of individual trees remains a cluster of individual trees and does not add up to a forest. The whole is not a sum of its parts. Each part is a whole.

This explains why some students with autism spectrum disorders are *specialists* but rarely generalists. They're good at facts, but they don't necessarily place the facts into a broader context. My son, at ten years old, was a *specialist* on the presidents of the United States. He could recall, instantly, the names of all the presidents, first ladies, and vice presidents, in order. He knew each of their birth and death dates and the dates of their terms. He was renowned at school for this impressive chunk of factual knowledge. But his expertise had no breadth: He had no interest in or recognition of a greater historical or political context so he did not know what national or global challenges any of them faced. He did not know the difference between a Democrat and a Republican. He did not know what any of these presidents stood for or how their actions influenced the development of our country. His information did not aggregate into a lush, multifaceted forest; instead each tall tree stood alone.

Smooth or Chunky?

Typical students organize their thoughts intuitively into fluid categories. New information flows in and is automatically sorted by category. It is then subconsciously assimilated into what students already knew, deepening and broadening their understanding and supporting the development of an abstract or generalized concept.

But students on the spectrum tend to learn new information in concrete chunks that remain discrete in their minds. Imagine chunks of actual solid concrete. They are fixed and immutable. This inability to meld the pieces or connect the dots makes it very difficult for these students to amass a meaningful picture from isolated bits of information; instead they end up with a randomly arranged collection of dots. This makes higher level skills, such as generalization, rule generation, complex problem solving, inferring, and extrapolating next to impossible. Learning from mistakes does not happen spontaneously or readily because students may make no mental

Chapter 10   Info In, Info Out: Making Curriculum Happen

connection between their erroneous action and its consequence, no correlation between the *cause* and its *effect*.

Temple Grandin says that when she saw her first dog and her first cat, she memorized that the difference between a dog and a cat is that "a dog is large and a cat is small." She noted only the one specific difference and neglected to make any big-picture generalizations. That worked for her until she saw a dachshund. Now nothing made sense. Any categorical match between a doberman and a dachshund went unnoticed.

Grandin had to study pictures of all kinds of dogs and cats to create a new file folder in her head to redefine dogs. Now, even to this day, as an adult, she has a list of features she must scroll through in her mind any time she sees a new four-legged animal. First she examines the nose—she has memorized that cats' noses tend to be pink or otherwise light-colored, whereas dogs' noses tend to be black. If, after the nose analysis, she's still not sure, then she'll examine the sound the animal makes and even the smell of the animal. Even with these carefully constructed sorting systems, Grandin is still mired in the details; she has never been able to assimilate a generalized sense of what makes a dog different from a cat.

Generally Speaking

Grounded as students on the spectrum are in discrete details, the notion of generalizing information may not even be on their radar. As we encourage them to generalize information, they may struggle to understand the very concept of generalizing, let alone apply it.

Some students on the spectrum do not generalize unless specifically told to. As author Ellen Notbohm describes, "If you teach [a student] to safely cross the street at the intersection of Main and Smith Streets, that 'learning' does not automatically apply to the situation that has him standing at the intersection of 23rd Avenue and Johnson Drive. To his way of thinking, it's not the same" (2006, p. 28).

Other students on the spectrum overgeneralize. They have been taught, by rote, to greet everyone with *Hi! How are you?* And now they use that greeting all day long, even when they just saw the person a moment before. Figuring out when and how much to generalize is a nuanced skill that will take time to develop.

Given the significant limitations of concrete thinking, students on the spectrum need to learn to organize isolated bits of information into open-ended categories and then synthesize those categories into a fluid body of knowledge.

ROLLING WITH RULES

As discussed in Chapter 3, setting clear, concrete, and consistent rules and expectations is helpful and comforting for students on the spectrum. Following rules may be an area of strength for these students and a way they can set an example for the whole class. In fact, they may be your best rule followers.

But students on the spectrum may also be rule followers to a fault. The extent to which rules can be generalized is not likely to be inferred by these students. If the parameters of the rules are vague or unclear, this will raise anxiety and compromise compliance. A student may not be able to infer whether *No running in the hall!* means *No running in the hall right now* or *No running in the hall, ever.*

- Try to spell rules out as specifically as possible.

- Be sure to check on a student's understanding or misunderstanding of a rule before jumping to the conclusion that he was willfully breaking it.

- Encourage students to think about *why* rules are what they are. This may help them prioritize conflicting rules and help them to apply rules more flexibly. If the rule is stated as *No running in the hall, ever,* guide students to figure out why that is a rule. Once they understand the purpose of some rules, they may be able to generalize the rule: *Now, can you think of any other places where we should never run? How about places where we can run sometimes?*

Getting Information In

Typical students naturally develop abstraction skills across the elementary years. As they move through third grade and beyond, they begin to notice patterns and make spontaneous associations that facilitate generalization. In their work and their play, they subconsciously test their assumptions and continually modify the categories that are emerging in their consciousness.

Students on the spectrum need to be taught how to mentally sort, label, categorize, file, and cross reference in order to abstract and generalize. They need to be taught to learn from their mistakes. Fortunately the routes to all of these abstract skills have concrete pathways.

Organization—From the Outside, In

If you have students who struggle with abstraction and generalization, the first step is to teach practical organizational skills to help them sort, label, and categorize elements of their physical environment. Most students on the spectrum need significant guidance and structure to organize both their external and internal environments.

This section will describe ways to support students' organization, both externally and internally, as an avenue toward flexible thinking and generalization. Your scaffolding skills are more important than ever here, as you erect permanent thinking structures onto which your students will build a lifetime of knowledge.

EXTERNAL ORGANIZATION

Some students on the spectrum are ultra-organized due to rigidity. They cling to order to maintain calmness and are intensely careful to keep their environment neat and predictable. But most are unable to create that kind of external order due to executive function challenges.

Organizing the Physical Environment

Create a clear, comprehensive, and sensible spatial structure in the classroom to reduce feelings of chaos in the larger environment. Most students will feel calmer inside when they can find certain elements of the environment to rely on for clarity and order.

For example, in Kamran Nazeer's *Send in the Idiots,* Nazeer writes about his friend Craig, an adult on the autism spectrum. Craig had to travel as part of his work and sometimes found it difficult to stay in other people's homes overnight. Nazeer recounts that Craig found

> *"there was always some idiosyncrasy to do with the shower ('pull the curtain all the way along to the left or the water'll drip on the floor'; 'turn the knob on the left-hand side a couple of times—if you turn it three times, you've gone too far—and then turn the lever in the middle counterclockwise.') . . . Staying in other people's houses, interacting with a different set of personal effects and a wide range of objects all with stories behind them that he didn't know, remained difficult . . . So he devised a strategy to help him manage. Every time he stayed with a friend, he reordered one thing. For example, if there was a pile of books on the coffee table, he might pick it up and alphabetize it. After he had done this one thing, introduced this coherence of his own, he came back to it every time he began to feel a little anxious"* (2006, p. 123).

✴ **Define Space:** Incorporate small, visually defined areas within the large room to make the space feel manageable. Label these areas clearly with signs such as *Quiet Corner, Writing Center,* and so on. A disorganized external environment fuels a disorganized internal environment.

✴ **Sensible Set-Ups:** Place the *Completed Homework* bin just inside the classroom door, so students can drop off their homework as they arrive in the morning, or just outside the coat closet so they can drop it off right after emptying their backpacks.

✳ **Say What You Mean:** Do not rely on students on the spectrum to intuit or remember that what you call *The Mailbox* is actually a folder that must be checked every day for outgoing notices. Supplement the cutesy name with real information: *Papers to Take Home Every Day.*

Organizing Workflow

✳ **Create Subject Sets:** Color-code all folders, notebooks, even worksheets according to subject. Students will have a much easier time taking home the correct sets of books if their social studies textbook, workbook, notebook, and worksheet all match. Color-code them with tabs or with wide strips of brightly colored tape on the bindings.

✳ **Use School-to-Home Checklists:** Laminate a school-to-home checklist. Attach it to students' desks and have them actually check off items with a dry-erase marker as they are completed. Consider enhancing this chart with photographs or line drawings, as needed.

Always prompt students to check the chart before leaving for the day or post a sign by the door asking, *Did you check your checklist?*

✳ **Home-to-School Checklists:** Suggest that parents or caregivers keep a home-to-school checklist, or other similar checklists for difficult times of day. Many families use checklists to help less-organized children get through the fast-paced morning or reluctant bedtime routine.

✳ **Forget Forgetting:** When necessary, allow students to keep extra copies of text books at home or an extra comfort object at school, if these important items tend to be forgotten.

✳ **Online Support:** Try to post each night's homework online, if possible, for students who recorded it incorrectly, cannot read their own writing in their planners, or cannot mentally reconstruct the assignment. This is also a welcome support for parents and caregivers as they try to help with homework.

SCHOOL-TO-HOME CHECKLIST

☐ Did you copy your homework assignment off the board?

☐ Did you put your homework books into your backpack?

☐ Did you put your planner into your backpack?

☐ Do you have your lunch box?

☐ Do you have your coat?

☐ Do you have your backpack?

Have a nice afternoon!

Chapter 10 Info In, Info Out: Making Curriculum Happen

A Homework Staple

Organizing a visual field can require only very simple adjustments. For example, Daphne gets utterly tangled up when trying to work on a packet of double-sided pages that are stapled in one corner. She never knows whether she is on the front or back of any page, and loses track of which way to flip: *Is it time to turn the whole packet over or just turn a page?* Inevitably, she either misses pages throughout or she does a couple of pages and then starts flipping backwards, coming to the erroneous conclusion that she has completed the entire packet when she hasn't at all.

Three staples down the left side of the packet, instead of only one in the corner, immediately turns an incomprehensible floppy mess into a neat booklet and eliminates this problem completely.

Organizing the Visual Field

✳ **Leave No Room for Doubt:** Keep pages simply organized, both visually and practically, by labeling items clearly with numbers or by drawing boxes around single elements.

✳ **Eschew the Curlicue:** Use a straightforward, highly readable font on worksheets, avoiding word art, outlines, shadows, elaborate curlicues, or other unnecessary frills on letters.

✳ **Instructions:** Label instructions by name: *Instructions.* Write instructions succinctly and in clear, unequivocal language.

✳ **Beginnings and Ends:** Use horizontal lines to separate sections when a new set of instructions is about to begin.

✳ **Guide the Eyes:** Create a clear visual connection between each question and its answer space, by using ellipses, dashes, or other visual connectors—for example: *Magnets have positive and negative poles . . . True or False?*

✳ **Curtail Clutter:** Be sure there is not too much information on any one page. Leave plenty of blank space to give the eyes a break.

INTERNAL ORGANIZATION

Though you can plainly see whether or not your students' desks are organized, their mental filing systems are more mysterious. But once the environment is clearly organized, students on the spectrum can make sense of it. Then they can begin to relax into the orderliness of their surroundings, recognizing that everything has its place. Ahhh.

Now, you can help them organize their thoughts and ideas similarly. As they have learned to view their physical environment through the lens of patterns and associations, prompt them to apply those same processes to more abstract concepts.

✴ **Organize to Categorize:** When discussing broad or abstract concepts, support concept organization by using graphic categorizing tools, such as charts, columns, grids, cluster maps, concept webs, Venn diagrams, character trees, sequencing activities, and timelines. These visually delineate what categories look like and organize what information fits where. Being able to see the parts that comprise the whole helps students recognize an abstract entity as a compilation of individual parts.

✴ **Cause and Effect:** Make cause-and-effect connections overt, demonstrating that for every action there is a reaction. Point them out wherever you notice them and state the lesson to be generalized from the experience. *Whoops! We forgot to feed Coconut this morning! She must be hungry because we forgot to feed her. Let's put "Feeding Coconut" on our jobs schedule so we won't forget to feed her again.*

✴ **Analogies:** Analogies help students make connections by encouraging them to examine relationships between various concrete objects.

Prompt all students in your class to articulate their reasoning: *Why do birds' nests remind you of doghouses? What do birds' nests and doghouses have in common?*

Guide thought processes if necessary: *Do birds' nests and doghouses look alike? Are they found in similar places? Are they used for similar purposes? What purposes?*

Making this process overt and conscious for students on the spectrum gives them the thinking tools they need in order to apply these organizational skills elsewhere: *What do birds' nests have in common with your house?*

✴ **Set the Scene:** Always begin new topics by putting them in familiar and meaningful contexts. If you are about to introduce world explorers, start by pointing out what wonderful things can happen when we pursue our curiosities. Ask the students to discuss what they themselves have explored and discovered. Setting the scene in this way opens the *curiosity* and *explorer* files in the minds of students on

Chapter 10 Info In, Info Out: Making Curriculum Happen

Person, Place, or Thing?

The game of Twenty Questions encourages the organization of facts into flexible categories. Suppose, for example, you begin the game with, *I'm thinking of a place that starts with* D. Immediately, students need to hone their thinking and sort all the places they know into a new category: *What places do I know that start with* D?

As students ask questions, possibilities narrow.

Is it in our town?

No.

State aloud what kinds of places are being eliminated based on the answers: *So we know it can't be Davis Elementary School, even though that starts with D, because Davis is in our town.*

Record the questions in *yes* and *no* columns in front of the class, so students can keep track and visually add and subtract information.

Would we take a plane to get there?

Yes.

Now students have to generalize all the places they can think of that are far enough to fly to that also start with *D*. They are challenged to make new associations and create brand new categories. This is fluid thinking.

Is it fun there?

Yes!

The most valuable part of the game for these students will be reviewing the overall process. Once the correct answer had been revealed, write it at the top of the chart: *Disney World.* Then review aloud all the steps taken toward discovery and discuss specifically how each answer modified your collective thought process.

the spectrum, allowing the upcoming information to be filed practically and cross-referenced appropriately.

At the end of the lesson, reiterate the context so that students walk away with a clear understanding of what this new information means to them. This whole-language approach, framing lessons in familiar and meaningful contexts, will support comprehension, retention, retrieval, generalization, and application.

✻ **Integrate Literacy:** Weave language use into reading and writing lessons, so that students will associate reading, writing, and language as integrated systems:

- Use language to support literacy by having students make predictions about what they will read, or discuss text-to-self and text-to-text connections after reading.

- Use literacy to support language by having students read their own writing aloud and comment on it.

✳ **More or Less:** The task of estimating invites students to step away from the concrete details and try to get an overall sense about a situation. But students on the spectrum may be quite comfortable mired in the precision of the details, thank you very much, and have a hard time stepping back to estimate. When you ask them to take a guess about how many people might be able to sit in the auditorium, they may find it much easier to count every seat or even to multiply by rows than to take a more abstract guess.

Affirm the value of counting, as you present the value of estimating. Compare situations that call for specific answers with others in which non-specific answers are more appropriate. The more students on the spectrum can recognize different ways to think, the more thinking strategies they will have at their disposal.

✳ **Create Continuity:** Collaborate closely and regularly with team members (including parents or caregivers, resource room teacher, reading specialists, aides, counselors, occupational therapists, and so on) to ensure that you all speak the same language. Because students on the spectrum will not generalize from person to person or moment to moment, seek to establish consistency and clarity of prompts and academic strategies across multiple contexts.

For example, Ian, a third grader, worked intensively with his occupational therapist to improve his very poor printing. Over time, his handwriting in his occupational therapy workbook improved dramatically. When the occupational therapist told the classroom teacher that Ian had achieved his handwriting goal, the classroom

What's the Point?

Many lessons and group activities are never put in any context, and students are left thinking, *That was fun, but what was the point?* For students who don't spontaneously generalize, it is especially important to describe overtly the purpose, relevance, and application of activities across their daily lives.

Chapter 10 Info In, Info Out: Making Curriculum Happen

teacher was astonished—she had seen no improvement in his handwriting at all. Ian had been returning to his classroom after each occupational therapy session and reverting immediately to his "old" handwriting! Ian was then instructed specifically by the occupational therapist and teacher together that he should use his "new" handwriting all the time now. Ian was happy to comply; it just had not occurred to him to generalize his new skill.

Vari-Sensory Instruction

Beyond their difficulties with abstract thinking and generalization, students on the spectrum face other obstacles to comprehending and processing information. As described previously in this chapter, they may be primarily visual, auditory, tactile, or kinesthetic learners. Bolster *everyone's* success by varying your style of instruction.

Demonstrating ideas via numerous senses at once, which is known as *multisensory instruction*, often helps students integrate new knowledge. For many students, having the opportunity to touch textured letters while seeing their shapes and hearing their sounds, all at the same time, enhances learning. Indeed, many students on the spectrum learn much better through some senses than through others.

However, due to sensory processing challenges, students on the spectrum may get overwhelmed by an abundance of sensory stimulation. Receiving input via multiple senses *at the same time* could be the worst approach for them.

For this reason, try not to require students to do two things at once, such as *Watch and take notes*; or *Listen to this story while you finish cutting*; or even, *Look at me when I'm talking to you.* Instead, think: variety and options. Expanded styles of instruction wake up the whole class and facilitate learning.

✳ **Show and Tell:** Get in the habit of supplementing your spoken words with visual cues. After you define a new term, explain it and then show it: *A prairie is a large grassy field or meadow that has hardly any trees. Can you imagine what that looks like? This is a picture of a prairie.*

Some teachers fade their use of visual supports toward the upper grades of elementary school, believing them no longer necessary. But students on the spectrum may continue to benefit from these supports to help compensate for their enduring challenges in other areas. Try to maintain your use of visual supplements for students on the spectrum throughout the elementary school years.

✳ **Switch It Up:** Consider that literacy and other skills can develop in nonlinear ways, facilitated by creative input. Know your students' sensitivities and learning styles and offer choices. Have a touch station, a look station, a listening station (with headphones), a performance station, a creation station, and so on. Some students will learn best by moving from station to station to reinforce in a multisensory way what you are teaching. Others will do best staying at one station and learning by repetition. Expose students to lessons using varied approaches, always seeking the one that flicks the switch, makes a connection.

For example, in her book, *You're Gonna Love This Kid* (2003), Paula Kluth, a former professor of education and special educator, describes having students "walk" a sequence or timeline. She suggests writing the names of important events on individual pieces of paper and having students place events in order as they walk, hop, crawl, skip, or jump along the sequence. At each step they might call out a detail or fact about that event or name an important player or element related to it. In addition to the academic reinforcement, this kind of kinesthetic learning experience can awaken interest and reinforce retention for most of the students in your class. It also provides valuable proprioceptive and vestibular input to students who need it.

But be aware that for some students on the spectrum, this same exercise could be an onslaught of too many expectations at once. Offer choices. Give students the option of simply placing the events along the timeline without speaking. Allow students to write the timeline on paper and draw pictures of the events. Appoint a fact-checker, who walks the timeline only after others have completed it and checks their work.

Getting Information Out

As described in the preceding pages, getting information into students on the spectrum depends upon the organization of both their external environment and internal thought processes. But another challenge remains: Once that information gets in, how do we get it back out?

Support Output

You will probably find that getting students on the spectrum to demonstrate their knowledge is an uphill battle. To be in your inclusive classroom, they are pushing up against their challenges all day long. With obstacles emerging around every corner, students on the spectrum frequently get impatient and frustrated just trying to get the words out. They may not dig in or persist with difficult work. Their impulsivity and

Chapter 10   Info In, Info Out: Making Curriculum Happen

prior failure experiences may cause them to give up as soon as the going gets tough. If you have students like these, any of the following strategies can help organize their efforts to help them hang in there long enough to get the job done.

✴ **Graphic Organizers:** To facilitate linear thinking and multi-step processes, experiment with templates such as paragraph maps, paragraph recipes, story outlines, and more. These will support organization and bolster students' feelings of progress as they work toward more complex tasks such as determining the main idea, writing a paragraph, and sequencing events.

To guide spatial judgment and process sequencing in math, offer graph paper to help students keep columns aligned as they work to identify place value, solve higher-order computations, make decisions, brainstorm, and approach other multi-step tasks.

You may find that certain students prefer one type of graphic organizer and some prefer another, so don't use a one-size-fits-all approach. Try to differentiate organizers that you believe will resonate with specific students and see how they respond. When you find something that works, stick with it. (See a list of graphic organizers at www. barbaraboroson.com.)

✴ **It's All About the Journey:** The more you incorporate graphic organizers into your students' work, the more access you will have to understanding and guiding their thought processes. Don't emphasize the final product; grade the *process*. This is a powerful intervention with struggling learners; by celebrating the value of effort over achievement, you will greatly bolster their willingness to try.

✴ **One Step at a Time:** Have students write down every step of each math problem, even the parts they do in their head, to prevent them from getting lost along the way.

✴ **Jot It Down:** Encourage students to make notes and keep lists. Many students on the spectrum have a fondness for lists. Lists are orderly and predictable and can be easily self-maintained.

✳ **Use Hand-Under-Hand:** Instead of the usual hand-over-hand support by which we help students manipulate materials, try *hand-under-hand.* Put your own hand directly on the material and let the student wrap his or her hand around yours. By having their own hands on top, students feel that they are making it happen, that they are in control of the action. This bolsters their confidence that they will ultimately be able do the activity themselves (Baker, 2009).

✳ **Any Which Way They Can:** The opportunity to demonstrate knowledge in a variety of ways can support students on the spectrum to demonstrate what they know. For example, when possible let them choose whether to use print or cursive, pen or pencil, or to type their work on the computer.

If writing paragraphs about independent reading books is too challenging for some students on the spectrum, for example, offer the options of creating a new cover illustration for their book, drawing cartoon versions of the story, acting out the plot, rewriting the ending, writing a poem about the story, crafting a collage about it, comparing one book to another using a Venn diagram, participating in a (school-sanctioned) online discussion forum, and so on.

All students may benefit from structured whole-class projects that allow for creative expression, such as performing a play for other classes, simulating historical events, presenting projects to parents and caregivers, performing a rap song, staging a debate, videotaping a documentary, creating a brochure, filming a commercial, and more.

Thinking Outside the Arteries

Linda, a fifth-grade teacher, collaborates with Keith, a physical education teacher, to set up a larger-than-life model of the circulatory system in the gym. Via four-wheeled scooters, students propel themselves across the floor, on their stomachs. Like individual blood cells, they glide along, circulating through veins, arteries, valves, ventricles, and atria, demonstrating their knowledge of the route on this sanguine journey they'll never forget.

✳ **Choice Boards:** When you present a choice of activities orally to students on the spectrum, they need to process what the options are, consider the variables related to each option, and then express their selection. By then, the moment of choice may have passed, the options forgotten. Supplement your spoken words with a choice board that demonstrates visually what the options are. Use PECS or make your own icons representing common choice activities in the classroom and place the relevant options on the choice board at any given time. This enhances students' ability to move through the choice process and express their wishes in timely and independent ways.

✴ **Follow the IEP:** In addition to whatever strategies you use in your class, students on the spectrum are (or should be) entitled to specific program modifications and/or classroom accommodations as mandated in their Individualized Education Programs (IEPs).

✴ **Assistive Technology:** For many students on the spectrum, alternative communication or educational devices may be necessary to accommodate specific challenges. When appropriately assigned, these devices augment students' ability to participate in the curriculum by facilitating independence, bolstering success, building confidence, reducing frustration, and improving behavior. These devices can include a tape recorder, large-key calculators, glare-reduction screens, word-prediction software, and much more. If adequate justification is presented to your district's evaluative team, use of specific assistive technology can be mandated on a student's 504 Plan or IEP and provided for the student's use at school.

✴ **Look at the Big Picture:** Consider the absolute value of certain skills. If a specific skill is not developing, despite longstanding and creative interventions and IEP accommodations, and if the effort is causing the student intense stress and anxiety, consider carefully whether the attainment of that particular skill is worth the battle. Collaborate with parents and caregivers to keep perspective on the necessity of attaining certain skills. For example, psychologist Tony Attwood (2009) views handwriting as a passé 20th-century skill, much the way saddling up a horse to go from New York to Boston is a 19th-century skill. In this high-tech era, there may be reasonable ways to compensate for certain skill deficits. If not, in some cases, achievement expectations will need to be modified on the IEP.

Assess Your Assessments

What are your tests actually testing? Sometimes what looks like poor comprehension on the part of students on the spectrum may actually be a problem *expressing* comprehension through traditional means. Consider that responding on a written test requires focus and organization; manipulating materials requires eye-hand coordination; participating verbally in class requires language processing and consistent engagement. In these cases, your assessments may not be assessing what the students know as much what they can produce. If you have students who struggle to process and produce information, try some of these strategies to create contexts in which all students can demonstrate their concept competence.

✴ **Cut to the Chase:** Be sure your content-area tests are testing only content, and are not dependent upon speed, vocabulary, working memory, word retrieval, organization, handwriting, or other isolated skills that could interfere with the demonstration of content knowledge.

✴ **Chew *and* Swallow:** Emphasize content comprehension over content regurgitation. For example do students need to memorize the precise longitude and latitude of the Amazon rain forest in order to understand the meaning of the word *tropical* and the relationship between tropical climates and the equator? Rather than test rote regurgitation of facts, reach for conceptual competence.

✴ **One Skill at a Time:** Try to test one skill at a time as skills are developing. If you are testing for structure, be flexible about length; if you are testing vocabulary, be flexible about punctuation; if you are testing for facts, be flexible about handwriting.

✴ ***Cloze* It Up:** Use multiple choice, True/False, and matching column question formats, as opposed to open-ended questions that require students to jump inside your head and anticipate your way of thinking—a very hard skill for students on the spectrum who may be limited by mindblindness.

If you must use fill-in-the-blank formats, stick with cloze sentences, such as *George Washington was the first _____ of the United States,* or starter prompts, such as, *Rainforests are located near the _____.* These are more specific in their expectations than wide open questions like, *Who was George Washington?* or *Where are rainforests located?*

✴ **Put It in the Bank:** *Always* accompany fill-in-the-blank questions with a small word bank. Word banks ensure that you are testing for word recognition and concept knowledge, rather than word retrieval.

✴ **Sounds of Silence:** When administering an assessment, implement some common-sense adjustments to the classroom environment. Shut down classroom computers to eliminate their distracting humming and hypnotic screensavers; turn off buzzing overhead lights; keep the classroom door closed. Choose another time to sharpen pencils, staple projects onto the bulletin board, eat your crunchy salad, and so on.

Chapter 10   Info In, Info Out: Making Curriculum Happen

✶ **Practice, Practice, Practice:** Since new situations are especially challenging to students on the spectrum, taking a test that is presented in an unfamiliar or unexpected format can set students back before they've even started.

Provide opportunities for students to familiarize themselves with the intricate workings and nuances of matching columns, word banks, analogies, and true/false questions. Clearly explain conceptual conundrums such as *None of the above* and *All of the above,* and organizational hazards such as bubble sheets. Do not assume that the use of testing formats is self-evident.

✶ **Read Between the Lines:** Just as you have learned to look beyond students' behaviors and reactions to see what they are really trying to communicate, examine your assessments through a similar lens. Read over your questions and instructions with the assumption that nothing is self-evident to students on the spectrum. They cannot read between the lines, but you can. Are you really saying what you mean? Are your expectations crystal clear? If you present information in simple, straightforward language, you just might get the same back.

This chapter offers strategies for getting curricular material into and out of students on the autism spectrum. You may feel that it took an awful lot of preparation and effort for you to get to this chapter and for your students on the spectrum to be "ready to learn."

But as you think back over what you've read in this book, realize that you have been teaching your students on the spectrum and they have been learning from you *every step of the way.*

✓ You have taught these students that others see and admire their strengths, which has boosted their self-esteem and inspired their belief in their own potential.

✓ You have taught them to trust in the safety and predictability of your classroom environment, optimizing their independence and capacity for flexibility.

✓ You have taught them how to monitor their own anxiety and sensory reactions, giving them tools and strategies to self-regulate and self-soothe.

✓ You have met them on their own terms and taught them how to expand their narrow horizons and risk moving out of their comfort zones to tune into new experiences.

✓ You have taught and learned from their families, establishing the vital link of school-home continuity and seamless support.

✓ You have taught your whole class life-lessons in diversity and acceptance by building a village that cultivates kindness and champions citizenship.

✓ You have created a responsive classroom, facilitating all kinds of communication and teaching students on the spectrum that their words and ideas are valuable and valued.

✓ You have shown these students that their team of supporters can capably sustain them through their most difficult moments and transform those moments into positive change.

✓ And, I hope, you have learned a thing or two along the way as well.

Best of all, the lessons you have taught your students on the spectrum are *skills for life* that they could not have learned on their own. These forever-lessons are now part of who they are and who they bring forward in the social world. You have imbued their futures with promise and their spirits with possibility.

Going forward, your students on the spectrum may always remember you as the teacher who gave out French fries during social studies. Or they may associate you with the 67 books in your classroom library, of which precisely five mention dinosaurs, four mention trains, eight mention baseball, nine mention presidents, four mention state capitals, eight mention inventions, seven mention computers, three mention autism, four mention airplanes, six mention holidays, five mention flags, three mention moon phases, and one mentions French fries.

But you can be sure that all of your students, whether on or off the spectrum, will remember you as a teacher who listened, understood, accepted, and believed.

References

American Psychiatric Association. (1994). *Diagnostic and statistical manual of mental disorders IV-TR Fourth Edition.* Washington, D.C.: American Psychiatric Association.

Attwood, T. (2009). *Making friends and managing feelings.* Presented at Autism/Asperger's Syndrome SuperConference. Guilford, CT: Future Horizons.

Baker, J. (2009). *No more meltdowns: Managing behavior in the home and classroom.* Presented at Autism/Asperger's Syndrome SuperConference. Guilford, CT: Future Horizons.

Baker, J. (2001). *The social skills picture book.* Arlington, TX: Future Horizons.

Baron-Cohen, S. (1995). *Mindblindness: An essay on autism and theory of mind.* Cambridge, MA: The Massachusetts Institute of Technology Press.

Baron-Cohen, S. (2001). Theory of mind in normal development and autism. *Prisme,* 34, 174–183.

Blanco, J. (2008). *Please stop laughing at us.* Dallas, TX: BenBella Books.

Bollick, T. (2009). Seeing the forest and the trees: Teaching concepts, principles, and higher-order thinking. *Autism Spectrum Quarterly,* Summer, 24-27.

Canter, L. (2002). *Assertive discipline—new and revised: Positive behavior management for today's classroom.* Santa Monica, CA: Canter & Associates.

Ernsperger, L. (2003). Developing proactive strategies for managing problem behaviors. In *The Best of Autism Asperger's Digest Magazine* (Vol. 1). Arlington, TX: Future Horizons.

Exkorn, K. S. (2005). *The autism sourcebook: Everything you need to know about diagnosis, coping, treatment, and healing.* New York: HarperCollins.

Frith, U. (2003). *Autism: Explaining the enigma* (2nd ed.). Hoboken, NJ: Wiley-Blackwell.

Gerould, L. (1996). *Balancing the tray.* Schnecksville, PA: Carbon-Lehigh Right to Education Task Force.

Grandin, T. (1992). An inside view of autism. In E. Schopler & G. B. Mesibov (Eds.), *High-functioning individuals with autism.* New York: Plenum.

Grandin, T. (2008). *The way I see it.* Arlington, TX: Future Horizons.

Gray, C. (2000). *The new social story book*: (Illustrated Edition.) Arlington, TX: Future Horizons.

Greenspan, S. I. & Wieder, S. (2006). *Engaging autism: The floortime approach to helping children relate, communicate and think.* New York: Perseus.

Grigorenko, E. L., Klin, A., & Volkmar, F. (2003). Annotation: Hyperlexia: disability or superability? *Journal of Child Psychology and Psychiatry. 44*(8), 1079–91.

Gutstein, S. E. & Sheely, R. K. (2002). *Relationship development intervention with children, adolescents, and adults.* London: Jessica Kingsley.

Heaton, P., Williams, K., Cummins, O., & Happé, F. (2008). Autism and pitch processing splinter skills. *Autism, 12*(2), 203–219.

Howlin, P. & Asgharian, A. (1999). The diagnosis of autism and Asperger's syndrome: Findings from a survey of 770 families. *Developmental Medicine & Child Neurology. 41*, 834–839.

Kranowitz, C. S. (2005). *The out-of-sync child.* New York: Perigee.

Koegel, R. L. & Koegel, L. K. (2006). *Pivotal response treatments for autism: Communication, social, and academic development.* Baltimore, MD: Brookes.

Kluth, P. (2003). *You're going to love this kid!* Baltimore, MD: Brookes.

Kübler-Ross, Elizabeth. (1997). *On death and dying.* New York: Touchstone.

Kuder, S. J. (2003). *Teaching students with language and communication disabilities.* New York: Pearson Education.

Kutscher, M. L. (2004). *ADHD book: Living right now!* White Plains, NY: Neurology Press.

Lavoie, R. (2005). *It's so much work to be your friend: Helping the child with learning disabilities find social success.* New York: Simon & Schuster.

Mandell, D. S., Novak, M. M. & Zubritsky, C. D. (2005). Factors associated with age of diagnosis among children with autism spectrum disorders. *Pediatrics. 116*, 1480–1486.

Mehrabian, A. (1980). *Silent messages: Implicit communications of emotions and attitudes.* Belmont, CA: Wadsworth Publishing.

Miller, L. J. (2006.) *Sensational kids: Hope and help for children with sensory processing disorder.* New York: Putnam.

Molloy, C. A., Manning-Courtney, P. (2003). Prevalence of chronic gastrointestinal symptoms in children with autism and autism spectrum disorder. *Autism. 7*(2) 165–171.

Nazeer, K. (2006). *Send in the idiots: Stories from the other side of autism.* New York: Bloomsbury.

Norris, J. A. & Hoffman, P. R. (1990). Language intervention within naturalistic environments. *Language, speech, and hearing services in schools,* Vol. 21, 72–84.

Notbohm, E. (2006). *Ten things your student with autism wishes you knew.* Arlington, TX: Future Horizons.

Owens, R. E. (2009). *Language disorders: A functional approach to assessment and intervention* (5th ed.). Boston: Allyn and Bacon.

Polimeni, M. A., Richdale, A. L., & Francis, A. J. (2005). A survey of sleep problems in autism: Asperger's disorder and typically developing children. *Journal of Intellectual Disability Research, 49*(4), 260-268.

Peale, N. V. (1996). *Have a great day.* New York: Ballantine Books.

Pychyl, T. (2009, March 5). Perseveration: The deep rut of change procrastination, [blog post]. Retrieved from http://www.psychologytoday.com/blog/dont-delay/200903/perseveration-the-deep-rut-change-procrastination.

Robison, J. E. (2007). *Look me in the eye: My life with Asperger's.* New York: Crown.

Saulny, S. (2009, February 25). Students stand when called upon, and when not. *The New York Times, p. A1.*

Schlieder, M. (2007). *With open arms: Creating school communities of support for kids with social challenges using circle of friends, extracurricular activities, and learning teams.* Shawnee Mission, KS: Autism Asperger Publishing.

Sundberg, M. L. (2008). *VB-MAPP: Verbal behavior milestones assessment and placement program.* Concord, CA: AVB Press.

Tammet, D. (2007). *Born on a blue day.* New York: Free Press.

Thompson, S. J., Morse, A. B., Sharpe, M., & Hall, S. (2005). *Accommodations manual: How to select, administer, and evaluate use of accommodations for instruction and assessment of students with disabilities* (2nd ed.). Washington, D.C.: The Council of Chief State School Officers.

U.S. Centers for Disease Control and Prevention, National Center on Birth Defects and Developmental Disabilities, corresponding author: Rice, C. (2009). Prevalence of autism spectrum disorders: Autism and developmental disabilities monitoring network, United States, 2006. *MMWR Surveillance Summaries, 58*(SS-10).

U.S. Centers for Disease Control and Prevention. (2010). Prevalence of autism spectrum disorders: Autism and developmental disabilities monitoring network, United States, 2006. MMWR Surveillance Summaries, *58*(SS-10).

Wetherby, A. (1986). Ontogeny of communicative functions in autism. *Journal of Autism and Developmental Disorders, 16,* 295–316.

White, Randall. (2005). Autism first-hand: An expert interview with Temple Grandin, Ph.D. *Medscape Psychiatry & Mental Health 10*(1).

Index

Note: numbers in bold indicate main discussions of topics.